The Research Student's Guide to Success

THIRD EDITION

The Research Student's Guide to Success

THIRD EDITION

Pat Cryer

 Open University Press

Open University Press
McGraw-Hill Education
McGraw-Hill House
Shoppenhangers Road
Maidenhead
Berkshire
England
SL6 2QL

email: enquiries@openup.co.uk
world wide web: www.openup.co.uk

and Two Penn Plaza, New York, NY 10121-2289, USA

First published 2006

Reprinted 2010

A catalogue record of this book is available from the British Library

ISBN-10: 0 335 22117 3 (pb) 0 335 22118 1 (hb)
ISBN-13: 978 0 335 22117 2 (pb) 978 0 335 22118 9 (hb)

Library of Congress Cataloging-in-Publication Data
CIP data applied for

Typeset by RefineCatch Limited, Bungay, Suffolk
Printed in Great Britain by Bell & Bain Ltd., Glasgow

Mixed Sources
Product group from well-managed
forests and other controlled sources
www.fsc.org Cert no. TT-COC-002769
© 1996 Forest Stewardship Council

FSC

The McGraw·Hill Companies

Contents

List of figures

Figures

Preface to the third edition

Since the previous edition of this book was published, the context in which postgraduate education operates in the United Kingdom has changed dramatically. Various policy reviews[1] have had major impacts, with the consequence that there is now much more structure and joined-up thinking in postgraduate research programmes. Thus a few additional chapters tagged onto the end of the previous edition would not adequately have reflected the quality of the guidance to which the book aspires. So this third edition has been thoroughly and completely revised, with more cross-referencing between chapters. In particular, I have kept in mind the QAA Code of Practice for Postgraduate Research Programmes (see QAA 2004).

The Roberts Review (Roberts 2002) has resulted in institutions of higher education setting up schemes by which research students can plan, implement and monitor their personal development. As institutions have the flexibility to formulate their schemes as they see fit, it did not seem appropriate for me to advocate any one scheme in preference to any other. Instead this third edition has a new chapter which concentrates on the general principles of skills development, and which outlines the broad features of personal development planning (PDP).

The Internet has increasingly enabled huge amounts of up-to-date information to be available in ways never previously dreamed off, and institutions of higher education and allied organizations have their own websites. So, in writing this third edition, I have been far more aware of the distinction between supplying information and providing guidance on its use. My emphasis has come down firmly on providing guidance, so that readers can better make their own more informed decisions. Short extracts from various websites are included for illustrative purposes.

The use of computers as everyday tools has become commonplace in research as in all aspects of life. So it seemed right to draw readers' attention to those uses that are generally applicable to research across all fields of study. I have, though, stopped at that. It was never an aim of any edition of this book to delve into the huge and ever-growing topic of research methods and techniques. There are numerous dedicated works elsewhere, including of course those on the Internet.

With such powerful search engines now available, readers can readily search the Internet for further information about anything in the book. So the 'Web-

---

[1] For a full list of policy reviews, see the National Policy link from the UK GRAD Programme website: http://www.grad.ac.uk

sites' appendix of the previous editions seemed redundant and has been omitted. A dedicated chapter-by-chapter 'Further reading' section seemed similarly redundant, as did the 'Select bibliography', and both have also been omitted. Useful further reading guidance can still be found from the References section. Also, where I can honestly and personally recommend particular works which are not specifically referenced, they are mentioned at appropriate places in the main text.

As early as the prepublication trials of the first edition, academic staff called for a dedicated chapter for overseas students. I resisted for the first two editions on the basis that (i) most of the challenges that research students have to face are grounded in the postgraduate experience rather than in their being of any particular country of origin, and (ii) those challenges which do stem from being of a particular country of origin do not affect all 'overseas' students equally. However, I have been persuaded to include such a chapter for this third edition and hope that it meets the expectations of staff and students alike.

Academic staff also called for more on ethics, on evaluating the quality of literature and on being a graduate teaching assistant. I have met these calls with a new chapter on research ethics, two new chapters on reading round the subject and enlarged sections on taking up employment while on a research programme.

Students in certain fields of study called for more help with what they regarded as their first significant hurdle. In response there is also a new chapter on developing the research proposal.

Although I am formally retired, I retain involvements with postgraduate research; and all sorts of conversations and observations have informed my thinking for this third edition. I am particularly indebted to the following colleagues: Dr Helen Baker, University of Manchester; Professor Paul Bridges, University of Derby; Dr Mike Carter, University of Surrey; Professor Pam Denicolo, University of Reading; Professor Gerald Hammond, University of Manchester; Jeremy Hoad, former General Secretary of the National Postgraduate Committee; Dr Charles Juwah, Robert Gordon University, Aberdeen; Professor Roger Kain, University of Exeter; Professor Peter Mertens, BBSRC Institute for Animal Health; and Dr Paul Walker, University College London. Their help and support has been invaluable, and I thank them sincerely. Any errors of course are my own.

I also wish to thank the UK Research Councils and QAA for permission to reproduce their list of skills training requirements for research students[2] – see the Appendix. It fits ideally with the general ethos of the book.

---

[2] The joint statement on skills training requirements for research students was first published in 2002 by the UK Research Councils and AHRB (Arts and Humanities Research Board) – see Appendix 3 of the QAA Code of Practice (2004) – and is reproduced here in the Appendix. At the request of Communications at QAA, the statement has been amended to reflect the fact that AHRB has since become a research council.

I enjoyed researching and writing this third edition, and I hope that it proves useful to the next generation of research students and their supervisors.

Professor Pat Cryer
Visiting Professor for the Development of Graduate Education
University of Manchester

1

Why and how to use this book

Fortune favours the prepared mind.

(Louis Pasteur at www.brainyquote.com)

Why use this book? • How and why the book can help, whatever your degree programme • How and why the book can help, whatever your background and experience • How and why the book can help in your topic and discipline • How and why the book can help outside the United Kingdom • How the book can help in the face of rapid changes in postgraduate education • How and why the book can make a real difference to your research programme • The best order to work through the chapters • What the book does and does not do • What else should you know?

Why use this book?

Research should be fascinating and fulfilling, packed with intellectual excitement. If this is to be your experience, you need to appreciate that ways of working which proved effective for taught courses, important as they still are, are no longer enough. New skills and strategies need to be developed. This book introduces them, as collected from students and supervisors across a range of disciplines and from a range of universities, colleges and other institutions of higher education throughout the world.

How and why the book can help, whatever your degree programme

This book is primarily for students undertaking research for a higher (post-graduate) award. Perhaps you are registered on a programme in which a research component is assessed alongside taught components, or perhaps your programme is 'entirely' by research. As a student on either, or a prospective student on either, you should find this book useful irrespective of your research topic, field of study, stage of work or institutional attachment. The book will also be useful if you are working on an undergraduate project requiring a dissertation.

How and why the book can help, whatever your background and experience

For you, some parts of this book will be more relevant than others. One reason is that to do its job properly, the book has to be designed for the hypothetical student who needs a great deal of guidance, help and support throughout the entire span of a lengthy research programme and who has a very wide range of uncertainties. You are not such an individual. You bring to your work your own unique background, experience and needs, and the research component of your programme may be relatively short. Furthermore, although the advice in the book does have a wide applicability, it is not made up of absolute rights and wrongs, and there is no reason why you should not reject what does not seem likely to be helpful for you and use or adapt what does.

How and why the book can help in your topic and discipline

This book can help you, whatever your topic or discipline. Although it is unquestionably true that different disciplines do require different strategies and skills, the differences are often only in terminology and emphasis. Where fundamental differences do exist, the book points them out. Your task is to continually bear in mind that you have to interpret the advice for your own needs.

How and why the book can help outside the United Kingdom

This book is based on small-scale studies in Australia, Ireland, Singapore, South Africa and Sweden, as well as more major studies in the UK. Additionally, individuals from a wide range of other countries were interviewed. So although the book is rooted in the UK, this by no means limits its usefulness elsewhere. Differences do exist for students in different countries and cultures, but these too are often a matter of terminology and emphasis. For example the terms 'postgraduate student' and 'supervisor', as used in the UK, are equivalent to the terms 'graduate student' and 'adviser' as used in certain other English-speaking countries (as well as in a few UK institutions). Examples of different emphases might be whether students studying part-time are permitted a formal and possibly cheaper 'part-time' mode of registration, as is common in the UK but not necessarily elsewhere; the various types of postgraduate programme; the nominal duration of the research components within them; the nature and extent of any associated assessed taught components; the administrative structure of supervision; and the form and even existence of the oral/viva examination.

Yet the processes of handling research itself are essentially the same worldwide. So is interacting effectively with people with whom researchers have to work. Consequently, provided that you accept the task of interpreting the terminology and modifying the emphases, you should find the book useful irrespective of the country in which you are based.

How the book can help in the face of rapid changes in postgraduate education

This book is being published at a time when the pace of change in postgraduate education – certainly in the UK – has never been greater. Some changes are completed or well underway, and they are consequently fairly well understood. One example is in credit transfer schemes by which students can, in certain circumstances, transfer from one institution to another; another is in the alternative routes to the doctoral award. Other changes, though, are in the process of development, and no-one can be sure quite how they will eventually be implemented. A significant example is the agreement to find ways of unifying postgraduate education across the European Community (European Ministers of Education 1999). Countries outside the UK are doubtless watching developments carefully, which will, in time, almost certainly stimulate related changes which may or may not mirror those in the UK.

Where the changes are already in place, the book addresses them. Where they lie in the future but are not yet clearly defined, the book considers possibilities. Either way, the fundamental requirements for postgraduate research remain unaltered, even where the 'wrapping' or 'branding' may be different. So the book will remain of use for many years to come.

How and why the book can make a real difference to your research programme

A criticism of many study skills books is that they merely give advice. They do not help readers to adapt the advice for their own personal requirements or to internalize it so that its use becomes second nature. To overcome the criticism, this book provides a number of breaks in the main text where readers are invited to involve themselves by applying or interpreting what they have read for their own personal circumstances. The breaks are flagged as 'Points to ponder' and/or 'Suggestions'. You may prefer to consider them in your head, or write a note in the margin, although a sound option would be to keep a dedicated notebook for responses which seem to merit something substantial. Such a notebook could form part of the documentation in personal development planning (PDP), as described in Chapter 12.

The nature of the 'Points to ponder' and 'Suggestions' is such that there are no 'right' or 'wrong' answers. Where certain responses may have implications that were not previously mentioned, a discussion follows in the main text.

You will be able to react to many of the 'Points to ponder' and 'Suggestions' as you come to them, but some will require talking to someone who may not be with you at the time, or referring to something which may not be to hand. In these situations, think about what your responses might be and mark the pages for returning to later. Peel-off stickers of the Post-It type are ideal for the purpose.

You may find it helpful to work through the book with other students. They need not be in the same field as you because the skills and strategies involved are either independent of field of study or are presented in such a way as to help you identify the norms in your own field. In fact, as later chapters will show, there are many good reasons for developing the habit of working in groups and forging links with researchers in other disciplines.

The best order to work through the chapters

If you are a new postgraduate research student, you will find that the order of the early chapters is roughly that in which you need them. However, as your work progresses, your needs are likely to open up along several fronts, because no part of postgraduate research can take place entirely in isolation from other parts. So, even though, at any one time, you may want to concentrate on one particular chapter, you will also need to have some idea of what is in the other chapters. In particular, your needs in the middle to later part of the research programme need to inform what you do from the outset. It would thus be a mistake to delay too long before studying the later chapters.

If you come across this book when you are some way into your research programme, you will probably want to start with the chapter about whatever is occupying you most at the time. If so, you would be well advised to follow all the cross references in the text, in order not to miss out on pertinent advice given in an earlier chapter or flagged up for a later chapter.

What the book does and does not do

It is important at the outset to be clear about what the book does not do:

- The book is not concerned with the sorts of work strategies and study skills which are generally accepted as helpful for students on taught courses. If you feel that you need a refresher course, there is no shortage of useful material.
- The book does not attempt to guide individuals through the design and implementation of their own research project. Apart from the obvious limitations of length, this is for two reasons. One is that the book is for students across disciplines, and research design and practice do, for good reason, vary considerably from one field of study to another. The other reason is that research design, with all that ensues from it, needs to be developed and refined over time, through face-to-face discussion with people who know all the aspects and ramifications of the work and who are experienced researchers in the general discipline area. These people are, first and foremost, supervisors. They are, or should be, closest to the work of the students in their care, and their advice should always take precedence over anything in any book.
- The book does not attempt to reproduce large chunks of information which is readily available on the Internet, however pertinent it may seem. Instead the book provides extracts from such material, as available when the book

went to press. From these extracts, it is a simple matter to pull out keywords for a web search on related and more detailed current material.

- The book cannot be a manual for the various uses in research of information technology (IT). IT is developing at an enormous rate on numerous fronts, so there can be no substitute for current manuals and local technical support. The book facilitates use of these by indicating the types of IT which are, or may be, helpful for particular purposes, so giving direction to enquiries.

- Where the administrative procedures associated with working for a particular award shape the strategies and skills required, the book touches on them, but it does no more. Administrative procedures always vary from department to department, from institution to institution and from country to country, and they are liable to change at any time. So do not rely on this book for them. Always check the current position at the institution concerned.

- Finally, the book does not address topics which depend crucially on the field of study or the nature of the research, or which are subject to regular updating. Common examples are health and safety, and the finer details of intellectual property rights and quality management. Responsibilities for these lie with supervisors and institutions.

In summary, the book is firmly and solely concerned with helping students involved in research to make sound decisions and to develop appropriate non-discipline-specific strategies and skills.

What else should you know?

Understanding the need for work strategies and study skills, and knowing what they are, are the two first steps towards developing them, but they are only first steps. You need to practise them continuously, think about how well they are working for you, adapt them to suit you better and then keep on practising them. This cannot be emphasized enough.

2

Exploring routes, opportunities and funding

A door that seems to stand open must be of a person's size, or it is not the door that Providence means for that person.
(Henry Ward Becher at www.quotegarden.com
(modified for sexist language))

The profusion of postgraduate awards • Credit rating at postgraduate level • Modes of postgraduate registration • Fees and sources of funding • Choosing the type of course or programme • Is postgraduate research right for you? • Making a short list of possible institutions • Towards a research topic

The profusion of postgraduate awards

The profusion of routes and opportunities for postgraduate 'research' would have been unrecognizable only a few years ago. Even where the term 'research' appears in the title or description, it may not be clear at first sight whether this applies to taught modules about research or supervised research-style investigations.

At one extreme of the profusion are the relatively lengthy and traditional PhDs (or DPhils) which are entirely by research. There may be occasional taught components, but these do not formally count for the final assessment.

At the other extreme, the research is in the form of short investigations or projects as part of otherwise taught programmes. A full listing of the routes and opportunities in institutions of higher education in the UK is available online from the Prospects website. Box 2.1 shows its menu for 'Postgraduate Study'. Moves are in hand to develop a common model for the PhD across the European Union – see the extract in Box 2.2.

This chapter explores routes, opportunities and funding for postgraduate study and research. Some parts will be directly useful worldwide – e.g. whether or not postgraduate research is a sound course of action for any individual; and how to go about choosing a suitable institution and research topic. Other parts of the chapter are orientated to the UK system. There are parallels elsewhere which can be followed up on institutional websites.

Credit rating at postgraduate level

Credit accumulation and transfer schemes enable students to build up credits by studying in a modular fashion. The idea is that credits can be either traded in for an award or accumulated towards another award at a higher level and possibly at another institution – although it is at the discretion of any institution whether or not it accepts the validity of credits from elsewhere. The scheme in the UK is known as CATS (Credit Accumulation and Transfer), and the European equivalent is the ECTS (European Credit Transfer System).

Box 2.1 The menu for Postgraduate Study on the Prospects website

Prospects is the UK's official graduate careers website where 'careers' are interpreted in the widest sense.

Find courses and research
Latest courses
Institutional profiles
Departmental profiles
International students
Why do postgraduate study?
Funding my further study
Work related courses
Explore studying abroad
Apply online

(Prospects undated)

Box 2.2 Towards a common model for higher education across Europe

In 1999, in the Bologna agreement, the UK signed up to the creation of a common model for Higher Education in Europe. This will include a three- or four-year first Bachelor degree, a second stage leading to a Masters degree, and a third stage leading to a Doctoral degree.

Many of the forty countries now party to the agreement have taken steps to institute a three-year first degree. In Berlin, ministers decided to specify degrees (Bachelor and Master) in terms of learning outcomes, rather than simply number of hours of study. '[Member states are encouraged to] elaborate a framework of comparable and compatible qualifications for their higher education systems which should seek to describe qualifications in terms of workload, level, learning outcomes, competencies, and profiles.' Co-ordination will be undertaken by a European Qualifications agency and there will be an 'overarching framework of qualifications'.

Where this leaves the path of a UK student to a PhD is unclear . . .

(Salinger undated)

Australia has a similar system, as do various other countries. Normally 'postgraduate certificates' require only a few months of full-time study – and correspondingly more part-time – and are worth 60 credits. 'Postgraduate diplomas' require up to twice as long and are worth 120 credits. Then come 'masters degrees' at 180 credits. The full research degrees of MPhil, PhD and DPhil are deemed to be different types of award and are not credit rated.

Modes of postgraduate registration

Two common modes of registration are 'full-time' and 'part-time'. Essentially they are distinguished by their fees (part-time being cheaper) and the minimum and maximum periods of allowed registration. There is not normally any formal expectation of how much time, proportionally, is meant by 'part-time'. The maximum limit on the period of registration enables institutions to limit the likelihood of the research becoming out of date. It is enforced quite rigorously, so students need to get down to work quickly and manage their time efficiently. Longitudinal studies (which monitor over a number of years) are no longer options, and original ideas which capitalize on the unexpected may be too risky to follow through. Extensions can be granted but they are by no means automatic and need to be backed by a good case. An even better case needs to be made if funds are to be extended to cover the extra time. Students can all too easily find themselves at the end of their research programme with no qualification and no funds to continue with their registration. The minimum limit on the period of registration prevents students from taking advantage of the cheaper part-time fees to complete as quickly as full-timers. For details consult the websites of individual institutions.

A part-time research degree is not to be taken on lightly, as it requires considerable energy and commitment over a number of years. Certainly many part-timers do succeed, but many also give up. So prospective students need to think carefully before going for the part-time route and be particularly careful to check that their integration into the academic community will be taken seriously by the institution. Additionally, the research programme should not be over-ambitious in terms of travelling and data collection and analysis. The challenges facing part-time students are considered further in Chapter 10, which would be worth reading before committing yourself to the part-time route.

Modes of registration are also available through collaborative programmes, through which students can undertake their research at another institution, which may or may not be academic, or split between different institutions. There are also modes of registration which allow students to spend long periods working away from the institution, although residential periods are also required. At the moment it is rare, but not non-existent, for institutions to run PhD programmes entirely by distance learning.

Fees and sources of funding

Funding issues are complex. Fees for postgraduate research are not uniform across disciplines or institutions. For up-to-date information do a web-search on keywords based on the extract in Box 2.3. Then, for detailed information, consult the websites of specific institutions, which often include helpful advice for prospective students. (Prospective students looking at institutions outside their home countries will also find it helpful to read the early sections of Chapter 11.) Remember that institutions require fees up front. Vague promises are unacceptable.

When looking for funds it is worth bearing the following in mind:

- Bursaries, scholarships, awards, grants or studentships may be available from some institutions in return for teaching, tutoring or assessment of undergraduates. However, do think carefully about whether you want to tie yourself down for the commitments involved, more on which is in Chapter 10. Some schemes come with no strings because they are designed

---

Box 2.3 Examples of advice on sources of funding on the Internet

See the actual website to follow through the links (underlined), or do a web search to locate comparable information.

The Prospects website is the official source of information on postgraduate study and funding and has information on funding your study including the latest funding opportunities.

The hotcourses.com website has a searchable database of funding opportunities for courses.

The Hobsons Postgrad website also has information on sources of post-graduate funding.

The Careers Group, University of London Online Careers Library has useful links to information on postgraduate study including funding.

The support4learning website has details of potential postgraduate funding sources.

The Scholarship Search UK website has a search facility for funded post-graduate studentships.

The scholarships and funding page on this site has details of some current funding opportunities for postgraduate study and research both in the UK and abroad.

The University of Leicester has one open research scholarship for students of any discipline. You should contact the Graduate Office for further details.

Postgraduate studentships are advertised on the jobs.ac.uk website.

The national and specialist press (for example the Guardian and the Times Higher Education Supplement) has details of funded research degree opportunities, especially in science and medical areas.

(University of Leicester Careers Service undated)

---

simply to boost the departmental or institutional research output by attracting research students.

- It is possible to be paid to do a specified piece of research under a contract which allows the contract researcher to be registered for a research degree. This provides a helpful source of funding and a ready-made research topic. However, before accepting contract research, do realize that it is not likely to last for the full duration of a doctoral programme and that it is normally to produce findings that are in the interests of the provider of the contract, which may not include original work of a doctoral standard. So contract researchers usually have to do additional work in their own time for a PhD.
- Some collaborative modes enable a student to receive a salary from an employer who may also contribute to the fees. Collaborative research

can be excellent from the point of view of funding, but, where the research topic is one which addresses a need of the employer, it is crucially important that the academic supervisor considers it suitable for the postgraduate level concerned, and that supervisors in the place of employment work well in a team with the academic supervisors. There is more on this in Chapter 6.

- Students looking for awards from institutions outside their home country may be able to arrange for their government or employer to provide funds. This normally carries severe time pressures, the implications of which are considered further in Chapter 11.
- Many funding bodies have strict deadlines for application, so it is important to explore options as early as possible.
- Fees do not cover the cost of living which can vary considerably from one location to another.

It is always worth raising the matter of funding during exploratory contacts with an institution, just in case there are untapped sources available.

Choosing the type of course or programme

A common factor in the choice of a postgraduate programme – research or otherwise – is how it can be expected to enhance career prospects and earning power. If this is in your mind, you need to weigh likely enhanced earning power against the costs of fees and any associated loss of earnings while studying. Loss of earnings are particularly important with full-time registration on the lengthier doctorates and for individuals who are not supported by an employer and who have debts accumulated from undergraduate study. Also bear in mind that although employers in some areas like to employ holders of doctorates to work at the frontiers of knowledge (such as in academia and research units), many prefer graduates of shorter programmes. Such individuals command lower salaries, and the employers can then afford to provide the training themselves, customized for their own requirements.

Postgraduate certificates and postgraduate diplomas are frequently orientated to a profession, and, being short, can be undertaken either on a part-time basis while in paid employment, or as a gap-filler between jobs.

Many 'taught' masters courses are also professionally orientated. They take longer than diplomas, but are increasingly becoming an expected qualification in the professions.

Professional doctorates and practice-based doctorates are undertakings of several years, which provide a rounded knowledge of investigative techniques pertinent to specific professions. As well as the taught modules, these doctorates normally include a short investigation for which the output can be a thesis/dissertation or a portfolio of work. The structure of the NewRoute PhD is broadly similar in that it too has taught modules with a thesis/dissertation. The doctorates are taught but still retain research training and elements of research practice. Doctoral programmes with a substantial taught element usually lead to awards that include the name of the discipline in their titles (e.g. EdD for Doctor of Education). The different 'branding' of these doctorates is supposed to make them more understandable to people overseas who are familiar with the United States system, but they do not appear to be as popular as the regular MPhils and PhDs/DPhils.

Awards entirely by research, such as the MPhil and PhD (or DPhil), can also be made to support the needs of a particular profession or place of employment if they research out answers to problems of particular concern to that profession or place of employment. They can also keep career options open, even in subject areas which do not seem to relate directly to employment – see Chapter 22. For a career in academia, they are increasingly becoming a requirement, and they remain the most popular postgraduate research route. When taken 'full-time', the lifestyle is flexible and students are very much their own bosses, which provides its own form of professional training. Registration for a PhD is normally three years full-time or six years part-time. Registration for an MPhil is shorter; the exact period depends on the institution. Both MPhil and PhD programmes can offer the option of an extension of one year for writing up a thesis. The normal required route to a PhD is to register for an MPhil and then, if progress is good enough, to transfer registration to PhD (see Chapter 18). The exceptions are normally for students who already hold a Masters degree in a relevant subject.

Another possibility which keeps options open is the MRes (Master of research) which has been gaining momentum in the UK in recent years. As its name implies, it provides a broad Masters level training in research. It also involves a wide range of activities across broadly related disciplines. Holders of MRes awards are reported to be attractive to employers and to 'hit the ground running' when they go on to do higher research degrees.

A route known as the '1+3' is becoming increasingly favoured, particularly by the UK Research Councils. It is designed for students wishing to go on to a PhD but without a prior Masters degree with appropriate research training content. The route involves a one-year taught masters in an appropriate subject area prior to progression to the standard three-year MPhil/PhD registration.

Because structure can be so confusing, it is important to check the details of a course or programme against your own requirements. Pay attention to the balance between taught and research components, what is to be taught, how the assessment works and whether academic or professional needs are primarily addressed. This book uses terms such as 'research' degree, or degree 'entirely by research' for programmes for which only the research component counts towards assessment. The most common examples are the PhD/DPhil and the MPhil, as they are commonly offered. The book uses terms such as 'other' to describe programmes for which the research component is assessed alongside other assessments, such as in most diplomas and Masters degrees.

Points to ponder

- What type of postgraduate programme would seem likely to suit you best?

Is postgraduate research right for you?

If you are thinking of undertaking a degree which is entirely by research, it is important to examine your motives before going ahead. Two categories can aid your thinking:

- motives which are essential if you are to succeed; and
- motives which will merely support your progress but which, alone, will not be enough.

Fortunately, many students who start out with motives in the second category do find that the 'essential' ones develop over time, as a natural product of trying to do the work well.

Motives such as anticipated career advancement or satisfying someone else are understandable and common. However, they are best regarded as supporting rather than essential, because, alone, they are unlikely to be enough. With a quite short research component in an otherwise taught programme, you may just get away with it. You certainly will not for a degree that is entirely by research. These degrees are seldom failed, but, not at all uncommonly, they are simply just not completed. Reasons lie either with detrimental personal circumstances – see Chapter 10 – or with lack of the right motivation.

Motivations which are essential are almost certainly intellectual ones, for example:

- developing a trained mind
- satisfying intellectual curiosity
- responding to a challenge
- experiencing an academic community
- contributing to knowledge
- fulfilling a lifelong ambition.

The extract in Box 2.4 underlines this.

Box 2.4 Reasons for doing a PhD, as expressed by students nearing the end of their programme

The verdict was unanimous. They did a PhD for love . . . They were doing a PhD because it made them happy. These are people who are not pretending when they say they are fascinated by [what they are doing]. Their eyes light up when the librarian brings them a big, heavy pile of dusty books . . . [In] the chemistry lab, things are, essentially, no different . . . They talk about the 'buzz of discovery' and 'loving what they do'.

(Taaffe 1998: vi)

If your sole aim is to get a postgraduate qualification as easily and quickly as possible, you would probably be storing up trouble for yourself by going ahead.

Points to ponder

- What are your reasons for wanting to undertake a research degree? Be honest with yourself and as specific as possible.
- How do these reasons fit into the above categories of 'essential' and 'supporting' motives?
- Turn to Chapter 10 and scan it to find out if there are any personal circumstances that might be detrimental to you on a postgraduate research programme.
- Hence, is postgraduate research right for you?

Making a short list of possible institutions

The choice of institution may be obvious for prospective students who are fortunate enough to have an institution nearby which happens to offer the programme that they want at a price they can afford. For the less fortunate, this section suggests some factors, in no particular order, which could influence choice.

- Where a bursary, grant, scholarship or other award is offered for research in the field of study of one's choice.

- Where a group of friends or compatriots are registered. This ensures the ongoing support of friends – and, for students from non-English-speaking countries, social interaction in their own language. (How far this may be beneficial is considered in Chapter 11.)
- Where one did one's first degree. Knowledge of the institution and department makes it easy to have informal exploratory discussions with the academic staff and prospective supervisors. One knows the locality and has friends there.
- Where one can live particularly cheaply, possibly with extended family or friends.
- Where there are attractive extramural facilities. Theatres, museums and galleries, for example, are most accessible from city institutions, whereas some types of sporting activity may be more accessible from rural and coastal institutions.
- Where the department appears particularly caring towards its postgraduates. Early signs of this may show up in clear and appealing websites and prospectuses and in fast and personalized responses to exploratory communications.
- Where there is an internationally renowned research group in the proposed research area. Such groups can be identified by recommendation or by checking through relevant research journals.
- Where one is already employed, so that one can take advantage of reduced fees for employees. (This may involve being supervised by a close colleague, which can bring both problems and benefits.)
- Where there is a Graduate School. (The existence of a Graduate School does demonstrate that an institution has given thought and resources to postgraduate research, but it demonstrates little else. Graduate Schools differ markedly in structure and responsibilities, and some excellent institutions do not have one.)

The first step in choosing an institution is to think carefully about relative priorities of these types of consideration. Useful general information is available on the Internet. Other sources include public libraries and careers offices of most educational establishments. Also check out advertisements in the national press and keep an eye open for any national postgraduate fair coming to your area where a large number of institutions are likely to have information stands. For prospective students from outside the UK, looking for an institution in the UK, the Prospects website and the local British Council office should be able to help, and some UK institutions send representatives overseas to meet prospective students. If you are spoilt for choice, see the extract in Box 2.5.

Box 2.5 Choosing the 'right' university

Recommending one Institution against another is not one of the services we [The National Postgraduate Committee] provide. I suggest you look up the Quality Assurance Association* for Higher Education website <www.qaa. ac.uk>, which gives details of reports on academic departments. You can also consult the Higher Education and Research Opportunities in the United Kingdom website <www.hero.ac.uk>, which covers all higher education institutes in the UK and carries their prospectuses. If the QAA has given the department a good grading, they'll mention it! You can also contact the Students' Unions at the institutions, to ask if there's anything you should know. If there is, they should tell you.

Note: ** Now the Quality Assurance Agency.*

(Ewing undated)

Points to ponder

- Bearing all the above considerations in mind, what you are particularly looking for in an institution for postgraduate study?

Towards a research topic

The choice and refinement of a research topic needs due consideration in discussion with the individuals who will supervise. Chapters 3 and 4 delve into the practical considerations, and you would do well to read them before committing yourself. This section is a brief orientation to set you thinking.

How a topic for research is selected and refined is likely to vary considerably from one field of study to another, and to depend on how, if at all, it is linked to organizations outside academia.

In the arts and humanities, for example, students will probably be given a free rein with their choice of topic, subject of course to the department's ability to supervise it. Such students have to put in considerable work in the library to identify and justify their topics and as worthy of attention.

In natural science subjects, on the other hand, the research may have to fit in with the availability of expensive equipment provided under a research grant and with what other members of a research group are doing. Then the research topic and the rationale for doing it are provided, and if prospective students don't like this, or think that appropriate enthusiasm is unlikely to develop, they should look elsewhere. It is never a good idea to commit oneself to years of something uninspiring, just because of the availability of a place to work on it.

The research topic is similarly provided, at least in terms of broad area, where employers are meeting the costs with the purpose of producing answers to questions of concern to themselves; or where the student is employed as a researcher under contract.

In the current climate of rapid change and resource reduction, a few departments in a few institutions may not be as careful as they might be about checking that they can provide a student with what is necessary to research a particular topic effectively. It is in your own interests to check for yourself that you have found a department that can provide a supervisor, resources and training commensurate with your personal needs and interests. Alternatively you can amend your topic to fit the department's ability to supervise it, although it is essential that you should feel comfortable about doing so. The decision should not be made lightly and it may require considerable discussion.

3

Making an application

Look before you leap.

(Proverb)

The importance of pre-registration groundwork • Timing first contacts with an institution • Being interviewed for a place • Checking out supervisory matters • Agreeing work with or for an outside organization • Handling other formalities • Making an application • Handling an offer • Using waiting time constructively

The importance of pre-registration groundwork

It is crucially important for research students to be in institutions which supply the kind of support that is necessary for their success and the kind of environment in which they can work comfortably and effectively. The choice of institution therefore needs very careful consideration. Pages 15–16 in the previous chapter gave pointers about drawing up a short-list, and this chapter moves on with suggestions about refining it, making an application, and handling an offer. The chapter concludes with suggestions on how to make good use of the time between accepting an offer and starting the research programme.

Timing first contacts with an institution

Ideally prospective students need to express their interest in a place well before the date they wish to start. The institution's website or prospectus will give details on how to go about this. Do be careful to follow instructions and to make all communications neat, to-the-point, grammatically correct and free of spelling and typing errors, as first impressions count. If necessary, get someone knowledgeable to help. If you are hoping for a particular named principal supervisor, it would be worth contacting him or her by email in advance.

Making an initial contact with an institution in no way ties you to applying there. In fact, it will be worth visiting a number of possible institutions to see for yourself which one is likely to suit you best – see the extract in Box 3.1. However your visit will involve staff in considerable work; so it is unreasonable to visit unless your interest is serious. Having visited, if you then decide against an institution, a short note to the effect would be appreciated.

Being interviewed for a place

A visit to the institution will involve an interview, even if it is not referred to as such. The extract in Box 3.2 suggests some of the points that an interview panel is likely be looking for. It will pay to work on them. Also prepare to explain verbally what you want to do and why. Depending on the nature of your funding – see pages 10–12 in Chapter 2 – you may be asked to produce a one or two page document about it, which may be called a 'statement of interest' or 'statement of purpose'.

Otherwise it is best to regard the interactions as two-way interviews. Try to interview the departmental staff as much as they are interviewing you, to see whether you feel you could work productively in that research environment.

Box 3.1 The value of visiting an institution before deciding whether to register there

If you can manage it, visit the institutions and pick the one where you feel most welcome. A warm welcome is no guarantee of academic brilliance, but it probably means that you'll get the most out of what the Institution has to offer – and a [grade 3 department] which gives you its all is better than a [grade 4 one] which takes your money and leaves you to fend for yourself.

(Ewing undated)

Box 3.2 How to impress at an interview for a research studentship

The following is a checklist of what an interview panel is likely to be looking for in the successful candidate:

- *Ability to grasp concepts and to reason analytically*
- *Motivation and perseverance in achieving objectives*
- *Capacity for independent thought*
- *Organizational skills*
- *Independence as a learner*
- *Self-confidence (but not over-bearance)*
- *Nature and extent of any relevant work experience*
- *Nature and extent of any previously undertaken training in research*
- *Likelihood of establishing a good working relationship with the allocated supervisor and others working in related areas*
- *Language skills, which are particularly important for overseas candidates who have never previously studied in the UK.*

(Adapted from Engineering and Physical Sciences
Research Council 1995: 5/4)

Make sure that you meet other research students to judge whether there seems to be a healthy and supportive critical mass of them and of research-active staff. Also take the opportunity to check students' office accommodation and the other facilities provided. The former is worth doing even if you will be part-time, because it indicates the department's values in connection with its research students. Chapter 5 considers office facilities in more detail.

Checking out supervisory matters

It is a rare institution that does not adopt a team or committee approach to doctoral supervision. The team can be anything from two upwards. This approach goes some way to overcoming the problem of students being left unsupervised if one supervisor is away or indisposed, because another can fill in the gap. It does, however, also bring its own risks – see pages 46–47 of Chapter 6.

On your visit, it is important to meet the person who will be your principal (i.e. academic) supervisor. It is often said that although a research student's formal registration is with an institution, it is, for all practical purposes, with a supervisor because effective supervision is the key to success. So talk to this person and ask yourself honestly if he or she is someone you feel you can work with over several years.

Depending on the nature of your proposed research and the norms of the department concerned, you may be asked for suggestions for additional people to include in your supervisory team. Such individuals do not need to play an academic role, but they must be able to provide ongoing guidance on some aspect of the work. They could, for example, have specialist knowledge of a particular research tool or a management framework in a particular organization, and they may be able to serve entirely at a distance.

The timing and location of supervisions do not necessarily have to be within working hours at the institution. There are all sorts of possibilities in this respect, but any which are at all unusual need negotiating in advance.

It is important to realize that good supervisors, like all good employees, are in demand elsewhere. They may move on, and their students may or may not be able or willing to move with them. Institutions will supply replacements, but how effectively they will be able to fill the gap must be open to question.

Agreeing work with or for an outside organization

Where the proposed research is to be conducted with or for an outside organization, there will need to be some sort of agreement between all the parties. Three issues in particular tend to cause problems if they are not openly addressed at the outset. They all concern potential conflicts of interest.

One is the issue of confidentiality, i.e. if and when the work can be published in journal articles and even in a publicly available thesis. The second concerns any financial advantages that the work may yield, as it is not unknown for commercial partners to make considerable money on the backs of students' research, while the academics and students get nothing. The third issue concerns ensuring that a project of value to an outside organization is at the appropriate level for the award concerned. For this, you must rely on the experience of supervisors in the academic institution. However, research is necessarily a journey into the unknown. So you may need to increase or decrease the scope of the project as it progresses, or give it a more significant or original slant. Advice on all of these is given in later chapters.

Handling other formalities

Before making an application, you need to check that the formalities are in order. These will certainly include entry qualifications, referees and funding arrangements, but there may be others. The special case for students from 'overseas' is considered in Chapter 11.

Making an application

Once you are certain that postgraduate work is right for you; that you have found the 'right' institution and research topic; and that the formalities are in order, you can go ahead with an application. This is normally straightforward, as it merely involves following the institution's instructions. It is important to stress again about getting someone to check over your application if you are at all unsure whether it will show you to advantage.

Handling an offer

Once you receive an offer from an institution, it is only fair to accept or reject it relatively quickly, rather than expect it to be kept open for an indefinite period.

A word of warning here about unsolicited emails which offer non-existent places for a fee. There is no way that anyone can bypass normal application procedures. A similar warning is in order about emails which offer certificated qualifications, without the buyers having to do anything but part with their money. Box 3.3 reproduces one of them. With communications so easy via the

---

Box 3.3 Worthless qualifications from non-accredited institutions available for a fee

A typical unsolicited email offering a worthless qualification for a fee, to be treated with the contempt it deserves:

> *Academic Qualifications available from prestigious NON-ACCREDITED universities.*
> *Do you have the knowledge and the experience but lack the qualifications?*
> *Are you getting turned down time and time again for the job of your dreams because you just don't have the right letters after your name?*
> *Get the prestige that you deserve today!*
> *Move ahead in your career today!*
> *Bachelors, Masters and PhD's* [sic] *available in your field!*
> *No examinations! No classes! No textbooks!*
> *Call to register and receive your qualifications within days!*
> *24 hours a day 7 days a week!*
> *Confidentiality assured!*
> *[Telephone number given, although it might just have easily have been a transient email or website address]*

(An unsolicited email which arrived on the author's computer, 2006)

Internet, qualifications can be readily verified, and anyone who tries to use a bogus one would be guilty of fraud. The only people who gain from bogus qualifications are those who make money by selling them.

Using waiting time constructively

Some institutions admit students for research degrees at any time. More usually there are several formal entry dates throughout the year, and it is best to aim for one of these, so as to take advantage of induction programmes. If there is a significant delay between accepting an offer and taking it up, you are fortunate, because you can do a great deal to make life easier for yourself later. Here are some suggestions:

- If you do not already have keyboard skills, acquiring them must be an early priority. You may have 'got by' until now by using only two fingers, and you may continue to do so, but you would be putting yourself at an unnecessary disadvantage. If you can learn on a regular course, all the better, but there are cheap and effective alternatives which can be used in one's own time. The best is probably one of the self-instructional tutorials, which may be bought on CD-Rom from various sales outlets and which run on personal computers.
- If you are not already adept with email and web searching, these should be your next priorities. You can expect your fellow students to be skilled in them already, so although some training will probably be provided by the institution, it will be worth getting up to speed in advance. The extract of Box 3.4 shows that there is no shortage of online help with web searching.

Box 3.4 Some examples of advice on how to search the Internet productively

See the actual website (www.cln.org) to follow through the links (below), or do a web search to locate comparable information:

- *Boolean Searching on the Internet*
- *Conducting Research on the Internet*
- *Evaluating Internet Resources*
- *How to Choose a Search Engine or Research Database*
- *Quick Reference Guide to Search Engine Syntax*
- *Searching the Internet: Recommended Sites and Search Techniques*

(Community Learning Network undated)

- The institution will almost certainly provide training in the use of whatever computer tools are necessary for your research programme. There are, however, basic tools which everyone needs, and if you are not already adept at them, it will be a good use of time to work on word processing with Microsoft Word and on spreadsheets with Microsoft Excel. In particular, explore how to use the time-saving tools of Microsoft Word, as explained on pages 165–167 of Chapter 16. It is probably best to delay on the other basic tools, because supervisors may recommend alternative packages better suited to your field of study. For information, though, commonly used ones, in order of ease of learning, are Microsoft PowerPoint for presentations, Endnote for bibliographic management and Microsoft Access for databases.
- It is also worth finding out more about what lies ahead. You can start by following links on the home page of the institution's website. Try to sort out banking arrangements and living accommodation well in advance. Where relevant, passports and permits, are also best organized sooner rather than later.
- If you have access to a good library, it is never too early to start reading around your proposed research topic. There is advice on this in Chapters 7 and 8.
- Finally, many of the suggestions in this book require elapsed thinking time (an incubation period) to generate the greatest benefit. So it would be a good use of time to peruse the rest of the book now.

4

Producing the research proposal

A research proposal is a piece of work that, ideally, would convince scholars that your project has the following three merits: conceptual innovation; methodological rigour; and rich substantive content.
(School of Advanced Study, University of London undated)

The requirement to write one's own research proposal • How the research proposal helps everyone concerned • The limitations of a research proposal • Essential elements of a research proposal • Fleshing out the research proposal • Putting boundaries on the research proposal • The writing style of the research proposal • Issues of time when preparing a research proposal • Adapting the proposal to apply for a small grant or other funds

The requirement to write one's own research proposal

In many cases, an institution will register students only when they have written and successfully submitted their own research proposals. This may or may not apply to you, and here are the reasons:

1 Where research is to involve expensive equipment or major collaborations, it is only realistic for institutions to take on research students after the funding is in place. By this time, the proposals have already been written (by academics) and the grants have already been awarded. A student who

is accepted for work on such research has to fill the niche for which the funding was awarded. There may be room for manoeuvre on details, but seldom in the early stages. Such a student is seldom required to write more than a short statement of interest or intent.

2 On the other hand, an institution can more readily take on students who wish to work on small scale research which requires negligible funding (apart of course from tuition fees) and whose research does not directly affect that of others. However, the institution does need to be convinced that the research is a practical proposition. Hence the need for a sound research proposal. If you have to write such a proposal, then this chapter is for you. Its suggestions are for 'full' research programmes such as the PhD and MPhil, but they can readily be adapted for programmes with only a component of research. The chapter closes with some advice on adapting the proposal as an application for a 'small' grant.

There is more on how research is different in different disciplines in Chapter 8.

How the research proposal helps everyone concerned

The value of the research proposal is twofold: to safeguard institutions and to help students to prepare themselves for what lies ahead.

Without a suitable research proposal, institutions might find themselves agreeing to take responsibility for research that would not be viable. There are all sorts of reasons, many of them unpredictable. Perhaps, for example, a vaguely defined research topic might subsequently prove difficult to clarify and refine. Or perhaps no suitable supervisor can be allocated. Or perhaps the methodological or ideological approaches of a supervisor and student turn out to be incompatible. Or perhaps language problems need addressing before the research can go ahead.

For students, the process of developing a research proposal should generate confidence about what lies ahead. If, instead, they find that it is making them feel progressively more uneasy, they need to establish why, while there is still time to do something about it.

The limitations of a research proposal

Useful as a research proposal is, it is, unfortunately, not a foolproof safeguard. One reason is that it can require prospective students to make decisions about research design before they have necessarily had adequate research training or read much around the subject. Another reason is that research, by its very nature, is unpredictable.

The limitations of research proposals are well known. So some supervisors in some institutions may pay scant attention to them or use them merely as discussion documents from which to develop students and progress the research. Even in institutions where students' proposals have to pass the close scrutiny of one or more committees before registration is permitted, more flexible attitudes are usually adopted afterwards.

Essential elements of a research proposal

Each institution will probably have its own terminology for its formal requirements for a research proposal. In general terms, though, students will be expected to show that the proposed work:

- Is worth researching
- Lends itself to being researched
- Is sufficiently challenging for the level of award concerned
- Can be completed within the appropriate time
- Can be adequately resourced
- Is not likely to be subjected to any serious constraints
- Is capable of being done by the student.

These criteria may seem deceptively simple, but each one can subsume a multitude of others and, depending on the nature of the proposal, there is likely to be cross linking between them. The detail and emphasis for your particular research proposal must depend on your topic, the department, school or faculty in which you are registered (particularly if your work is multidisciplinary) and the rigour required by your institution, which will be the final arbiter. So use the points to set yourself thinking. You will soon see how some depend on others, and then suitable headings and cross-references will probably present themselves naturally. It is very unlikely indeed that the headings that you end up with will directly reflect the above bullet points.

You may find that a technique known as a 'mind-map' is helpful in developing the ideas about what to include in the proposal. On the other hand, you may not. Mind maps do seem to generate strong feelings, one way or the other. If, having read what follows, you prefer to find your own alternative ways of developing content, there is no reason why you shouldn't do so. A mind map is a technique for freeing the mind from the constrained and ordered viewpoint from which it has been seeing a problem or issue. It provides an overview, which shows at a glance all the components of the problem or issue and the links between them. This tends to stimulate new and creative ideas. The technique is best explained by trying to develop one yourself, based on Figure 4.1.

Suggestions and points to ponder

- To illustrate the use of mind maps to develop the content of a research proposal, copy Figure 4.1. The spokes are already labelled with the bullet points mentioned above.

1 Look at any one of the spokes and let your mind wander over its topic and let sub-topics occur to you.
2 For each newly identified sub-topic, draw a new spoke and label it.
3 When no more such sub-topics occur, move on to the next spoke. Let your mind continue to wander, and draw and label additional spokes for each sub-topic.
4 Continue like this until you run out of ideas.
5 You will probably find that some sub-topics occur on more than one spoke. If so, link them together. Your final result will look something like Figure 4.2, although hopefully containing more information. Figure 4.2 has had to be edited for size, and anyway, does not apply to your particular research proposal.
6 Do you feel that the technique has helped you to develop the content of your proposal?
7 Now read on for further ideas about 'fleshing out' the content.

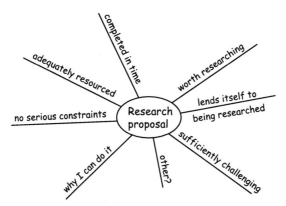

Figure 4.1   A mind map with spokes labelled to aid thinking about the content of a research proposal.

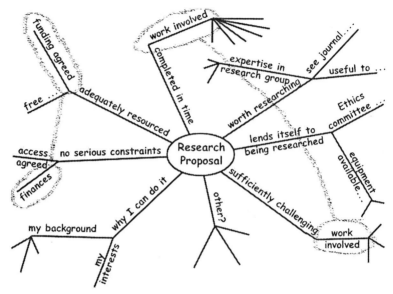

Figure 4.2 A more fully developed mind map showing common ideas linked.

Fleshing out the research proposal

A sound research proposal requires much more than the orientation in this chapter. Obviously supervisors will help, but they are busy people, who will expect you to do your own groundwork. So you would do well to dip into other chapters of the book now.

To show that the work is worth researching, you will need to set it into a context of other work that has and has not been done in the general area. This requires a literature survey, for which Chapters 7 and 8 give advice. Chapter 8 also flags up issues of methodology and terminology which should guide your thinking. It will also be important to scan forward to Chapter 9 to alert yourself to ethical considerations which, depending on your particular research topic, may vary in importance from minimal to very considerable indeed; and to Chapter 19 on claiming originality . . .

Regarding length and detail, you will need to look at the requirements of your institution, as listed in the student handbook or the website. For the norms of your field of study, look at some research proposals which have previously been accepted.

The extract in Box 4.1 lists some of the things to avoid. Use it as a checklist for further thought and discussion. It was written for one particular discipline and you may need different terminology. Page 68 in Chapter 8, for example, points to alternative terminology for terms like 'research question'.

Box 4.1 Common mistakes in writing a research proposal

1 *Failure to provide the proper context to frame the research question.*
2 *Failure to delimit the boundary conditions for your research.*
3 *Failure to cite landmark studies.*
4 *Failure to accurately present the theoretical and empirical contributions by other researchers.*
5 *Failure to stay focused on the research question.*
6 *Failure to develop a coherent and persuasive argument for the proposed research.*
7 *Too much detail on minor issues, but not enough detail on major issues.*
8 *Too much rambling – going 'all over the map' without a clear sense of direction. (The best proposals move forward with ease and grace like a seamless river.)*
9 *Too many citation lapses and incorrect references.*
10 *Too long or too short.*
11 *Failing to follow the . . . [style required].*
12 *Sloppy writing.*

(Wong 1997)

Research design, methods and techniques are highly discipline-specific and are outside the scope of this book. An excellent general introduction for short research projects is Bell (2005).

Putting boundaries on the research proposal

Additional or alternative research methods or avenues to explore may keep emerging from reading or from the advice of individuals and committees. So students may want – or feel they ought – to include all these in the proposal and the eventual research. Doing so may be a useful, but, on the other hand, it may not. Remember that there are countless ways of looking at a topic, and accordingly there are countless ways in which a statement of interest can be expanded into a research proposal. You only need one, or possibly several inter-related ones. You cannot afford to be too ambitious or to take on anything that doesn't appeal to your own interests. Pages 157–158 and 161 in Chapter 15 consider ways of recognizing the helpfulness or otherwise of suggestions and ways of reacting to them.

It is also possible that your proposal will need boundaries put on it because you are too committed to something all-embracing which is close to your heart.

You need to keep an open mind and listen to your supervisors' advice. Remember that the aim is to get that research award. There will be the opportunity afterwards for other things, particularly with the backing of your qualified status.

The writing style of the research proposal

A good writing style is something that is expected of all postgraduates. Whatever the quality of their academic work, it is on their writing that they will be primarily judged. Later chapters elaborate, but there are certain points to bear in mind as particularly pertinent when writing the research proposal.

The research proposal should be written in language that is understandable to an intelligent lay person as well as to a subject expert. Remember that it will probably have to go to a committee which may consist of members from different backgrounds. They all need to be able to understand it. So any terminology that an intelligent lay person could not reasonably be expected to understand should be edited out or, less preferably, explained. (Theses are different, as they are examined by subject experts.)

Spelling, sentence structure and punctuation must be sound. Obviously supervisors will help, but it is only fair that you do your bit first. It should be worth asking family and friends to check the proposal over too. It is never too early to involve them in your work. Intelligent lay people can be an enormous help throughout the programme with spotting inconsistencies, suggesting leads and general encouragement.

If the research proposal is to be of any significant length, it will be worthwhile now to look at the word processing tools that can aid writing efficiency. They are introduced on pages 165–167 of Chapter 16.

Issues of time when preparing a research proposal

How long a research proposal takes to write can depend on the background and experience of the student and the formal requirements of the institution. Six months is not unusual. For students with no research background, this is hardly surprising because developing a viable proposal is a form of research in its own right. There are a range of considerations which should not be rushed.

Time spent preparing the proposal is time well spent, however, because the material should serve as source material for the thesis.

Adapting the proposal to apply for a small grant or other funds

Students who want to boost their finances may like to try adapting their research proposal for the purpose. However, although quite a number of small funding bodies do exist (see pages 10–12 in Chapter 2), the funds that they offer are usually quite modest. So in making the decision to apply, you have to balance the loss of time searching them out and making applications against possible benefits if successful. Ask supervisors to advise.

If you do decide to go ahead, the crucially important point to bear in mind is that criteria for spending money tends to be highly specific, and it is no use applying to any funding body if you cannot precisely meet their criteria. Do read their small print. If, for example, they want to give money for 'younger' researchers, don't waste everyone's time by applying if you are a mature student. If the grant is to support a particular type of work in a particular city do not apply if you are envisaging work in another city. All this ought to be self-evident, but reports from funding bodies indicate that they have to reject a large proportion of good applications out of hand, just because they do not meet some basic criteria. There may, though, be room for manoeuvre, in that you may be able to show how your work will help whatever it is that the funding body is aiming to achieve. With care, a surprising number of applications can be framed to meet criteria that you hadn't previously considered. Do take care, though, not to commit yourself to anything that you don't think you can reasonably achieve within acceptable time limits.

Larger grants are in very short supply. Leave them for the academics, who are more experienced at what is involved and should have more persuasive track records. Even academics, though, in the current financial climate, do not have guaranteed success.

5

Settling in and taking stock

We were forming a group of people who'd be working together and learning together, going through similar experiences, creating together. I thought it was terrific.
(Leonard Nimoy, speaking of the original series of Star Trek, where he played Mr Spock; quoted in Shatner 1993: 204)

The importance of settling in quickly • Using induction events profitably • Taking advantage of 'office' facilities on-campus • Setting yourself up with office facilities off-campus • Getting to know the academic staff • Getting to know the people in the 'community' • Getting to know how things work in the department • Using public and other libraries • Identifying national and international sources of support

The importance of settling in quickly

Once you formally start your research programme, the sooner you can settle in, the sooner you can set to work productively. This chapter is about speeding up the settling-in process. It considers what you will need and the people who can help you – informally as well as formally.

Using induction events profitably

Institutions invariably pay a great deal of attention to helping new students to settle into the academic community. It is, for example, a rare institution that does not put on induction events, campus tours and welcome gatherings, and arrange for library cards and Internet access – all supplemented with folders of useful information. Nevertheless, if you are to make best use of your time as a research student, you need to realize that you too must take your share of the responsibility. No better time to start than with settling in.

If you are a full-time, on-campus student, much of the responsibility is taken off you. In addition to the induction events, you will almost certainly be supplied with the essentials in terms of (shared) office accommodation, regular office equipment and anything else that is specific to your particular research topic, such as laboratory space or access to archives. You will thus have less need of this chapter than part-time or off-campus students. Nevertheless, you may find it useful to scan the chapter quickly.

Similarly if your research is a part of an otherwise taught programme, the chances are that you will already feel at home in the department before the research starts. You will know the staff and students who will want to support you, and you will feel relatively comfortable in utilizing that support. You too may, nevertheless, find it helpful to scan this chapter, as there is much in it that you can adapt for your own situation.

This chapter is primarily aimed at students who are on degree programmes which are entirely by research and who have to spend significant amounts of time off-campus, either because they are part-time or because they are 'working away'. They have to take upon themselves a larger chunk of the responsibility for settling in.

Taking advantage of 'office' facilities on-campus

Every full-time postgraduate research student can expect the institution to provide: shared office accommodation with after-hours access; a sole-use desk; a lockable filing cabinet; a bookshelf; access to computer facilities for data analysis, bibliographic management, writing and Internet access; general office facilities, such as printing, phone, fax, photocopying, post, pigeon hole and stationery; and limited administrative and secretarial support.

For part-time students, there are normally bookable spaces on the institution's computers, either in the main library or in various computer suites.

Points to ponder

- What is the institution's or department's attitude to using its facilities (such as emails, printing and the phone) for personal use?
- If you do much of your work from home, what are you doing to ensure compatibility between your computer files and departmental ones?

Institutions often 'turn a blind eye' to students' personal use of institutional facilities such as email and printing, provided that the use is 'limited' – a term which they do not define. However some institutions do have strict restrictions. It is worth finding out what the position is in your institution, as it is not uncommon for institutions to present students with unexpected bills for unauthorized use of facilities. Note, too, that emails can never be totally private, as is highlighted in the extract in Box 5.1.

Setting yourself up with office facilities off-campus

Even if you are a full-time student, you may prefer to set yourself up with office facilities at home. It may even be possible to set off costs of new equipment against tax if you have, or have recently had, an income. Or maybe, if you are doing some of the research for an outside organization, they may be persuaded to contribute.

If your main office is off-campus, it is crucially important to get reasonable access to all the institution's Internet services and other resources to support your research. You need to set this up sooner rather than later. You will have access to a free email account while you are a registered student. Obviously you

---

Box 5.1 The security (or otherwise) of the Internet

One useful lesson to learn from the Clinton scandal is that emails do eventually catch up with you. Too many PC users have been lulled into a false sense of security by the 'delete' command. Because you are accessing the internet through the university's computers and networks, details of every website visited and every email sent are stored and can be retrieved by administrators. The information is often kept on file for months or, in some cases, years.

(Times Higher Education Supplement 1999: 11)

can use another if you prefer, but you need to make sure that those who need to know it do know it, as the institution will use it to send you important information.

If you can possibly manage it, upgrade your home computer (or buy one if you don't have one). It will save a great deal of time and hassle in the long run. All students will be expected to produce word-processed reports and theses and to be able to use certain software tools. Most educational institutions have licence agreements for their most commonly used computer applications, which allow students to buy software at a discount. These are not always well advertised; so you may have to ask around for them. Some basic application packages can also be downloaded free of charge or on a trial basis from the web.

Whereas your institution probably has an automatic daily backup procedure which is invaluable in preventing lost work, files on one's own computer are very vulnerable indeed. Only someone who has lost everything on a hard disk without an up-to-date backup can fully appreciate the enormity of the loss – see the extract in Box 5.2. If it happens to you, you will have allowed yourself to have your work put back by many months, and it is your responsibility to sort out preventative procedures from the outset. Free firewall and anti-virus software are downloadable over the Internet. The simplest way of backing up if you have only minimal resources is probably a stack of re-writable CD-Roms. (Using the normal sort of CD-Roms that record only once would result in getting through an unmanageably huge number if you back up as often as you should.) Using the re-writable method, put the day's work into a dated file and copy it onto the CD-Rom. Then place that CD-Rom at the bottom of the stack. Similarly for the next day's work use the next CD-Rom, back up in the same way and place it at the bottom of the stack. Any one re-recordable CD-Rom will hold quite a number of separately dated text backups, particularly if zipped up first, although figures and diagrams generally take up more memory. By the time any CD-Rom reaches the top of the stack again, its contents will be somewhat out of date, so if it should corrupt, it is not the end of the world. Other methods of backing up do of course exist, but depend on the resources available. Never be tempted to throw CD-Roms away or over-record on them, as experience shows that one never knows when one is likely to need something later.

Box 5.2 Keep back-up copies of work! Sheila's story

From the start I was aware that I should keep a copy of my work on back-up disk in case of accidents. However, perhaps as with plague, famine, war and terminal illnesses, we like to imagine that they happen to other people but never to ourselves. It was only after I lost a whole week's work, which simply disappeared from a disk, that I now make not only one but three back-up disks of each chapter.

(Salmon 1992: 112)

Points to ponder

- If you do much of your work on your own computer, what are you doing to ensure compatibility between your files and departmental ones?
- Are firewall and anti-virus software up to date on your own computer?
- What are you doing about backing up files?

Getting to know the academic staff

Each member of academic staff in the department will have his or her own personal area of research, possibly with a group of paid researchers and research students. It can be useful for all students to know the general nature of this expertise, and it will certainly be useful to know the individuals concerned. Post-doctoral researchers and technicians can be a considerable help with routine matters on which one may not want to bother a supervisor. It is also important to find out about the other departmental staff such as the secretaries and the administrators. Their friendship and support can be invaluable.

Points to ponder

- What are the areas of research in the department and who heads them?
- Where, if at all, do all the other departmental staff fit into these research areas?
- If you are to be part of a research group in which one or more research students work on parts of a single large topic, where, in general terms, are the boundaries between your work?
- Do any research groups have activities which it could be worth keeping informed about or being involved in?
- What links are there between research groups?
- What are the areas of responsibility of the secretarial, administrative and, where appropriate, library and technical staff in the department?
- Do they ask that research students follow any particular procedures when requesting their services?

Getting to know the people in the 'community'

It is obviously worthwhile to get yourself on good terms with everyone who you will be working alongside. Of all the staff outside the department, the one that is likely to be of most use in your research programme is the subject specialist in the main library. If you introduce yourself personally and explain your needs, he or she can be invaluable. If you are working on contract or collaborative research, there are bound to be additional people who it would be worth cultivating.

It is important to find out fairly urgently about the institutional health centre and how, if necessary, to register with a local doctor. If you are outside your home country, it will pay you to look forward to Chapter 11 which raises a number of questions, with answers, for students living away from home.

Various institutional service units exist to provide help when or if students need it, for example: the students' union; computing services; print services; counselling services; financial services; services to help with language problems; centres for major religions; accommodation services; careers services; shops; eating places; and so on. Some institutions also have a research students' support group and a nursery for students' young children. All should be contactable via the institution's website.

Getting to know how things work in the department

Every department and institution has its own way of doing things. Some will be documented as formal procedures, and students will almost certainly have been informed of them at induction, However, much will be implicit and undocumented, and students will need to find out about these either gradually through experience or by sensitively asking around.

Points to ponder

- At induction, students may be provided with departmental or institutional procedures on the following, although the headings will probably be different:

  1 Notes of guidance for students undertaking research
  2 Roles and responsibilities of supervisors and students

> 3 Procedures for monitoring research students' progress
> and traversing hurdles such as the transfer from MPhil
> to PhD
> 4 Complaints and appeals procedures
> 5 Health and safety regulations (where appropriate for the field of
> study)
> - Are any of these missing and what other useful or important and
> relevant documents have you been given? At what stage do they
> seem worth studying in detail?
> - How do people feel that decisions seem to get made in the
> department?

Departments may operate a form of study contract (also commonly called 'learning contract') which documents the results of negotiations between a student and supervisor, and which is amended, by mutual agreement, over time. Such contracts form a sound basis for understanding what is required of students and what they have a right to expect. Contracts are not, however, used everywhere, as some people feel that they are too trivial and patronizing for work between mature and independent adults and that they could have unpleasant legal consequences. Most supervisors, though, would probably institute some form of informal contractual working if their students requested it.

Using public and other libraries

Of particular value to part-time students are public libraries. They may even be more readily accessible than the institutional library for students working off-campus. Libraries generally have their own websites, which can be immensely useful throughout a research programme. Not only do they offer a quick and relatively easy way to find out about the library's stock and mode of operation, they almost certainly link to other useful websites. Internet access to certain libraries may, however, depend on the subscription arrangements and on having an appropriate card – see Box 5.3.

Supervisors should advise on any departmental resource areas which house reading material of particular interest to their students, for example, past theses, conference literature and any journal articles to which the department or departmental staff subscribe.

There may also be nearby libraries which are open to members of the institution, and there may be specialist libraries elsewhere which can be used by arrangement, possibly on a fee-paying basis.

Box 5.3 How to get a library card for libraries that may be more convenient

There is no charge to join the SCONUL (Society of College, National and University Libraries) scheme. Simply . . .

1 *Check that your home institution is participating in SCONUL Research Extra. Discover which other libraries are participating in the scheme. Download a SCONUL Research Extra application form (PDF or MS Word) – or ask in your home institution library.*
2 *Submit your completed SCONUL Research Extra application form (PDF or MS Word) to staff at your home institution library. If eligible for the scheme, you will receive a SCONUL Research Extra card.*
3 *Check the websites of individual participating libraries for their opening hours and other local conditions (for example, new tickets may only be issued during office hours, also it is possible that you will need to supply a passport sized photograph). If you think you may need specialist help during your visit, it is best to contact libraries in advance. Then take your SCONUL Research Extra card and your library/ID card (from your home institution) along with you.*
4 *Start borrowing!*

(SCONAL 2005)

Points to ponder

- What is the name of your subject specialist in the institutional library?
- How can your library's on-site catalogue be accessed via the Internet to find out what is in stock or on loan?
- How can the site be used to link to similar information about other libraries?
- What, if anything, is the cost to you of using the library's inter-library loan services? Is there a limit on the number of such loans allowed without charge?
- How can you access:
    1 Catalogues of works currently 'in print' worldwide (or capable of being acquired if they are media-based)?
    2 Catalogues of all works that have been available in the recent past?
    3 Journals available online?
    4 Online citation indexes?
    5 Databases available online?

All institutional libraries (and good-sized public libraries) have their own catalogues on the web. Specialist catalogues should also be accessible from regularly updated CD-Roms, although their use may require a personal visit. Of related interest are the websites of bookshops and publishers. The former are widely advertised and the latter can be readily located using a simple web search. Also of related interest is the service provided by some journal publishers by which one can request and receive the current contents of certain journals to see what articles seem worth the time to seek out. Advice should be readily on hand in your institution.

Fortunately there always seems to be a member of staff in any library who is more than happy to help with a query.

Identifying national and international sources of support

One of the most useful supports outside the department and institution may come from the learned or professional society for a field of study, particularly the postgraduate section if one exists. It can provide access to all sorts of useful information and support, such as email discussion groups, newsletters, journals and conferences. It may also provide certain facilities free or at a reduced charge.

There are also national and international organizations which exist to support and/or develop policies for research students, and they too provide access to information, such as email discussion groups, newsletters, journals and conferences. It would be useful, in due course, to familiarize yourself with their remits. The National Postgraduate Committee (of the UK) is particularly worth noting, as it is run by students for students, and it represents the interests and aspirations of all postgraduates whether on taught courses or undertaking research. Box 5.4 shows the idea. It lists some of the topics that have been aired by students in email discussion, and contributors come from outside, as well as inside, the UK.

For specialist support for students from outside the UK, see Chapter 11.

Suggestions and points to ponder

- Find out (possibly by enquiring of your supervisor, other departmental or library staff or by searching the web), whether there is a learned or professional society for your field of study and, if so, how it may be contacted.
- Use its website or take advice from your supervisor about what the society has to offer in the way of help with your research.

Box 5.4 Examples, in no particular order, of the wide range of topics considered in the email discussion group of the National Postgraduate Committee

- Bank loans
- Employment vacancies
- Funding sources for postgraduate study
- Career development
- Insurance
- Intellectual property
- Printing costs
- Fees while writing up the thesis
- Institutional status of research students (students versus staff)
- Induction (departmental and institutional)
- Electronic databases
- Types of postgraduate qualification
- Modular postgraduate programmes
- Research Council funding
- Appeals and complaints procedures
- Library loans (allowances, loan periods, costs of inter-library loans)
- Procedures of oral/viva examinations
- Teaching undergraduates (training and rates of pay)
- The British Library
- Institutional postgraduate societies
- Binding theses (timing and costs)
- Pensions and pension contributions
- Commercial thesis editing (for style and grammar)
- The research proposal
- What makes an award a research award

As a programme of lengthy research progresses, a major complaint from research students is the feeling of isolation. So unless you are working on a group project or as part of a large and active research department, you would be well advised to put effort into warding off isolation. You need to be on the constant lookout for people who know enough about your field to be able to discuss it meaningfully, while also having the time to do so. You may find such people in your family, in your social group or in your department. Visiting staff on sabbatical leave are ideal, as are email discussion groups.

6

Interacting with supervisors

It is important that supervisor(s) and student are fully aware of the extent of one another's responsibilities.

(QAA 2004: 16)

The importance of student–supervisor relationships • The composition of supervisory teams • Points to watch for with team supervision • Roles and responsibilities of supervisors and students • The developing nature of supervision • Arranging meetings with a supervisor • Making the most of meetings with supervisors • Keeping records of meetings with supervisors • Asking a supervisor for feedback and advice • Responding to feedback and criticism from a supervisor • Handling dissatisfaction with supervision

The importance of student–supervisor relationships

The relationship between a research student and a supervisor can be a precious thing, particularly where supervisors and students work closely together over a number of years on something which fascinates them both. Mutual respect and trust can and should develop, together with a working relationship that can continue, as between equals, long after the research is completed. It is in every student's interests to develop and nurture this relationship. Only highly unusual students successfully complete their research degrees if relationships with their supervisors are poor. A research degree is about research training as well as contributing to knowledge, and although it is not impossible to find ways of training oneself, the whole process is designed to be guided by supervisors. This chapter is about interacting with them.

There are two aspects to developing and nurturing the relationship with a supervisor, and they are valid irrespective of the award for which you are registered and how many supervisors you may have. One is administrative and starts with finding out the respective roles of students and supervisors, as laid out formally by the institution. The other is interpersonal and involves treating a supervisor as a human being who has strengths and weaknesses, personal satisfactions and disappointments, good days and bad days, just like everyone else.

The composition of supervisory teams

Normal practice is for MPhil and PhD students to be supervised by a team of supervisors. The following are some of the common ways in which a team may be made up:

- There may be two academic supervisors: the single academic who has day-to-day responsibility for a student, henceforth called the 'principal' or 'main' supervisor (or just supervisor where the meaning is obvious from the context), plus a back-up supervisor whose main role is to keep a watching brief over what is happening and to step in if the main supervisor has to be away. The title of mentor, adviser or 'personal tutor' may be used, to reflect the fact that the back-up supervisor can be turned to for impartial advice and support. A variation is that the adviser can be an impartial third party.
- Where a main supervisor has not yet supervised a doctoral student through to completion, a second experienced supervisor will almost certainly be part of the team. This individual may be overseeing a number of research students and new supervisors, and may, in some institutions, have a formal position. The term 'director of studies' is a common title.
- Where the research is collaborative or contract research with or for another organization, the supervisory team will probably be made up of an academic supervisor plus someone employed at a reasonably high level by the industrial or commercial partner. That individual can advise on matters relating to the context of the research, but not necessarily on the scholarly matters that distinguish straightforward data-collection from research at doctoral level.
- Where the research requires an expertise that no-one else in the team has, someone with that expertise may be asked to join the supervisory team. An example might be someone from the home country of an international student. Such teams are normally put together at the outset by the main supervisor, but students may be invited to make suggestions. New members may join the team as needs arise.

• Variations and combinations of the above.

However the team is made up, it must include the single, main or principal supervisor who is the student's primary point of contact and who takes full responsibility for the overall management and direction of the research programme, plus administrative matters relating to registration and progress. Institutional regulations normally require teams to meet a specified number of times every year. The nature of the meeting may be flexible, with perhaps the student meeting individuals separately. All members of the team are expected to keep up to date with the progress of the student's research.

Points to watch for with team supervision

Team supervision was devised to overcome a number of problems associated with single supervisors. However, it is not necessarily without its own problems.

It is a fortunate student whose team members have entirely common understandings of what the research is to be about. Academic supervisors should be primarily concerned with keeping the research to manageable proportions for the award concerned, but it is understandable that they may also like the fees that consultancy work brings in. Outside supervisors will be primarily concerned with using the research to solve problems in their workplaces. These sets of concerns may not always overlap.

The problems are compounded where the research is multidisciplinary, which is increasingly common these days because it more readily attracts money. Not only may team members not fully understand the expertise of one another, they will inevitably have slightly different ideological or methodological understandings about what good research ought to be. Remember that 'research is different in different disciplines'. Students need to appreciate that they will be submitting their thesis in the field of study of the department in which they are registered, not from that of any other team member.

All this can put considerable burdens on students who try to satisfy everyone. The worst scenario is that they end up satisfying no-one and compromising the progress of the research. It is crucial that students keep a wary eye open for signs that the implicit expectations of co-supervisors are conflicting. Then they must use their interpersonal skills to bring these matters into the open while keeping everyone on good terms. Once made explicit, differences can be openly discussed and dealt with at an early stage. Implicit differences, which are not recognised and handled early, can escalate.

It would be totally inadvisable for students to rely on one member of the team to the exclusion of others, just because that person happens to be more approachable. The advice of every member of the supervisory team has a part to play, but it is the guidance from academic supervisors in the department in which students are registered that can make or break success in the research degree.

There are two useful booklets on joint supervision, where students are working respectively in industry and in public sector organizations. Although in a series produced for supervisors, they may also be of interest to students. They are in the References section under Smith and Gilby (1999) and Denicolo (1999b). A well-regarded book specifically for supervisors and which is also in the References section is Delamont et al. (2004).

Roles and responsibilities of supervisors and students

Essentially, a principal supervisor's primary professional responsibility is to develop his or her research students so that they can think and behave as independent academic and scholarly researchers in the field of study concerned.

It is crucially important that students know what they have a right to expect from their supervisors and from the institution generally. It is also crucially important that students understand and act on what supervisors have a right to expect from them. Your institution will have these rights and responsibilities documented, almost certainly on the institutional website, under a heading such as 'Handbook', 'Code' or 'Regulations'. It will be worth your while to become familiar with them. In general terms they will follow the *Code of Practice* published by the Quality Assurance Agency (QAA undated) – see Box 6.1. The full code can be downloaded from the web by following links from the main QAA website (www.qaa.ac.uk). However, since the QAA

Box 6.1 The Quality Assurance Agency for Higher Education

Our mission is to safeguard the public interest in sound standards of higher education qualifications and to encourage continuous improvement in the management of the quality of higher education.

We do this by working with higher education institutions to define academic standards and quality, and we carry out and publish reviews against these standards.

We were established in 1997 and are an independent body funded by subscriptions from UK universities and colleges of higher education, and through contracts with the main UK higher education funding bodies.

(Quality Assurance Agency undated)

specifically leaves interpretations to individual institutions, those of your institution will differ in detail and they will probably also differ from one subject area to another.

It is only reasonable that supervisors themselves may find it best for the unique partnership of themselves and any one of their students if they interpret the code in their own way while still abiding by its principles. You will, anyway, easily be able to recognize if your supervisor is doing a professional job. Most do, as the extract in Box 6.2 shows. Nevertheless it is always a good idea for student–supervisor partnerships to discuss and agree their expectations of each other, although, for fear of litigation, they may not want to enter into a formal contract.

The extract in Box 6.3 gives a 'trite but true' way of checking out how a supervisor–student partnership is working.

The developing nature of supervision

New students tend to expect supervisors to tell them what to do. Indeed, this may be justified for very short research projects or where the work is tied into a group project and bounded by the efficient use of expensive and heavily utilized equipment. Where this is not so, students may wait for their supervisors

---

Box 6.2 Student satisfaction with supervisors

Postgraduate students are overwhelmingly satisfied with the quality of their supervision . . . In an online poll carried out for the Times Higher *by the National Postgraduate Committee, MA and PhD students from around Britain gave the quality of their supervision an average mark of seven out of ten. Nine out of ten was the most common score.*

(Wainright 2005)

Box 6.3 How to recognize an outstanding supervisor

The following conclusion was reached in an Australian research project which looked at postgraduate work in a range of academic departments. It has a face validity which suggests universal applicability:

One of the hallmarks of outstanding supervisors appeared . . . to be that their students felt driven very hard to impress them.

(Parry and Hayden 1994: 75)

to tell them what to do because they think that demonstrating dependence in this way also demonstrates respect. Fortunately, good supervisors realize that they have to wean many students gradually into independence; so they may provide a well-defined task, as something on which supervisor and student can both build – perhaps a pilot project of some sort. If this is what your supervisor does, it may give you a sense of security, but things are unlikely to carry on that way. Many people would argue that they ought not to carry on that way.

At the other extreme, some supervisors toss out a multitude of ideas at the first meeting, which can be overwhelming. If this happens to you, just realize that the ideas are merely possibilities for you to consider, not tasks that you necessarily have to do. Your best course of action is probably to make a note of them and then take them away to think about, to decide which ones comprise essential groundwork and which ones are merely alternative possibilities. There is no single best way to research a topic, although there are numerous bad and non-viable ways. It is you and you alone who have to be intimately involved with what you are doing over a considerable period. So, for all but the shortest of projects, it is essential that you design yours so that it appeals to you as well as being acceptable to your supervisors.

As your work progresses, supervisions should become two-way dialogues. Your supervisor will expect you to develop your own ideas – which may have to be bounded for various reasons – but will want to discuss them with you, to give advice and to warn in good time against possible dangers. It is not a sound interpretation of 'independent work' for students to continue along their own way, on the mistaken assumption that they do not need supervisions.

Since research means going beyond published work and developing something new, your relationship with your supervisor must accommodate the natural and inevitable fact that you will eventually come to know more about your work than your supervisor. You will need to become comfortable with this and with engaging him or her in academic debate as between equals.

Arranging meetings with a supervisor

It is important to distinguish between formal supervisions and informal meetings. There will be specific policies about the timing and duration of the former, probably around a minimum of eight meetings per year. The dates may be roughly laid out for an entire programme of research and require specific documents to be completed and signed at each meeting.

Traditionally students have had right of access to a supervisor or his or her nominee at any time in an emergency. However, you should play this carefully. One person's emergency may not be another's, and it is in no-one's interest to upset a supervisor unnecessarily. It is important to talk access through with supervisors and come to some agreement in advance of any emergency occurring.

Informal meetings can also form part of the supervisory process, more so in some subject areas than in others. Supervisors may be torn in two directions as far as scheduling these is concerned, and it is helpful to understand why. On the one hand supervisors want to do what they can to be supportive, but on the other they do not want to interfere on the grounds that independent students ought to take the initiative when they need to discuss work which should, after all, be their own. This latter view is reinforced by the formal dictate of most institutions that it is the responsibility of the student to take the initiative in raising problems or difficulties, however elementary they may seem, and to agree a schedule of meetings with the supervisor.

The practical way forward is for you to take steps early on to find out how scheduling supervisions is likely to work best for the unique partnership between you and your supervisor. It is polite to wait a while, to give your supervisor time to raise the matter.

Suggestions and points to ponder

- Find out how comfortable you and your supervisor are with the following ways of interacting:

  1 Dates and times of meetings are arranged a considerable time ahead according to departmental requirements. In this case, are there distinctions between formal and informal meetings?
  2 You take the initiative by emailing or phoning a request for a meeting.
  3 Your supervisor timetables regular meetings irrespective of whether there is anything new or special to discuss.
  4 You submit something in writing in advance of the meeting so that your supervisor can consider it before you meet. Or your supervisor prefers to cut down the burden of non-essential reading and react to you on the spot when you meet.
  5 If either you or your supervisor think there is any reason to meet, one of you arranges it when you next happen to see each other.
  6 Much of the informal interaction is provided without meeting, via email. If so, how much?
  7 You simply turn up at your supervisor's office in the expectation of him or her having time for you.
  8 Some other arrangement. What?

- How are you expected to go about setting up an additional meeting in an emergency?

Each of the above possibilities will suit some partnerships of students and supervisors, but some will be intensely disagreeable to some supervisors. So you and your supervisor must develop a mode of working that suits you both.

Supervisors are busy people, and their workload is increasing all the time. So be sensitive about taking up a supervisor's time. Remember, though, that legally the responsibility for not raising significant matters with your supervisor is likely to be yours. Also, if you neglect to communicate ideas and findings to your supervisor, you may overlook obvious interpretations, waste your time pursuing something that is not viable and wander into dead-ends. Supervisors who feel that they are being worried unnecessarily will say so.

Some students are based where there are no departmental requirements about frequency of supervisions. Then supervisions can be very much at the discretion of the supervisors. Some such supervisors may choose to see full-time students three times a term and part-time students twice a term. Some supervisors like to have two or more meetings booked ahead in diaries, on the proviso that they can be cancelled nearer the time if there is no need to meet. Some supervisors feel that meetings should be set up flexibly, according to the needs of the student, which are likely to be greatest when the direction of the work is being decided and during the final stages of the writing-up. As the relationship develops and confidence in each other grows, some supervisors may welcome forgoing the time outlay of a meeting in favour of interaction by email.

The location and timings of meetings is particularly important for part-time students, and most supervisors are sensitive to this.

Making the most of meetings with supervisors

Regular meetings between students and supervisors are not enough to ensure effective progress with the research. The meetings must be productive. This starts with conscientious preparation on the parts of students. In particular work that is to be discussed, along with any other papers for the meetings, must be handed in or circulated in time to be given due attention. This is only fair to supervisors who need to schedule their own commitments, but it is also only fair to the students themselves if they want supervisors to take them seriously. The extract in Box 6.4 reiterates this point.

Quite generally, handing work in on time is part of students' personal and professional development, as considered in Chapter 12. Time management, in particular, is considered on pages 143–148 of Chapter 14. Perhaps, though, the most important reason for submitting material on time is to learn that most tasks take far longer than expected. The best advice in this connection is to impose a personal deadline some days in advance of the actual one.

Box 6.4 Supervisors are not easily fooled

Supervisors are not idiots – at least not many of them – and they are not fooled by absent students who leave messages saying that everything is fine and they will soon be needing a meeting or sending in a written draft. Neither are they taken in by the student who does put in an appearance from time to time, talks volumes about work in hand, new ideas and the next steps about to be taken in practical work, and then disappears again, never submitting anything tangible.

(Phillips and Pugh 2005: 100)

Keeping records of meetings with supervisors

Students need to have a sufficient record of what takes place during supervisions to be able to think the discussion over before taking action. Memory may not be enough. The record needs to be of the same form as minutes of meetings generally, i.e. to include:

- The date, time and location
- Names of everyone present
- Review of objectives achieved, as agreed and documented in the previous meeting
- Decisions made about future work, distinguished in terms of firm objectives and possible ideas for consideration
- Any other business
- Date, time and location of the next meeting.

It is normally the students' responsibility to take the minutes. It is an important transferable skill which is well worth developing – see Chapter 12 – and it focuses students' minds. Everyone at the meeting should receive their own copy.

Students may find that it gives them confidence to ask their supervisors if they may audio-tape supervisions, even if, in the event, they never find it necessary to replay the tape. Not only does this give a verbatim record of ideas and conclusions, and the strengths of feelings behind them, it also records forms of expression and explanation which may be ideal for reproducing in reports and the thesis.

Records of supervisions form part of the PDP documentation described in Chapter 12.

Asking a supervisor for feedback and advice

Most students are entirely satisfied with how their supervisor responds to their requests for feedback and advice; and any initial problems tend to sort themselves out as the relationship develops. Students can help by understanding some of the pressures that supervisors may be under, and acting accordingly.

Supervisors are human beings who are exceptionally busy and who may also be shy or inexperienced. Any of these may be reasons for unhelpful, throw-away remarks rather than considered responses. There are other possible reasons. For example, a supervisor may not want to stunt the development of students' independence by rejecting their ideas. Or a supervisor may feel embarrassed because a mature student has an impressive career record or is a colleague in the department. If you think that any of these may be reasons for unconsidered responses from a supervisor, a good technique is not to ask for a reaction to a single idea, but to put forward several alternatives. Then there is something to discuss and an implicit ground-rule is that some ideas will have to be rejected.

Overwork could be affecting a supervisor. If you think that this may be so, be sensitive about how you raise issues for discussion. Busy people may react most favourably to a written outline of ideas, to study and respond to at their convenience. On the other hand, an informal chat, to ease interaction with burgeoning paperwork, may be more acceptable. In your own interests, you should find out.

It is a well-researched and accepted fact that people tend to reject ideas if they feel forced into quick decisions. If you think that this may be a problem when you interact with a supervisor, give him or her plenty of thinking time by outlining the situation and then suggesting that he or she might like to mull it over in readiness for talking again in a few days.

If you think that a supervisor may be suffering from the shyness of inexperience, put him or her at ease by asking for answers to simple questions, to which you may even already know the answers. If, of course, the problem is also overwork, this tactic would make matters worse rather than better.

Responding to feedback and criticism from a supervisor

It is students' own interests that supervisors give full and comprehensive feedback on their work. This is difficult on both sides where the feedback is critical, and students need to help in every way they can.

Start by accepting that certain emotions are normal. You may be embarrassed at what you think your supervisor is seeing as your inadequacy, and you may be angry at how he or she appears to be misunderstanding you.

Understandable as these emotions are, it is counter-productive to let them show, and the chances are that, when you calm down, you will realize that they were somewhat unjustified anyway.

So, if necessary, mask negative emotions. Try to show gratitude that your supervisor is going to so much trouble to give the feedback, and to show interest in its content.

It is not necessary to agree with all the criticisms, either while they are being made or later. Only you know the ramifications for your own work and situation. So only when you have taken time to consider can you decide how much to accept, reject or adapt. Agreeing instantly with criticism indicates compliance and lack of independent thinking. Seek clarification if necessary and say that you will go away and do some thinking, ready for talking again about any points that may need further discussion.

Only in exceptional circumstances is it sensible to launch into a justification of why the criticism is inappropriate. You may want to justify some points, but do this only when your supervisor has finished his or her say on that point. Then ask if he or she would like you to explain why you did what you did.

At the close of the meeting, reiterate your thanks. Say nothing more, other than general pleasantries.

Handling dissatisfaction with supervision

Although most student–supervisor partnerships work well, there are those which do not. Perhaps there is some sort of unprofessional behaviour, or a clash of personalities, or a lack of interest. Perhaps a supervisor does not seem to have adequate expertise in the subject area; perhaps he or she does not seem to respect arguments and judgement when the student, after genuine and lengthy consideration, feels that they are valid. Perhaps a supervisor is regarding a student as cheap labour for personal research or is 'too busy' too often. If giving it time does not work, diplomacy is needed. Not only is it impolite to compromise a supervisor, it is probably pointless and is likely, however justified, to discredit the person doing it in the eyes of others.

If a change of supervisor does seem inevitable, someone else in the supervisory team is the person to approach about it. Other sources of advice are the member of staff, if he or she exists, who has departmental responsibility for research students, the head of department, formal institutional documents and the students' union. The final recourse would be raising the matter in an annual review and ultimately legal action. All institutional codes of practice explain how to go about the steps involved.

However, it is crucial to do whatever one can informally early on, rather than formally later, once things seem to have got out of hand. Whatever the validity of complaints and appeals, they are stressful, time-consuming and usually public; and sadly in the eyes of the world, 'mud sticks', even to inno-cent parties. At best, students will recover no more than lost fees.

In particular it is formally the responsibility of the student, not a supervisor, to decide when the thesis is ready to be examined, even though of course the supervisor will give an opinion. There is thus no recourse, other than the formal appeals procedures already mentioned, if the degree is not awarded. So, if you see things going wrong, it is in your own interests to act in good time to do something about them yourself.

7

Reading round the subject: working procedures

To do their work well, workmen must first sharpen their tools.
(Chinese proverb, quoted on http://www.bartleby.com
modified for sexist language)

Why the work of others is important • Identifying and accessing relevant material • Reading purposefully and effectively • Bibliographic management software • Systems and styles for citing sources • Using literature in your own work • Implications for a 'Literature survey/Review' • The distinction between a 'References' section and a 'Bibliography'

Why the work of others is important

All research, by its very nature, is based in some way on what other people have done before. As far as research students are concerned, an early task is to explore the context of what they want to do, i.e. to find out enough about what others have done to identify gaps in knowledge that their own research can fill. This is part of refining the topic of the research. Research students also need to find out how others have gone about gathering and using data, so that they can make decisions about how to gather and use their own data. In fact, throughout the whole research programme, research students need to look to the work of others for answers to questions that keep arising. This is known as 'reading round the subject'.

This chapter is about locating relevant material, recording it and citing it in one's own work. The next chapter, Chapter 8 is about evaluating the quality of the material. Both chapters need to be read before you spend very much time reading round your subject.

Identifying and accessing relevant material

Access to information has never been simpler:

Journal articles (and possibly other material) will be listed on one or more of the subject databases, i.e. electronic indexes of publications. The subject librarian should be able to advise which one or ones are most suitable for your field. Access to all databases worldwide is just a few clicks away via your institution's intranet. Logging on, just requires a valid user name and password. If an item seems likely to be of use to you, check to see if the institutional library has it in stock. If not, it can almost certainly be borrowed on an inter-library loan.

Websites may provide a way in to relevant material. So, if necessary, you will need to polish up your search techniques by finding out which search engines are most helpful for your area of research and their use of the Boolean operators, i.e. AND, OR and NOT, etc. Again, the subject librarian will be able to advise.

Some of the most productive reading takes place on a casual basis, perhaps while relaxing with books or articles away from the workplace. Important points and ideas can then easily get forgotten or lost. A way of marking a page for processing later without seriously interrupting the flow of the activity or causing damage is with a peel-off sticker of the 'Post-It' type. It is worth keeping a pack readily to hand for the purpose, along with a pen or pencil.

Similarly productive reading can take place on a casual basis, while surfing the web, and it is helpful to be able to mark a site for attention later so that one can carry on with the original activity. One way is to save the site directly onto the desktop. Another way is to record the site temporarily under 'Favorites' (Internet Explorer, which uses the American Spelling) or 'Bookmarks' (Netscape and Firefox) and set them to be available off-line. This saves the web page, its reference address (URL) and any links and graphics.

Reading purposefully and effectively

Sadly there is no completely satisfactory way of processing what one reads because it is seldom possible to know at the time precisely how the item or quotation might best be used, if indeed it can be used at all. Hence difficult decisions have to be made about how much to record and with what key-words. There is no formalized procedure which can entirely support the burden of this, and there is no substitute for a mind that can provide a partial retrieval system of its own.

An increasing amount of material is available online, and there can be the feeling of being swamped. It can be helpful therefore to remind yourself about reading skills.

Suggestions

- If necessary, do a web search on such terms as 'reading skills', scanning, 'skim reading', 'reflective reading', 'critical reading', 'rapid reading' and 'speed reading' to see if the advice is helpful.

The extracts in Box 7.1 offer some suggestions about coping with information overload.

Box 7.1 Some ideas for helping with information overload

The library is the first port of call in the search for ways to deal with information overload. Solutions can range from traditional methods, such as reading reviews or journal articles rather than entire books, to electronic alerting services and the subject-specific filters of web material available through JISC* . . . You should not ignore more basic methods of sorting information such as speaking to people.

(Toby Bainton)

You should approach your library for information about e-mail notifications for the tables of contents of your favourite journals or search alerts from a bibliographic database for new papers published in your subject area. Book, patent and conference alerts are other options as are the RSS** news web feeds that alert you to news from websites and services that you have specified.

(Melissa Highton)

(Both quoted in *Times Higher Education Supplement* 2005: 42)

Notes: *Joint Information Systems Committee; **The Royal Statistical Society.

Bibliographic management software

Bibliographic management software can help keep track of what you read. Users input references in their own unique 'library' or database, which they can then search according to various criteria, format in a particular style and manipulate in various ways. A number of bibliographic software tools are available, of which Endnote is probably the best known. Some are more suitable than others for certain fields of study and your supervisor will recommend one that is particularly suitable for you. The extract in Box 7.2 lists some of the criteria on which to base the choice.

The adage about 'garbage in; garbage out' is particularly pertinent when using bibliographic management software, as indeed when using any method of recording what one reads. One can never recover from poor inputting. However, bibliographic management software does help prevent it because once the user has confirmed the type of reference (such as book, article,

---

Box 7.2 Choosing a bibliographic software tool: a checklist for consideration

- *The tool would need to be able to incorporate multiple bibliographic styles, to switch easily between styles, and to choose styles appropriate to a particular discipline.*
- *It should be able to pull information from online sources and from online bibliographic databases.*
- *It should have an easy-to-use 'cite while you write' functionality, with excellent integration into word processing software.*
- *The personal database of sources generated should be easily transportable or available on a server, so that students can access the information no matter where they are. However, the user should be able to access bibliographic references and add to his/her personal database of sources while offline.*
- *Good documentation and technical support need to be available for the product, along with a clear commitment by the manufacturer/creator to maintain the software over time.*
- *The tool should be available for the PC and Macintosh platforms.*

Other possible features:

- *Non-Western character sets*
- *'Direct connect' feature that allows you to access multiple databases via one interface*

(George Mason University undated)

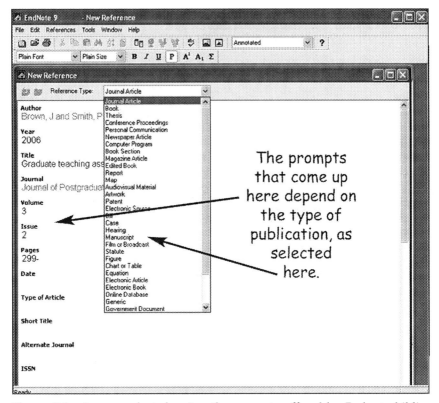

Figure 7.1 A screen shot showing the prompts offered by Endnote bibliographic software.

website, etc.), prompts appear for all the necessary input information. Figure 7.1 shows the prompts in an Endnote screen for a journal article.

Many academics manage well without bibliographic management software, and your supervisor may be among them. Some still use index cards and some use simple text files, like Word. For your own work, you must obviously be guided by your supervisors. If you do decide against bibliographic management software, you will need to be particularly careful to record all the elements of any reference. It is, for example, all too easy to forget to record page numbers when examining a text; and it can be very time-consuming and irritating to have to find them again later.

When making your decision for or against bibliographic management software, do bear in mind that there is an inevitable compromise between the ease of putting information into whatever device you choose for keeping your records and the ease of retrieving it. For example, a particularly straightforward way of inputting information would be to keep hand-written notes on scraps of paper. Yet this would be the least straightforward for quick and easy retrieval, as it would require sorting through to find what is there and interpreting handwriting. The choice is personal: to go for ease of inputting, ease of retrieval or a balance somewhere between them. You will not regret investing time and effort in looking for and setting up systems that seem right for you.

When making your decision it will also be worth bearing in mind that current government emphases are very much on skills development in a research programme (see Chapter 12), and that competence with bibliographic management software is a valuable and transferable skill. Furthermore, it is a rare research student who, at the time of writing up the thesis, does not bewail the wasted days of following up references that were not fully recorded earlier. Institutions are certain to offer training in bibliographic management software and may be able to find a way of easing the cost of purchase for students' personal computers.

Bibliographic management software interfaces directly with word processing software.

Systems and styles for citing sources

References to the work of others in your own work must provide sufficient detail for anyone else to be able to check the sources, if they wish to do so. There are established systems and styles for this. Three are in common use, all of which can be restyled as required with bibliographic management software. The styles are:

- Sources are indicated in the text as they occur, solely by the author's surname and the year of publication. They are then listed fully in a dedicated final section in alphabetical order by author. This system is known as the Harvard system. (Note that whereas bibliographic management software can style and sort automatically, word processing software can only sort.)
- Sources are numbered consecutively in the text, normally as superscripts. They are then listed fully in a dedicated final section in numerical order. (Word processing software can take care of the renumbering automatically when another source is added mid-text.)
- Sources are shown as footnotes on the page where they appear, denoted by a symbol or number. (Word processing software can also take care of this automatically.)

You will be told which of these methods is the norm for your particular field of study. Further details on all of them are readily available on the web. See, for example, the website referred to in Boxes 7.3 and 7.4, which are respectively for text-based sources and electronic sources.

Box 7.3 Referencing paper-based publications

See the actual website to follow through the links (below), or do a web search to locate comparable information.

- *One author*
- *Two or three authors*
- *Four or more authors*
- *No author*
- *One volume of a multi-volume set*
- *Two authors with the same surname*
- *A chapter in an edited work*
- *Personal communications*
- *A work described in another work*
- *Information found in more than one source*
- *Two or more publications with the same author and date*

(Flinders University Library undated a)

Box 7.4 Referencing electronic sources

See the website to follow through the links (below), or do an Internet search to locate comparable information.

1   *General rules for referencing electronic sources*
- *The statement of availability*
- *Date of access*
- *Page numbers*
- *The webpage title*
- *Determining the webpage author*
- *Publication dates on webpages*
2   *Electronic journal articles in fulltext databases & journal collections*
- *A journal article from Expanded Academic ASAP*
- *Ovid*
- *A journal article available on the CINAHL database*
- *A journal article abstract on the CINAHL database*
- *A journal article from the Blackwell Science collection*
3   *Electronic journals available on the World Wide Web*
4   *A World Wide Web page*
- *A webpage with an author*
- *A webpage with no author*
5   *Email*
6   *CD-Roms*

(Flinders University Library undated b)

Suggestions and points to ponder

- What system are you expected to use when citing and referencing sources?
- Do a web search on this system and make a mental note of the different ways of citing and referencing different types of publication.

Using literature in your own work

In your own work, you will frequently need to refer to what you have read. For some students, this starts as early as the research proposal, but it applies for all students for progress reports and ultimately the thesis.

When you come to use literature in your own writing, it is helpful to think of yourself in the role of a barrister in a court of law having to argue the case for something. What you have read in the literature is 'evidence' in that case. Use literature primarily to support argument or counter-argument and to move understanding forward. Mere lists of sources, as in a 'catalogue' of vaguely relevant items, are pointless and will do you no credit. Direct quotations should be used only for purposes of illustration, never as a replacement for a soundly argued case. If you find yourself quoting more than a few sentences, think again, as you are probably losing the thread of whatever argument you are trying to put forward.

Sources should additionally be used to show a thorough knowledge of the field, which is particularly important in PhD theses. Where seminal works are not directly pertinent to the thrust of the argument, skill and thought are required to bring them in meaningfully.

The absence (or apparent absence) of literature on certain topics can also serve as evidence, provided that this is set in a wider field of knowledge and is clearly not a ploy for an inadequate literature survey.

It is worth a reminder here that you should never attempt to pass off what you have read as your own work. That would be plagiarism which pages 89–91 of Chapter 9 and page 112 of Chapter 11 consider in some detail.

Implications for a 'Literature survey/Review'

The emphasis placed on a separate literature survey chapter a thesis or report depends on the field of study or nature of the research. Where it is usual to define a research problem early on and to keep it relatively unchanged, much of the source material may seem most appropriately presented in a single chapter which may even be entitled 'The literature survey'.

In fields where it is usual for the direction of each stage of the research to rely on findings of an earlier stage, new literature will need to be incorporated at each stage. Most theses will require some, at least minimal, references to literature to run through all the chapters, even if one chapter contains more than others.

The distinction between a 'References' section and a 'Bibliography'

It is common practice in many fields of study for there to be a distinct difference between a Reference section and a Bibliography section. The first lists sources cited in the main text and the second lists sources which were consulted during the work and which fed into the author's thinking. It is important to find out whether this distinction is standard practice in your subject area. Whether it is or not, there should be no literature alluded to in the main text which is not fully referenced later.

Points to ponder

- In your field of study, is it normal practice for there to be a Reference and a Bibliography section at the end of a research report?

8

Reading round the subject: evaluating quality

If I have seen further than others it is by standing on the shoulders of Giants.

(Isaac Newton at www.saidwhat.co.uk)

The importance of being able to evaluate the work of others • Issues to consider when evaluating the work of others • How do they use terms like 'research area', 'topic', 'theme', 'focus', 'hypothesis' and 'problem'? • How do they use research methodologies? • How do they demonstrate academic argument, academic discourse and scholarship? • How do they use literature? • What is their claim for original work? • What is their claim for significant work? • What is their claim for the reliability of their work? • What is their claim for the validity of their work? • The nature of 'truth': research paradigms and frameworks • The 'traditional' research paradigm • The 'interpretivist' research paradigm • How appropriately are works of others set into research paradigms? • The benchmark for quality • Where next?

The importance of being able to evaluate the work of others

Not all the information that comes one's way is of any value for serious research. Some can actually be misleading. Newspaper hype is an obvious example, but there are many others. So, if students are not to risk wasting their time by building on foundations that may be shaky, they need to be able to judge the quality of what they read – i.e. to 'evaluate' it. This chapter makes a start on a journey that never entirely ends: that of learning what constitutes quality in research. The chapter takes a general approach that should be valid across all disciplines, although obviously it will need to be developed through the advice of experienced researchers in the subject area concerned. The chapter thus provides guidance to students embarking on their 'literature survey' or 'literature review'. Ways of locating relevant material, recording it and citing it were considered in the previous chapter.

Issues to consider when evaluating the work of others

This chapter will introduce the issues by taking you on a guided tour of various types of publication. You would be well advised to take the tour, even if you feel that you already have research experience from elsewhere. Before starting, though, a word of warning. The tour will introduce terminology for discussing research. However, each field of study has its own norms, which have been built up over many years through dealing with the types of research with which the discipline is concerned – see the extract in Box 8.1. There is thus no way that this chapter can give specific guidance which would be acceptable across all fields of study. Nevertheless, the general guidance should be useful as a starting point for discussions with supervisors and others in your discipline. Later chapters will elaborate.

For the tour, you will need access to some Masters level theses and a few PhD theses in your area, as well as to some published refereed journal articles and published or unpublished conference papers. All should be available in your institutional library or departmental resource centre; alternatively supervisors may be prepared to lend out personal copies. Most libraries do not allow theses or journals to be loaned out, but they can be studied on site. Even if your own research is less ambitious than doctoral level, do include the PhD theses because only at that level can certain points be illustrated. It will help you to be aware of these, even if only to know that they need not necessarily concern you. At this stage, resist the temptation to use online journal articles or theses because you will need to lay out the materials together for comparison purposes.

Box 8.1 Postgraduate research is different in different disciplines

In science, research education is strongly shaped by the conditions required for maximising the productivity of specialised research groups. Students are recruited to a research group geared towards defining discrete sets of problems. Students will undoubtedly contribute to their solution. But sometimes the needs of the research are difficult to combine with those of the student. It might, for example, be in a highly competitive and rapidly changing field where speed is of the essence . . . Students' contribution to the work of their group may often be substantial. But their contribution to disciplinary knowledge is normally predefined by their supervisor and expectations of originality are limited.

. . . In the humanities the traditional emphasis has been on individual modes of inquiry and on the importance of the freedom of the student to select his or her research topic. Originality and independence are strongly held values . . . Claims of substantial contributions to knowledge on the part of PhD students are still made, but only from the most prestigious institutions.

. . . In the social sciences . . . the ideal remains that of the individual pursuing the problem of his or her choice and making a more or less original contribution. Concepts of originality are usually but not always fairly modest . . .

(Becher et al. 1995: 13–14)

Suggestions

- Collect together a sample of literature from your own discipline. It should include published, refereed journal articles, unpublished conference papers and theses at PhD and Masters level. You won't need conference articles until the end of the tour.

How do they use terms like 'research area', 'topic', 'theme', 'focus', 'hypothesis' and 'problem'?

Researchers always begin their work with a general area of interest or concern. It may start out vague or it may be clearly defined. There are various ways of expressing it. Possibilities include:

- A research area or topic (or set of linked topics)
- A research theme (or set of linked themes)
- A research problem (or set of linked problems)
- A research question (or set of linked questions)
- A hypothesis (or set of linked hypotheses)
- A focus (or set of linked foci).

The terminology used tends to depend on the nature of the research, which in turn tends to depend on the discipline. It is useful to understand why, irrespective of what your own discipline or research happen to be.

Sometimes the precise purpose of the research may be known fairly clearly from the outset. Then the whole research programme can be mapped out in some detail and the boundaries of the work are fairly neatly defined. It usually then seems natural for researchers to think of themselves as working towards solving a 'research problem', and the term 'project' may be used to describe what they are doing. This way of working, with its associated terminology, is usual in the natural sciences.

At the other extreme, researchers may start out with only a general area of interest, and the emphasis is on exploring that interest. Each new phase of the work takes up and further explores interesting or significant parts of what emerged from previous stages (which is known as 'progressive focusing'). Over time, the research tends to focus on specific and significant issues, which may not have been identifiable at the outset, and it is these that form the foci or themes of the research report or thesis. These have to be written, or at least edited, with hindsight to make a feature of the foci or themes that have emerged, and the title is finalised at quite a late stage so as to encapsulate these foci or themes. At the outset, the research is not neatly contained inside obvious boundaries, and it does not have a clear end-point. Indeed part of the skill of the researcher is to create and impose boundaries so that the work can be rounded off within the time and resources available and presented as a self-contained package. (Chapters 19 and 20 elaborate on the implications for research students.) Since neither the scope of the work nor its eventual focus (or foci) or theme (or themes) are precisely known until the work is considerably underway, the terms 'project' and 'research problem' tend not to be used. It is as if the purpose of much of the research is to identify a problem which it can solve or which it has already solved. Then the processes of identifying the problem and solving it both feature in the report or thesis. The well-known saying about 'the solution looking for the problem' captures the idea. This way of working, with its associated terminology, is common in the social sciences.

The drawings in Figures 8.1a and b capture these two extremes. The way one normally thinks of going about hitting a target with an arrow is to start by noting where the target is, then to develop the skills to hit it, and then finally actually to hit it – as in Figure 8.1a. That is analogous to conducting research which is neatly defined and contained by a pre-specified research problem and which researchers direct their energies to solving. Yet the woman in

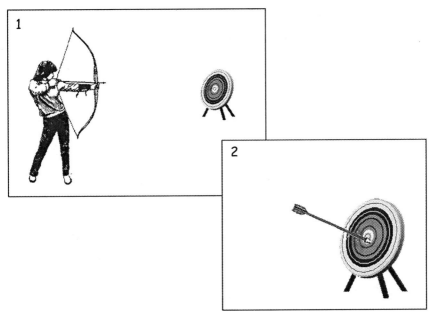

Figure 8.1a   Success by noting where the target is and using one's skills to hit it – analogous to addressing a pre-specified research problem.

Figure 8.1b   Success by aiming in a pre-decided general direction and using one's skills to make the landing point into a target – analogous to exploratory research where nebulous research studies need to be consolidated into a self-contained piece of work.

Figure 8.1b merely shoots her arrow in the right general direction, notes where it lands and then paints a target around it. So it is with identifying the research problem (or theme or focus) once a viable solution has become apparent, and then putting time and energy into ring-fencing various possibly nebulous studies so that they can appear as a self-contained piece of work.

You will now be invited to get a feel for how the terminology of 'research problems', 'hypotheses', etc. tend to be used in your field of study. The purpose is to raise issues to discuss further with supervisors and other research students. Make sure that you do so, and don't be surprised if they prefer alternative terminology.

Points to ponder

- Scan the theses in your sample. (Don't attempt to read them in full, and don't for the moment look at the journal articles.) Does it seem usual in your field to define a research problem explicitly, possibly in terms of a list of specific research questions or hypotheses? Alternatively, does it seem usual for the focus (or foci) or theme (or themes) of the research to emerge as the work progresses?
- Does there seem to be any indication in the theses that the research problem, topic, theme or focus, etc. changed in direction or in emphasis during the research?

The usual starting point to defining a research problem – and this is true irrespective of whether the term is used explicitly or implicitly and whether the research problem is identified early or late in the research programme – is to read round the subject to get to know the background and to identify unanswered questions or controversies. Small-scale investigations or pilot studies may also be conducted, to identify significant issues for further exploration. Where the research problem is identified early on, a common way forward is to break it down into a set of questions or hypotheses. Then care and attention are given to make these so detailed and specific that the research design falls naturally into place. The process of getting the research questions or hypotheses into a form which has the right amount of detail is known as 'operationalizing' them.

How do they use research methodologies?

In general terms, a 'research methodology' is a rationale for the methods used to gather and process data. A research methodology is not a grand term for a list of methods, but an informed and properly argued case for designing a piece of research in a particular way. A research methodology needs to be appropriate for the research problem (or 'project', or 'piece of research', or whatever is the terminology in the field of study concerned), and the justification that this is so must form part of a thesis. Some quite general definitions of 'methodology' are given in Box 8.2. The suffix '-ology' means 'the study of'; hence the terms sociology, psychology, etc.

It takes experience of research in a discipline to comment on the appropriateness of a research methodology for any piece of research. Nevertheless you should be able to see how well methodologies are argued for in the theses and how reasonable they seem in the articles. Good argument involves paying attention to counter arguments. So, at PhD level at least, the theses should show a familiarity with alternative methodologies, and an argument in favour of one should include arguments, however brief, against others.

Box 8.2 Some dictionary definitions of 'methodology'

The science of method.

(*Shorter Oxford English Dictionary*)

A body of methods, procedures, working concepts, rules and postulates.

(*Webster's International Unabridged Dictionary*)

Points to ponder

- How well do you feel that the research methodologies in the articles and theses are argued for?
- If a research problem was formulated early on in terms of fully operationalized research questions or hypotheses, how well do these seem to lead naturally and easily to decisions about how the research had to be designed?
- Do others in your discipline feel that a research methodology for a particular piece of work is so obvious that it doesn't need arguing for?

How do they demonstrate academic argument, academic discourse and scholarship?

Quality theses, journal articles and research reports go much further than merely describing what was done and listing the data collected. They provide a well-documented and well-argued case for one or more specific solutions to a research problem (or whatever is the appropriate alternative terminology). The idea of a thesis, journal article or report being a 'case for something' is helpful, because it shows that researchers have to adopt the role of a barrister, rather than a journalist, in their writing. In order to make a sound case, evidence has to be collected and presented so as to take argument forwards. The evidence can be taken directly from literature or it can be the data collected in the research. It must be made clear which is which.

Theses almost certainly contain a number of streams of argument, which may be intertwined. Minimally they may be how the research problem or gap in knowledge was identified; how it was investigated; what the solutions or outcomes were and their importance and limitations. Arguments need to be convincing, and counter-arguments need to be explored and dealt with rigorously and fairly.

Before accepting the validity of any research it is always worth asking yourself whether it would be reasonable or difficult to try to prove or argue for the opposite; where there might be flaws in the reasoning; and what impression the findings make on your expectations. Without such checks, it is quite possible for unscrupulous researchers to seem to prove anything they like. There is an example in the extract in Box 8.3.

The language in which the case is argued has to be precise with relevant evidence and unblurred with irrelevancies. This is part of what is known as 'scholarship' and 'academic discourse'. 'Scholarship' is explained in Box 8.4.

Box 8.3 An example of the flaws in seemingly sophisticated research

Hans Eysenck has the following to say of the psychologist Cyril Burt:

Burt, while outstanding in his ability to use statistical methods in the analysis of data relating to intellectual or personality differences, was rather careless about the quality of the data he analysed. As I once told him: 'You use the most advanced methods of psychometrics in your analyses, but you use them on data that are quite dubious – tests done unsupervised by teachers, for instance . . .' This did not increase his liking for me . . .

(Eysenck 1994)

As the extract in Box 8.5 points out, one has to keep a watchful eye open for research that may seem to be of high quality at first sight but is actually lacking in scholarship and academic discourse. Chapters 16 and 23 give advice for your own writing.

Box 8.4 The meaning of 'scholarship' from an encyclopaedia

Scholarly method – or as it is more commonly called, scholarship – is the body of principles and practices used by scholars to make their claims about the world as valid and trustworthy as possible, and to make them known to the scholarly public. In its broadest sense, scholarship can be taken to include the scientific method, which is the body of scholarly practice that governs the sciences.

(*Wikipedia Free Encyclopaedia* undated)

Box 8.5 When academic discourse and scholarship are lacking

One may give all the stylistic indications of setting out a case in a rigorous fashion, using devices such as 'it follows from what I have just said', when in fact nothing follows; 'I have argued that . . .', when in fact no argument has been offered; 'I refute the suggestion that . . .', when the suggestion is merely contradicted, not argued against; 'it has been shown that . . ., when nothing of the kind has been done and so on, without setting out a case.

(Fairbairn and Winch 1996: 169)

Suggestions and points to ponder

- How far do you feel that the articles and thesis draw meaningful conclusions rather than presenting the data as an end in itself?
- Try to identify the cases that are being made in each thesis in your sample. The places to scan are the abstract, preface, introduction or overview (whatever is the norm in the subject area), contents list, the first and last paragraphs of each chapter and the final chapter. (At PhD level there will almost certainly be more than one case in each thesis, and the streams of argument are probably intertwined. Disentangling and identifying them could take some considerable time and is probably not worth attempting in any detail at this stage.)

- Summarize the main case that is being made in each of the research articles in your sample.
- To what extent do you feel that the theses in your sample have cogent, convincing arguments? Do you feel anywhere that the cases being made are blurred with 'padding'?
- To what extent do you feel that the theses in your sample acknowledge and deal fairly with counter-arguments?
- In terms of quality of argument, scholarship and academic discourse, can you identify any significant differences between the masters level and the PhD theses? What about in the journal articles?

All the theses in your sample should be logically and convincingly argued, but some will inevitably be better argued than others. You may feel that the PhD theses are more soundly argued than the masters ones. Certainly inability to argue is one reason, but only one, why students are not permitted to pass through certain probationary hurdles – notably in the transfer from MPhil to PhD.

How do they use literature?

Properly written-up research should cite source material in a consistent manner according to the norms of the discipline and as explained on pages 61–64 of Chapter 7 and page 169 of Chapter 16. This is an important aspect of quality, as it is the only way that others can realistically check the validity of the evidence supplied.

Suggestions and points to ponder

- Do all the articles and theses in your sample use the same style for quoting literature sources? (In many fields of study, the answer will not be a straightforward, yes, and you will need to query the implications for your own work.)
- If there is both a Reference section and a Bibliography section at the end of the theses, what appears to be the difference between them? (This was discussed on page 64 of Chapter 7.)

What is their claim for original work?

Institutions require theses to demonstrate originality, particularly at doctoral level. Chapter 19 considers originality at some length with the purpose of helping students to incorporate it into their own work. Here it is mentioned primarily as one of the criteria for evaluating research.

What is their claim for significant work?

Significance is another criterion for evaluating research, and again it is normally an institutional requirement at PhD level. That some theses demonstrate it is beyond question. With others, however, it can be a matter of opinion and debate, guided by normal expectations in the field of study concerned.

Points to ponder

- Do the articles and theses in your sample appear to make much of a point of claiming originality and/or significance?

What is their claim for the reliability of their work?

Where researchers can repeat a piece of research and obtain precisely the same results, the results are said to be entirely 'reliable'. In practice, though, reliability can never be total, and it is important to understand why.

Consider first the type of research that is concerned in some way with small numbers of people, animals, plants or other living organisms. Their individual vagaries all come into play. With people, variables, such as 'hungry', 'happy' or 'slept well', are highly influential on behaviour. They vary from one point in time to another; they cannot be measured numerically; and different observers may interpret the signs differently. Similar arguments could apply to studies on animals; and even plants and the lower organisms. Consequently, unless the numbers are large enough for the vagaries effectively to cancel each other out, the research cannot be entirely reproducible when conducted on different occasions by different researchers. It cannot therefore be totally reliable.

Reliability is less complex where the research is with inanimate objects and the data is numerical (i.e. measurable), as is usually the case in the natural sciences. To a first approximation, the research is reproducible – although there are still issues of competence and minor perturbations. All measurements have an error associated with them, which limits reliability.

What is their claim for the validity of their work?

Where a piece of research does what it is intended to do, it is said to be 'valid'. The achievement of good validity at the same time as good reliability may be feasible, but it may not be. Figure 8.2 shows some of the possible combinations of reliability and validity in an archery analogy. An example in research could be the use of examinations as a research tool to judge or grade students. The most reliable form of examination consists of tick-in-boxes types of question, marked by computer, because all suitably programmed computers would come to the same judgement about the same student, given the same script. However, if the purpose of the examination is to grade and understand students' thought processes, as well as the outcomes of their thinking, then tick-in-boxes questions are not particularly valid. Essay questions would be more valid. Unfortunately, though, they are inevitably less reliable, since examiners' judgements are involved in the marking, and these are always somewhat subjective. The reliability of essay questions can be increased through double marking, but in the end it has to be accepted that the reliability cannot be total.

Where there has to be a trade-off between reliability and validity, validity must always be the more important. Achieving it starts with an understanding of the nature of 'truth' as it can be revealed by research. This, in turn, leads to the choice of an appropriate 'research paradigm' in which to set the research. Both are considered in the next section.

The nature of 'truth': research paradigms and frameworks

Just as a paradigm, quite generally, is a viewpoint which shapes ideas and actions, a 'research paradigm' is a 'school of thought' or 'a framework for thinking' about how research ought to be conducted to ascertain truth. Different writers use different terminologies when discussing research paradigms, even when the paradigms are broadly similar, and consequently it is impossible to say how many there are. This book will simplify them into two, which it will call the 'traditional' research paradigm and the 'interpretivist' (Denzin and Lincoln 1994: 536) research paradigm.

Figure 8.2   An archery analogy for possible combinations of reliability and validity.

The 'traditional' research paradigm

The 'traditional' research paradigm relies on numerical (i.e. quantitative) data and mathematical or statistical treatment of that data. The 'truth' that is uncovered is thus grounded in mathematical logic. The traditional research paradigm lends itself to highly valid and highly reliable research, but only where the variables that affect the work can be identified, isolated and relatively precisely measured – and possibly, but not necessarily, also manipulated. This is how research in the natural sciences normally operates. Researchers who can work in this paradigm are fortunate because high reliability and validity are held in high esteem. The proponents of the paradigm tend to take it for granted, and theses grounded in it generally take the high reliability and validity as self-evident.

The traditional research paradigm can lend itself to research touched by human and other animate behaviour if the data is numerical and if the sample is sufficiently large for the effects of individual vagaries effectively to cancel one another out. An example could be the performance of school leavers in national examinations across a country over a period of years. Another example could be an investigation into the yields of a hybrid crop using large fields of control and experimental plants. Research set in the traditional research paradigm can answer questions about what is happening and the statistical chances of something happening in the future, but it cannot directly answer questions about why something is happening or may happen, nor about the existence of anything else that may be relevant. Answers to such questions may, however, be provided by an established theory within which the research fits.

The 'interpretivist' research paradigm

The traditional research paradigm is generally not appropriate for research involving small samples of living beings. Then, the variables which stem from individual vagaries and subjectivity do not cancel one another out; neither can variables be readily identified or measured, let alone isolated and held constant while others are varied. Even with a large sample there are sometimes ethical or pragmatic reasons why variables cannot be held constant or manipulated experimentally. Then research has to be set in the 'interpretivist' research paradigm (Denzin and Lincoln 1994: 536). What this involves is more like in-depth investigations to establish a verdict in a court of law than experiments in a laboratory. The evidence can be circumstantial and even where there are eye-witness accounts, doubt can always be cast on the veracity or reliability of the observers. A verdict must be reached on what is reasonable, i.e. the weight of evidence one way or the other and on the power of the argument. Data gathered within the interpretivist research paradigm is primarily descriptive, although it may be quantitative, as for example in sizes of living areas, coded questionnaires or documentary analysis. The emphasis is on exploration and insight rather than experiment and the mathematical treatment of data.

Research set in the interpretivist research paradigm can answer questions about how and why something is happening. If it also addresses questions about what is happening in a wider context and what is likely to happen in the future, it can seldom do so with statistical confidence, because the 'truth' is not grounded in mathematical logic. The 'truth' has to be a conclusion in the mind of a reader (or listener), based on the researcher's power of argument, and different recipients of the research may come to understand different 'truths'. So it is important for those who use the interpretivist research paradigm to present their work as convincingly as possible. The workshop handout in Box 8.6 offers some advice, and, if you are working in this paradigm, your supervisor will advise you further.

Box 8.6 Towards making a thesis convincing

The following is part of an unpublished discussion document used in training supervisors of postgraduate research students at the University of Reading.

CHOICE OF RESEARCH PARADIGM

All research inevitably requires the selection of an appropriate philosophical and methodological framework. Since all such frameworks have limitations, this choice involves selecting the one which fits the questions and objectives of the research best while rejecting others even if they may have some salience. In order to demonstrate that this selection has been grounded in understanding, rather than being an arbitrary decision or one based on habit, it is important that the rationale for the selection includes both the argument for selecting a particular one and the reasons why others were deemed unsuitable for this research.

SELECTION OF RELEVANT LITERATURE

The literature section(s) of a thesis is/are intended to demonstrate that the student is conversant with the field and can use evidence from the literature to focus enquiries. This is most effectively achieved by:

- *The selection from what might be a plethora of authors, those who are significant in the field*
- *The provision of a critical review of the works, with particular respect to the focus of and relevance to the current research*
- *The support, or illustration, of statements and contentions made by the student using apposite quotations from the literature.*

To elaborate on the last point, since quotations out of context can be misleading, it is important that exact references, including page numbers, are provided so that readers can check both their accuracy and the intent in the original works. Similarly, it is good practice to provide some context to quotations, such a 'in a debate about such appropriateness, Bloggs (1999;123) provided the following critique: . . .'

DEMONSTRATING THE SALIENCE OF THE DATA

The source, context and relevance of data used to justify interpretations is critical. It should be clear that evidence has been assiduously collected, compiled and reviewed, with alternative perspectives given credence and weight, and attributed suitably to origin. This is especially important when the data is derived from an interpretive framework with sources such as interviews and other narrative material. A data trail should be explicit, including for instance: a table of sources (participant, method, location in the temporal frame of the fieldwork); samples of transcripts showing the style and contextual structure; lists of categories derived from the data; lists of quotations used to determine particular categories, including a miscellaneous category to include material that does not fit into any other category. Much of this material is most appropriately contained in referenced appendices so that the reader can audit the instances cited for illustration in the text of the thesis, find other examples of the category and check on the validity of the interpretations drawn.

(Denicolo 1999a)

Research students who use the interpretivist research paradigm normally have to do a considerable amount of justification. In contrast those who use the traditional research paradigm often never even mention the fact.

How appropriately are works of others set into research paradigms?

Research paradigms tend to be associated with particular disciplines, because of the sorts of questions that research in those disciplines tends to address. Nevertheless even within the same disciplines there can be intense rivalries between individuals who have loyalties to a particular research paradigm because of the nature of the truth that it uncovers.

Different parts of a complex investigation may need to be set in different research paradigms. For example, research into the effects of a new drug may involve the measurement and statistical treatment of, say, blood pressure, but the subjective views of patients have to be taken into account in the search for side effects.

Alternative terms for research paradigms which are broadly similar to the traditional research paradigm are: quantitative, scientific, experimental, hard, reductionist, prescriptive, psychometric – and there are probably others. Alternative terms for research paradigms which are broadly similar to the interpretivist one are: qualitative, soft, non-traditional, holistic, descriptive, phenomenological, anthropological, naturalistic, illuminative – and again there are probably others. It must be emphasized that the similarities are in broad terms only. Many academics would argue fiercely about the significances of the differences.

Points to ponder

- If the articles and theses in your sample are concerned in any way with the vagaries of human behaviour, check on the various ways in which they deal with these.
- If the articles and theses in your sample are concerned with animals, plants or other living entities, how are individual differences addressed?
- Do any of the articles fall into the trap of ignoring subjectivity and other individual vagaries by focusing on what can be measured and measuring it, even though the central aspects of the research ought in fact to be variables which cannot be isolated and measured?
- Do you feel that the articles and theses are convincing in their treatment of reliability and validity?

Because the traditional research paradigm is so highly esteemed, researchers often try to use it even where it is not appropriate – in other words to sacrifice validity for reliability. This is reminiscent of a well-known analogy which is reported in various forms, about someone looking for what he has lost under a lamp post, because that is where the light is, even though he knows that he lost it somewhere else. Working inappropriately within the traditional research paradigm is no less absurd, even though it is often done.

The benchmark for quality

This chapter has introduced some of the criteria that are widely used when evaluating research. In theory, these can be simplified down into just one: whether the research has been published (or is worthy of being published) in a refereed journal article or an encyclopaedia. In practice, however, new journals seem to be popping up all the time, and it is very difficult indeed to find experienced and knowledgeable reviewers prepared to spend their time and energies on refereeing. So, although research students should be able to accept the reliability, validity and general quality of research that is written up in any refereed journal article, they should make it their own responsibility to weigh up quality. The same is broadly true of the confidence that they can place in a thesis which has been successfully examined.

Suggestions and points to ponder

- Now is the time to turn to the conference articles in your sample, i.e. to work in progress that will not have reached the stage of peer-review.
- Using all the criteria introduced in this chapter, how would you judge the quality of the research in the conference papers?
- Look up a few items on the web. Bearing in mind what you have read in this chapter, how far are you convinced by their claims?

The conference papers probably appear somewhat lacking on some of the criteria mentioned so far. Where they are 'work in progress', written to accompany a conference presentation, there is nothing wrong with this. The websites are likely to be highly variable.

Where next?

This chapter has over-simplified a complex topic in order to present a grounding that is understandable to new researchers in all disciplines. The purpose is to raise awareness and to stimulate discussion. Make sure that this happens, and remember not to be surprised if modifications in terminology and perspective turn out to be necessary for your field of study.

You may feel that the chapter leaves you with a sense of frustration that it does not say more. However the 'more' that individuals seem to want always turns out to be intimately associated with the requirements of their own particular field of study or programme of research. This book is cross-disciplinary; so it does not consider aspects of research which could be seen as irrelevant in some disciplines, however important they may be in others. Fortunately there is no shortage of books on research design, research methods and research techniques appropriate for particular fields of study, and you can readily find out what they are and study a selection. Then, under the guidance of others in your field of study and, in particular, your supervisor, you should extend your journey into recognizing and conducting quality research. It is a journey that will never completely end.

9

Handling ethical issues

Ethics is nothing else than reverence for life.
(Albert Schweitzer at www.brainyquote.com)

The place of ethics in research • Towards an ethical research proposal • Getting the research proposal approved for ethical considerations • The ethics of ownership in research: conflicts of interest • The ethics of ownership of the work of others: plagiarism • Avoiding 'unintentional' plagiarism • What to do if you meet malpractice and fraud • Subject-specific ethical guidelines

The place of ethics in research

There is no shortage of definitions of 'ethics'. Here are three taken at random from the web:

a system of moral principles, rules and standards of conduct

with regard to professions, a code of professional standards, containing aspects of fairness and duty to the profession and the general public

a system or code of morals of a particular religion, group, or profession

Essentially therefore ethics in research might seem to be no more than the simple matter of doing what is 'right'. However, it is not always as simple as that, because what seems right to one individual or group may seem quite the opposite to another. Much depends on viewpoint, as exemplified in Box 9.1.

Box 9.1 Common idioms which illustrate how there are (at least) two sides to most viewpoints

- One person's junk is another person's treasure
- One person's terrorist is another person's freedom fighter
- One person's meat is another person's poison
- One person's gaffe is another person's truth
- One person's junk is another person's antique
- One person's vice is another person's virtue
- One person's security is another person's prison
- One person's blessing is another person's curse

So even researchers who consider themselves ethical might hurt others without realizing. Furthermore it is not unheard of for unscrupulous researchers to know quite well what they are doing when they hurt others. Their driving force may be financial gain or they may feel that small discomforts for a few individuals are acceptable for the greater benefit for the many. In a society where litigation is becoming increasingly commonplace, such research is fraught with dangers, and could cause considerable financial hardship to researchers if a court of law finds against them.

For all these reasons institutions invariably require research done under their auspices to be approved from an ethical standpoint. This has implications for everyone in their employ, including postgraduate research students. The policy applies to all research where there could be ethical considerations, and it tends to be strictly enforced with disciplinary procedures for infringements. The overarching purpose is to respect the rights and responsibilities of everyone in any way concerned. Animal rights are necessarily included.

Ethical considerations have a wider coverage than most students appreciate, and they can often crop up quite unexpectedly in the guise of plagiarism, fraud and intellectual ownership – to quote just a few of the areas of malpractice in research. This chapter aims to prepare students for spotting issues with ethical overtones and for handling them acceptably.

Towards an ethical research proposal

Most if not all institutions have ethical guidelines for students' research proposals. The same is true of professional bodies representing particular disciplines. There are invariably common features across the guidelines, but the details may vary and will necessarily develop somewhat with time. So here is not the place to attempt a full list of all the ethical considerations that you should consider in your research proposal, and, anyway, every proposal needs to be considered on its own merits. In the case of research on a grant which has already been awarded, the ethical approval may already have been sought and obtained. Either way, your part as a research student is a matter of common sense and then, with the help of those more experienced in the field, to explore where unforeseen ethical consequences may lie. Supervisors can and will help, but you can have a good stab at getting your proposal ethically acceptable by yourself.

Points to ponder

- If your research involves human subjects, imagine yourself in the position of the individuals being questioned, monitored or analysed. What might you feel unhappy about? Consider the experience of being used and how the results might be publicized? What protections would you want?
- Repeat the exercise from the point of view of your funding body. Is it funding a search for 'truth' or a verification of something to its commercial advantage which may turn out not to be verifiable?

Often simply foreseeing likely reservations on the part of a research subject is enough to suggest ways of circumventing them. For example, you may be able to offer individuals the freedom to withdraw from the research, or that their involvement may be kept anonymous.

Postgraduate research has to be a search for 'truth' rather than an attempt to verify an 'untruth'. This is particularly pertinent for contract research where those providing the funding may require the research to show some-thing to their commercial advantage. If they are not to feel let down, this needs early discussion. A way forward could be that the results of the research may need to be kept confidential, as is frequently the case where something of commercial value is being developed. Then, although there are implications of confidentiality for publishing and examining the thesis, the registration and work for the postgraduate award can still go ahead.

Getting the research proposal approved for ethical considerations

The procedure for ethical approvals varies from one institution to another, from one discipline to another, and from one funding body to another. If your proposal is considered in any way at risk ethically, at some stage you will probably need to supply:

- A brief statement of the purpose of the research
- A brief statement on the proposed methods of data generation
- A brief statement of how you plan to gain access to prospective subjects or research participants
- A draft information sheet for the prospective subjects or participants to explain what they are being asked to involve themselves in
- A draft form for them to sign to confirm their informed consent.

The extract in Box 9.2 shows how one institution assures itself that research subjects/participants give their informed consent to the research.

Obtaining ethical approval for a research proposal can take time. Much depends on the nature of the research. Agreement in principle has to be obtained from everyone involved; lengthy documents may have to be completed; and they may have to pass through committees. Nevertheless, research students should welcome the fact that their work is to be scrutinized so thoroughly. They can use the time to further their research in other ways, like reading round the subject as described in Chapters 7 and 8, and they can relax in the knowledge that, once the proposal is approved (and the research keeps strictly to the proposal), the responsibility for ethical matters will be borne by their institutions and not themselves.

Points to ponder

- In the true case summarized in Box 9.3, a certain amount of disappointment and embarrassment could probably not have been avoided, but how could the 'informed consent' form have been framed to minimize disappointment and embarrassment and cover the university and its staff against accusations of reneging on commitments?

The donors should have been asked to sign a form of informed consent including the simple statement that although the university would do all that

---

Box 9.2 The procedure for gaining the 'informed consent' of research subjects/participants – an example from one institution

- *The subject . . . must know the purpose of the study, what it entails for the subject and whether there is any risk to the subject (including psychological pain).*
- *The subject . . . must have the right to withdraw consent once given at any stage.*
- *The investigator must undertake to protect the confidentiality of the subject.*
- *In the event that the results are published, the investigator must protect the identity of the subject, unless the subject consents to be named.*
- *Applicants for approval from RGEC [Research Governance and Ethics Committee of the University of Salford] should prepare a short, accessible statement for the subject to read containing the above.*
- *Accompanying this, the information sheet, should be a form asking for signed consent, and spelling out conditions 2–4.*
- *The RGEC needs to see the information sheet and consent form.*
- *The RGEC also needs a completed ethics approval form and a copy of the protocol (proposal) in which is highlighted for its attention a consideration of the ethical issues raised by the proposal and how the investigator proposes to resolve them.*

(Bellaby undated)

Box 9.3 A true story of subjects/participants of research being left in the lurch

Back in 2000 I was asked if I would co-operate in a PhD study on the frequency of a common Y chromosome in folk with a common family surname. I agreed and after a number of meetings with the researcher and her supervisor I submitted a selected number of names across the varying spellings of the name using a set of criteria provided by the University. These folk were contacted and most submitted samples. The lab examination was completed and folk were sent their results which of course could only be revealed to them. Then the problems began. The researcher had a couple of pregnancy absences and when she returned her supervisor had developed cancer. The PhD seems to have disappeared into the distant future. Meanwhile those who know I was responsible for their names going forward keep asking me when they will get the definitive report on the results, as five years plus seems a long time. None of these delays could have been avoided but one might think that there could have been a strategy for dealing with this sort of situation.

(A colleague of the author who wishes to remain anonymous)

is reasonable to progress the research to conclusion, it could not be held responsible for unforeseen circumstances which might prevent this. Institutional ethics committees can suggest forms of wording in such situations, which is why it is crucial that they be involved.

The ethics of ownership in research: conflicts of interest

The rights and safeguards of individuals can be important in connection with who owns a student's research. When students first register for a research degree, ownership may not seem to matter very much. However it can matter a great deal later, in two ways in particular.

One way is due to mismatched assumptions between students and supervisors. This shows itself when supervisors require their names to go on journal articles where the students, rightly or wrongly, feel that they, themselves, merit sole authorship. Both feel that their claim to ownership, either joint or sole, is justified. The supervisor advised the research throughout, probably made suggestions at the publication stage and needs publications for appraisal and career advancement. However the student did the work. Clearly this is a matter which should have been resolved early on, before it came to a head, through discussion, negotiation and agreement.

The other facet is also due to mismatched assumptions, but this time between the academic partnership of students and supervisors and the funding bodies (usually the industrial partners of collaborative research). It shows itself when the outcome of the research can be capitalized on for commercial gain, particularly when the true extent of that advantage was not predicted at the outset. The collaborative partner feels that having funded the research, all outcomes belong to the company. Without prior negotiation and agreement, academics and students probably have to agree, but tend to feel very badly done by. Again the lesson is obvious: Find a form of words that encapsulates the financial advantages that may emerge from any research and negotiate agreement on them at the outset.

Suggestions and points to ponder

- What are your assumptions about whose name(s) goes on publications that arise from your research? Do your supervisors agree?
- If your research results in something of financial value, who will hold the patent or copyright and what are the financial implications?

> - If these matters have not already been addressed, check them out on your institutional website or with supervisors and funding bodies. Where there may be financial implications, get a written and signed agreement.

The best way to show that work is yours is to publish it in a journal article, but this is a slow process. The work has to be packaged in a 'complete' form, and then more than a year can elapse before a submitted article gets to press. Peer-reviewed electronic journals may be a little quicker, but not much. One way forward is to put down an ownership marker by presenting your on-going work at a conference (see Chapter 17). Another is to publish something about it yourself on the Internet in the form of what has come to be known as an e-portfolio (see Box 12.5 in Chapter 12). Neither are particularly valued academically, but they do provide public markers of ownership. Sadly, though, where the work is of commercial value, it does of course have to be kept under wraps.

The ethics of ownership of the work of others: plagiarism

Everyone has what is known as 'intellectual copyright' or 'intellectual property rights' on what they write. No formal patent is necessary. Plagiarism is taking the written work of others and passing it off as one's own – although the meaning is increasingly becoming blurred to include passing off the ideas of others as one's own. It is not plagiarism to quote short passages, provided that one points out where the quotation comes from and uses it for illustration or criticism. It is plagiarism to copy a chunk of material and present it without indicating its source as if it is one's own. Plagiarism is a form of fraud and malpractice.

The Internet, particularly online academic journals, may seem to provide considerable scope for taking the written work of others and passing it off as one's own. Cases are even reported of students with short research projects buying complete theses or dissertations on the Internet. This is something they could never get away with on a full research programme like a PhD, as there are too many checks along the way, which would immediately alert supervisors. In particular supervisors can often spot plagiarized chunks of text because the different authorship of the various sections is so obvious from the different writing styles. To add to the armoury against plagiarism, there are online tools which take only minutes to analyse and compare text – see the extract in Box 9.4. Supervisors can run the software themselves, but common

---

Box 9.4 Plagiarism detection software

The JISC*-funded TurnitinUK plagiarism detection software is an online service hosted at www.submit.ac.uk that enables institutions and staff to carry out electronic comparison of students' work against electronic sources, and other students' work. The service is based in the UK and accessed via standard Internet browsers. JISC hopes that this service will be a valuable support tool for institutions, staff and students in their efforts to prevent and detect plagiarism.

Note: **The Joint Information Systems Committee (JISC) supports further and higher education by providing strategic guidance, advice and opportunities to use Information and Communications Technology (ICT) to support teaching, learning, research and administration. JISC is funded by all the UK post-16 and higher education funding councils.*

(JISC Plagiarism Advisory Service undated)

---

practice is to ask students to do it as part of their personal development, and to produce the downloaded report as evidence.

Blatant plagiarism is being taken very seriously indeed, as pointed out in Box 9.5. Do it at your peril. Not only would you be risking the most severe of penalties, you would also be destroying the educational value of your programme of work.

Avoiding 'unintentional' plagiarism

Although plagiarism is simply wrong, students from some backgrounds do it in good faith – to indicate that they have studied what the 'experts' have written and to honour those experts. Understandable as this may be, it cannot be allowed to continue. It is unlikely to remain unnoticed for long, and no-one would ever accept that a student of more than a few months into a research programme is anything but fully aware that plagiarism is unacceptable. The penalties can be very severe indeed, and can be applied retrospectively, even after students have graduated.

The way to avoid this sort of plagiarism is simple. Every time you use someone else's work, simply say so and cite the source as shown in Chapter 7. If you feel uncomfortable about this or find that your work is consisting of too many quotations or citations from elsewhere, you are probably not subjecting the material to your own independent thought. Your personal critical analysis is what is important. So try to present the work of others in terms of what they 'consider'/'describe'/'suggest'/'argue for'/'explain'/'conclude' ... etc. and then add how much confidence you feel that their work generates and why.

**Box 9.5 Plagiarism at one of the UK's top universities –
experiences and policies**

*Prof Alan Grafen, the senior proctor, who is the [University of Oxford's] chief
disciplinary officer said [that] the number of students copying other people's
work without acknowledgement threatened to undermine the worth of the
Oxford degree. He said that the problem had become so serious that all
students should be required to sign an affidavit for every piece of work they
submitted . . . Writing in Oxford Magazine, the dons in-house journal, Prof
Grafen said: 'Plagiarism can be defined in a variety of ways but the dominant
form that reaches the Proctors' Office is simple copying. Hard though it may
be to believe, students type word-for-word, increasingly copy-and-paste from
the internet, and submit essays containing whole pages of this verbatim
material.' When a case was suspected, it was referred to the proctors who took
it before a disciplinary court. This had the power to reduce a mark, fail the
student, or permanently expel him or her – all sanctions that had been applied
in the past year . . . 'Vigilance is required for the sake of the education our
students receive and also in order not to create implicit understandings that
plagiarism is acceptable in practice' [he said]. A number of recent cases
had involved students whose first language was not English and who had
'unfortunately gained the impression' that copying was tacitly accepted. Dons
should also resist 'siren voices' claiming that in a scientific DPhil, for example,
it was the science that mattered, not the words. 'An employer is entitled to
assume that the holder of an Oxford DPhil can explain in his or her own words,
in English, the background to the research carried out' he said.*

(Clare 2006)

Another plagiarism-avoidance technique is to rewrite what someone else
has written, but concentrating on leaving out what is peripheral to one's own
argument (while not misrepresenting); and then stressing where it is in agreement, where it is in disagreement and where it is particularly fascinating from
your point of view. By the time you have done this, you may feel quite comfortable that what you have written genuinely is your own and that all you
need to do is to cite the source material and put direct quotations inside
quotation marks.

Points to ponder

- If you come from a culture where direct copying from experts is
  acceptable, how can you use the suggestions in this section?

What to do if you meet malpractice and fraud

The chances are very high indeed that everyone in your department or research group will conduct themselves responsibly and professionally, and that you will never come face-to-face with the decision of having to decide what to do if malpractice or fraud rears its ugly head. The initial decision is whether or not to do anything, as it is somehow more comfortable to tell yourself that you are imagining things. The story in Box 9.6 is a true example.

Box 9.6 The dilemma of whether or not to expose suspected malpractice or fraud

This true story is based on a contribution at one of the author's workshops for research students.

Paul, * *a PhD student was a guest overseas in the house of Anna,* * *another PhD student who held a prestigious position in her home country. As part of Anna's research she was measuring blood sugar levels in a group of local people. Paul was somewhat surprised at how quickly Anna seemed to be making these measurements. Then, during Ramadan, not only did she again come back with her measurements quickly, but they were not significantly different from the previous measurements, even though the individuals concerned were fasting during the day. He strongly suspected that she had not really made any measurements at all, but had invented them on the basis of her previous measurements. He asked the other workshop participants what he should have done.*

This story polarized the workshop participants. Some hotly defended Anna, suggesting reasons why the measurements should not have been significantly different anyway. Others felt equally strongly that Paul had a duty to his discipline and the academic community to check the matter out to ensure that academic standards were not being compromised. Yet others felt that he had a duty to himself because, if the measurements were in fact fraudulent and Anna were found out, then his own academic professionalism and position would be at stake. No-one felt that he should have ignored the matter. Yet, the outcome was, as he told the workshop, that, neither at the time nor since, had he found the courage to question Anna about her measurements, and that he had worried about it ever since. Fortunately for him, the professional community had not noticed anything amiss.

Note: *Names have been changed to protect individuals.

Points to ponder

- What would you have done if you had been Paul in the situation of Box 9.6?

If you genuinely, after much thought, feel that you are witnessing or have witnessed malpractice or fraud, the institution's code of practice will document what to do first and what to do after that if you don't get satisfaction. Whatever happens don't yield to the temptation of circumventing official channels by, for example, speaking to journalists or gossiping in such a way that it gets repeated. Doing so will only count against you, and it will not be to your advantage to have enemies in academia. Your aim should be either to remedy the situation if that seems possible, or, if it does not seem possible, to ensure that any action is delivered through official channels. It is a sad fact that whistleblowers seldom do themselves any good.

The subject of ethics in research can be pursued further in Oliver (2003).

Subject-specific ethical guidelines

Most professional organizations issue their own guidelines on ethical research. Your supervisor will probably be able to advise on these for your field of study, or suggest that you find them from a web search.

10

Managing influences of personal circumstances

Circumstances do not determine individuals, they reveal them.
(James Lane Allen at www.brainyquote.com
(modified for sexist language))

The influences of personal circumstances and the need to adjust • The full-time/part-time divide • Being a 'mature' student • Working away from the institution • Undertaking research with or for an outside organization • Undertaking teaching in the institution and being a 'graduate teaching assistant' • Staff or student status? • Fitting research into and around other paid employment • Handling effects on family life • Handling effects of living accommodation • Coping with disability • Handling illness, financial difficulties and other emergencies • Other influential personal circumstances • The three necessities: health, motivation and support

The influences of personal circumstances and the need to adjust

Undertaking a long research programme has to be a way of life, not just a job, because it can't simply be locked away into office hours inside the institution or other place of work. Remember that research degrees are seldom failed. In general, students either pass them or simply drop out and have their registration terminated. Causes of drop-out normally lie either in lack of the right motivation – see pages 14–15 of Chapter 2 – or in personal circumstances which do not permit the work to be given the attention it requires.

This chapter focuses on some of the more common personal circumstances that may affect the efficient and effective conduct of the work and lives of research students. Not all, if any, will apply to you. You, like everyone else, have a unique personal background, expectations, needs, responsibilities to others and implicit assumptions about how you expect to lead your life. The aim of this chapter is to help you to recognize potential problems at an early stage so that you can head them off before they become serious. Those that can accompany being a student in a 'foreign' country are considered separately in Chapter 11.

The chapter is primarily for students on the longer research programmes, although students on shorter ones may also find it useful.

Points to ponder

- Identify all the circumstances in the following checklist which apply to you now or may apply to you in the future:

    1 Studying full-time
    2 Studying part-time
    3 Studying 'at a distance' from the institution
    4 Recently graduated from first degree
    5 Not straight from first degree
    6 Not comfortable with IT
    7 Employed in work outside academia
    8 Employed in work inside academia, such as teaching
    9 English not first language
    10 In a 'foreign' country
    11 Living with parents
    12 Living with a partner
    13 Living at home
    14 Living away from home
    15 Living with other students
    16 Having to spend significant time travelling each day
    17 Not in the best of health
    18 Caring for children
    19 Caring for aged relatives
    20 Finances likely to be a problem

- Now add any other of your personal circumstances which may possibly have an influence on your way of life during your programme of research.

The checklist does not include items like 'lack of background or experience in research'. That is an underlying theme of the rest of the book and is not to be confused with the personal circumstances which sap one's time and energy. There can, at times of course, be an overlap.

The full-time/part-time divide

In the UK, more than half of all postgraduate students are registered on a part-time basis. The statistic is probably similar elsewhere, and it is widespread practice to categorize students according to whether they are full- or part-time. However such a sweeping two-way divide is not particularly helpful for highlighting the adjustments that students need to make in their lifestyles, because everyone has such different reasons for wanting or needing to study full- or part-time. Part-time students may, for example, be caring for children, in which case child-minding care needs to be sought, either from the institutional nursery (where one exists), or from a relative or partner, or on a paid basis. Part-time students may be caring for elderly relatives who may require different and progressively increasing degrees of care. Part-time students may be in employment, which can provide anything from a great deal of support to none at all, and which may or may not impose restrictive office hours. Part-time students may have financial responsibilities for others. In fact, the only circumstance that all part-timers have in common is the difficulty of finding extended blocks of time for their programme of research and to attend associated training. Chapter 14 should help.

Many part-time research students tend to be in fields of study where the next stage of the work grows out of previous stages rather than being envisioned as a whole at the outset. So it is very important that they keep a wary eye open to prevent the work from becoming over-ambitious. Chapters 19, 20 and 21 are worth early attention in this respect because they highlight ways of ring-fencing or integrating seemingly nebulous studies into a unified whole of PhD standard.

Another piece of advice is to make sure that supervisors realize when students are part-time. This may seem obvious and hardly worth a mention, but it does happen that busy supervisors unwittingly overlook such matters and are consequently less helpful than they might otherwise be.

The following sections consider the implications of some of the most common personal circumstances that influence the lifestyles of postgraduate research students, whether full- or part-time. In practice, though, no personal circumstance occurs in complete isolation from any other. Personal circumstances interact with each other in complex ways. So you will have to think carefully about the strategies you will need to handle your own lifestyle as a postgraduate.

Being a 'mature' student

An increasing number of postgraduate students have had a break between their undergraduate and postgraduate work. They may, for example, have spent time 'out' to develop themselves and make decisions about their lives; they may have set up home and started a family; and they may have started a career which they wish to run in parallel with their study or continue later.

'Mature' students are normally at an advantage in as far as that they know their own strengths and weaknesses; they know what they want and they are dedicated to achieving it. Yet their greater life experience may not be directly relevant to the research and they may need time to get back into the routine of studying, and to put effort into bringing themselves up to speed with IT. Some 'mature' students may also have to come to terms with what they may perceive as a loss of prestige in being treated as a student rather than a relatively senior member of staff or an autonomous adult. If this applies to you, do realize that supervisors, too, may be uncomfortable with the situation and that you, through your own attitude, can do a lot to help. There is more on this in Chapter 6.

Working away from the institution

If you are to spend periods working away from the institution, you will need to set yourself up so as to make your working life as straightforward as possible. You will require somewhere quiet and comfortable to study, appropriate IT facilities and, ideally, access to the Internet and a good library, as described on pages 35–37 of Chapter 5. The library at a nearby institution may, for a fee, extend membership to outsiders, or may be part of the SCONAL scheme, whereby one card gives borrowing privileges in other libraries – see Box 5.3 in Chapter 5. Local public and specialist libraries are likely to be worth investigating.

It is also important to do everything possible to combat isolation, which could have a seriously detrimental affect on your life and health. One way is via support groups with other students. You may like to ask supervisors if they can recommend a suitable one, or you may like to set one up yourself or to join the email discussion group of the National Postgraduate Committee – see Box 5.4 in Chapter 5. Subject associations and professional bodies normally have their own email lists, some of which are specifically for postgraduates.

You will almost certainly have to spend time at the institution for a period of research training. You should obviously try to make the most of this by meeting staff and interacting with other students. Afterwards email and telephone will be the main means of keeping in touch. Some supervisory teams are comfortable with tele-conferencing, and some supervisors even agree to organize their commitments to travel to their students rather than the other way round. It is not reasonable to expect any of these things unless specifically agreed at the time of accepting your place, but given goodwill, a great deal can be done to minimize difficulties associated with travel.

Undertaking research with or for an outside organization

Students who are funded externally or are on contract research are under a particular set of pressures. They may be expected to produce findings that suit employers or funding agencies; they may be on the receiving end of conflicting advice from academic and work-based supervisors with differing loyalties and value systems; they may find themselves working on topics that are not readily suitable for research degrees; and they invariably find that they have to put in considerable time of their own to extend and develop a research report into a viable thesis at research degree level. All these issues are considered more fully elsewhere in this book, but it is worth mentioning here that if your research supports your paid work in some way, it should be possible to negotiate some measure of flexitime with your job, or time off during the day.

Points to ponder

- What issues in the previous sections seem likely to be relevant to you?
- What strategies might you consider for dealing with them?

Undertaking teaching in the institution and being a 'graduate teaching assistant'

It is not at all uncommon for postgraduate students to be employed as undergraduate tutors or laboratory demonstrators. Even regular departmental academics may enrol as postgraduate students while continuing to carry out their teaching duties. Such dual roles can be excellent for ready access to facilities and personnel, and there are usually also beneficial financial implications. However, there are pitfalls which this section aims to outline.

Students who teach part-time, on a paid basis, while working on their own higher degree research programmes are called graduate teaching assistants or GTAs. There are costs and benefits of becoming one, which students need to weigh up very carefully. Benefits are subsets of the following:

- Adding teaching to one's portfolio of skills, particularly if there are aspirations of a career in academia
- Satisfaction of using one's knowledge
- Satisfaction of helping others
- The money that it earns

Yet there are strong arguments against and only you can decide on which side your cost-benefit analysis will come down.

A major argument against rests on the time that the teaching preparation can take. Clearly this is negligible where the work involves merely being in a laboratory to respond to queries from undergraduates. However, it is a different matter where significant preparation is involved. Some students take the latter so seriously that they have little time left over for their research. Another argument against, for some students at least, is that a 'teaching session' overshadows the complete day. The students work themselves up for it and then need time to unwind afterwards. So, before anyone agrees to take on teaching work, they need to think about how it suits their disposition. It might be better to boost their earnings in less emotionally-sapping employment that has fixed hours.

It is not uncommon for institutions to rely on their GTAs in order to function. So it is understandable that pressure may be put on postgraduates to take on teaching. However, in the interests of successfully completing the research programme within the given time constraints – which is, after all, what students are there for – they must be free to refuse. The extract in Box 10.1 may guide your decision.

If you decide to go ahead with teaching, bear in mind that you only need to acquire a 'flavour' of what teaching is about in order to add it to your skills inventory. Also bear in mind that a generally accepted maximum teaching load for GTAs is 6 hours a week; and that you need to be adequately trained and financially recompensed. Box 10.2 gives an extract about the rights of GTAs. The extract in Box 10.3 summarizes recommendations from the UK Council of Graduate Education.

Staff or student status?

The jury still seems to be 'out' on the issue of whether or not PhD students should have staff or student status. Staff status would be more in line with

---

Box 10.1 The pros and cons of being a postgraduate teacher

One of the good things about being a postgraduate teacher is that you have a better idea of what your students might be thinking and of how to reach them. One of the bad things is that many will choose to go to you with a problem rather than one of the older lecturers. You have to be strict in limiting the time you spend with them. I now say 'You have three minutes.' If they say they generally don't understand, I tell them to go away and read their notes and come back with a question.

(Smith 2005)

[My] advice would be even more ruthless – you should avoid teaching altogether. Universities encourage postgraduates to teach to further their careers, but most find out when applying for academic jobs that what really interests selection panels is how much you have published . . . Because of the time involved in finding out what to teach and preparing a lecture, financially you may as well do a menial task that involves less intellectual effort. If you must teach . . . be ruthless about the amount of time you spend on it.

(Francis 2005)

Box 10.2 Advice on being a graduate teaching assistant

- *Ask as many members of your department or faculty as possible if they know of any relevant teaching that is available. Most posts are unlikely to be advertised formally.*
- *Send your CV to other universities in the locality. They may be looking for some part-time staff. The Open University also appoints part-time tutors throughout the UK.*
- *Make sure you are aware of exactly what any teaching you are offered entails. Find out how much preparation you will be expected to do, whether the payment includes marking and what the real hourly rate is.*
- *Ensure that you receive a written contract detailing exactly the tasks you are expected to perform and the payment rate for them.*
- *You should receive a training course in teaching skills before setting foot in a classroom to teach.*
- *Ensure that you will be provided with appropriate support facilities such as access to a room in which to meet students, staff access to the library and computing centres, free photocopying and administrative support.*
- *Establish at the outset which academic members of staff you will be working with and ensure that they brief you fully and make you aware of what they expect of you, and vice versa.*

- *Never undertake teaching you don't feel entirely comfortable about.*
- *Always ensure that you are fully supported when marking students' work. A member of the academic staff should second mark any assessments that count towards the final degree score.*
- *Remember that most students are supportive and keen to learn. Design your teaching with this in mind and don't be afraid to be innovative.*

(Prospects undated)

Box 10.3 Recommendations on preparing postgraduates for teaching

The following responsibilities in connection with preparing postgraduates for teaching are summarized from a report produced by a working party.

- *Postgraduates with teaching responsibilities should be appropriately prepared for teaching.*
- *Every department should appoint a mentor to offer guidance and support.*
- *A member of staff should also be involved with the outcome if GTAs* are engaged in any form of assessment that contributes to the award of a degree.*
- *Appropriate bodies – for example the UK Council in association with ILTHE** should develop a Code of Practice for GTA contracts of employment.*
- *Preparation for teaching should be integrated into the study programmes of research students.*

(UK Council for Graduate Education 1999: 2)

Notes: * Graduate teaching assistants; ** Institute for Learning and Teaching in Higher Education, now the Higher Education Academy.

European norms and the ideals of the Bologna Agreement of Box 2.2 in Chapter 2. Some UK institutions seem to be moving in this direction, but most seem to be keeping the student status, at least for the time being. The extract in Box 10.4 indicates some of the pros and cons.

Difficulties always tend to arise at boundaries between roles, and the roles of research student versus staff member are no exception. Some such difficulties are embedded in policy, such as whether the students are allowed the 'staff' or 'student' allocation of books from the institutional library and whether students are allowed to attend staff meetings. There can also be interpersonal problems in terms of shifts in where power is perceived to lie. These have to be handled with sensitivity all round.

Box 10.4 Employee versus student status for PhD students

Employee status:

- *Pension and national insurance contributions can be made*
- *Social security and other benefits available*
- *Better for mortgages, tenancy agreements and banking*
- *The right to be in a trade union*
- *Better family and childcare support*

Student status:

- *Exemption from council tax*
- *Eligible for student discounts*
- *Possibility of tax-free earnings for teaching done in addition to research*
- *Implications over intellectual property not restrained since they do not work for an institution*
- *Supervision provided*

(Sanders 2004)

It is a matter of speculation as to whether employment status would really improve the lot of PhD students in the UK.

(Cameron 2004)

Fitting research into and around other paid employment

It is common and usually necessary for most students, whether part-time or full-time, to boost their finances through some sort of paid work.

One option is to fit the research around the paid employment, such as in the evenings or at weekends. Even where the research does not require access to facilities outside normal working hours, this option has become much less viable in recent years now that institutions are so strict about limiting registrations to a maximum time span. Anyway, being tired at the end of a full day is not conducive to starting productive research. Neither is having to keep switching one's mind between one thing and another. Successful research at doctoral level is not a mechanistic process. It requires a fresh and creative mind, which in turn requires spare time to relax in reasonable blocks of uninterrupted time. If you must choose this option, at least go for a research topic which is closely allied to your day-to-day employment – or vice versa – so that your creative energies and abilities can work on both together.

Another option for bringing in extra cash is through casual 'unskilled' or 'manual' work. Although this does not have the advantage of being closely allied to the research, it seldom saps one's creative energies and the hours can be very much of one's own choosing.

However you decide to boost your finances, do remember that your first priority must be the research degree. It may be better to go without than to compromise that. Box 10.5 gives some ideas for making your money go further. Although most of them are obvious, they may nevertheless have slipped your mind.

Before taking on any paid work as a postgraduate research student, you need to talk to your supervisor to find out how much is reasonable. Additionally students funded by any of the UK Research Councils are subject to clearly defined limits to how much paid work they may take on. If you are in the UK on a visa, you should also seek advice.

Box 10.5 What to do when the money runs out

- *State handouts. There are not many left! If you are a UK citizen, you may get free prescriptions, eye tests and dental checkups. It is worth asking about them.*
- *Watch those transport costs. If you travel by public transport, don't just assume that buying a travel card/season ticket is the cheapest option. Often it is not if you don't have to come in every day. Don't forget that a bicycle or walking is the cheapest form of transport.*
- *Don't live at the Ritz. It is always worth looking to see if you can move somewhere cheaper or nearer. Halls of residence are often cheap, if you can get a place. The most important advice is to seek help from the institution's accommodation office. Finally, living with relatives may be unbearable, but it can be cheap!*
- *If you can get some kind of job, it will help your situation considerably. It is worth visiting the careers service on a regular basis. If you have any special talents, this is a good time to discover them.*
- *Shopping for bargains. Supermarket own brand items are often considerably cheaper than branded products and often just as good. Try markets and second-hand shops for clothes and CDs.*
- *Managing your money. Don't put £2000 under the bed. Don't put it in a student bank account either. Put it into a high-interest building society account or – if you are brave (or foolhardy) – a unit trust (which can go down as well as up). Use credit cards to buy items like books and travel cards. Pay when you get a statement; under no circumstances pay any interest charges. Remember that heating bills are related to how much you use your heating!*
- *Be nice to people. You may wonder what this has to do with finance. However, it is very important – especially with parents or spouses. If you want people to support you or make sacrifices for you, you need to be nice to them. Remember birthdays (particularly your mother's) and make people*

think that you appreciate their help. That way they are likely to go out of their way to help you. Bank managers also appreciate being told that you want to go into overdraft before you do.

- *Do they do a student discount? A surprisingly large number of places do. Don't be afraid to ask – many places do not advertise the fact. It is also worth using any money-saving vouchers you can get your hands on. If you have not got a Student Union card, it is worth getting one for discounts.*
- *Selling the family silver. Many people plead poverty but appear wealthy. Each of us has various bits and pieces we keep in a cupboard somewhere. Books are especially prone to sitting idly on bookshelves. Remember that second-hand bookshops buy as well as sell. Virtually everything can be sold for a price.*

(Adapted from University College London Graduate School 1994: 4)

Note: Issue 2 of the University College Graduate Society Newsletter elicited responses from staff which flagged up the existence of hardship and travel funds of which postgraduates could take advantage. These were specific to University College London, but this suggests that it would be worth finding out what other institutions can offer.

Handling effects on family life

Only rare individuals undertake postgraduate study without some sort of disruption to their families. Lack of money may mean going without, quality contact time may be curtailed or even disappear and day-to-day problems may have to be handled without the support of the now preoccupied student. It is crucial to discuss these matters with all the adults in the family and to agree in advance some form of informal agreement about what they are prepared to take on or go without, for how long and with what ultimate benefits.

There is a related matter about which this book can do no more than forewarn. It is that students on the longer research programmes, living with non-academic partners need to be sensitive to any signs that their partners are feeling threatened or 'left behind' at not being able to keep up academically. The likelihood and significance of this cannot be over-emphasized, and the fact that problems tend not to surface until some time into the research programme can produce a false sense of security.

Handling effects of living accommodation

Where students live or stay has an impact on the progress of their work.

Living at home, for example, is comfortable, companionable and relatively cheap, but skills and strategies have to be developed to cope with the distractions there. Chapters 14 and 21 offer suggestions. As mentioned above, there is also the need to negotiate a form of agreement with respect to effects on family life.

Living with other students has advantages and disadvantages. The advantages, apart from cost-sharing, lie in the easy interaction which counters loneliness and isolation, and which can stimulate productive help and discussion. The disadvantages are being distracted from work.

Students whose research base is away from home need to find living accommodation that is convenient and congenial. The institution may have its own accommodation on or close to campus, and there should be an accommodation office to advise on seeking private rented accommodation and formalizing tenancy agreements. Once in some sort of accommodation, a good way to find something better is to take advantage of informal networks to hear about anywhere to be vacated.

Coping with disability

Institutions normally welcome students with disabilities. However it is the student's responsibility to declare their disability along with any special requirements at the time of applying.

Handling illness, financial difficulties and other emergencies

Supervisors need to know about any major events that are occupying or distracting their students. Otherwise they can't help or suggest courses of action. It is not necessarily the role of supervisors to solve students' problems, but they should at least be able to suggest who else to turn to.

Illness, changes in family circumstances or financial difficulties sometimes make it necessary for students to take a break from their research. In view of the requirements that theses must be completed within a given time period, it is important to obtain a formal extension if the break is to be of any significant duration. There should be no problem in agreeing this, given due cause, and it relieves the burden of time pressures.

Other influential personal circumstances

You may have – or imagine that you have – special circumstances which could affect your being taken seriously or fully accepted in your academic community. You may, for example, be considerably older than the average research student and think that you could be a target for ageism; or your previous experiences could make you think that you could be the target for sexism. There are many other such '-isms', and all sorts of terms could be coined for what is imagined to cause or genuinely does cause prejudice in others. Although genuine and deep-rooted prejudice does exist, most of it is either imagined or can be negated over time by appropriate professional behaviour. If you think that an '-ism' is likely to bother you, make resolutions to get advice from others who seem to be coping well with the same 'handicap', and possibly to set up or join self-help support groups, either on campus or electronically at a distance. These groups can be as large or small, formal or informal, transient or long-lasting, as you and other members find appropriate for your own needs.

This book is not the place to advise on what to do if other personal difficulties arise. Most institutions provide all sorts of sources of help which can be readily accessed through their websites.

Suggestions and points to ponder

- If you think that you need skills or strategies to meet any special circumstances now or in the future, make a note of the problems now. Then ask around for suggestions.

The three necessities: health, motivation and support

A recurring theme of this chapter is that postgraduate students, particularly those on long research degrees, need to set themselves up in a way of life that supports their work. This chapter has made some suggestions. However, the vagaries of life affect everyone differently, and have to be handled individually as they occur. The three necessities are health (or stamina); motivation, i.e. the wish and determination to succeed; and the right sort of personal support, both financial and interpersonal (i.e. from friends, parents, partners, children, etc.

11

Succeeding as an 'overseas' research student

Travellers are active; they go strenuously in search of people, of
adventure, of experience. Tourists are passive; they expect interesting
things to happen to them.

(Daniel J. Boorstin at www.annabelle.net
(modified for sexist language))

*The challenges of being a postgraduate research student outside your home
country • Preparing yourself while still at home • Selecting a suitable
institution • Funding issues and their implications • Timing the application
• The challenge of working in another language • The challenge of thinking
independently • Other possible challenges*

The challenges of being a postgraduate research student outside your home country

Research students have a great deal in common with one another. They
are bound together by the needs and interests of their research programmes
and, in general terms, they face the same types of challenges, and experience
the same kinds of highs and lows. This is true whatever their countries
of origin. Yet research programmes do involve some challenges that are

more pertinent for students from some countries than from others. This chapter explores them and suggests sources of advice and help. First, though, some terminology.

Fees for higher education in the UK depend on whether students are UK/EU nationals or from elsewhere. In this connection, the students from elsewhere are referred to as 'overseas students'. For other purposes the term 'international' is more common. It tends to be used to describe the societies, support groups and social events which can be so helpful for students who are away from home in a foreign country.

Preparing yourself while still at home

The extract in Box 11.1 lists some of the common questions that prospective international students want answered before committing themselves to study outside their home countries. The questions come from the Council for International Education (known as UKCOSA, the initials of a previous name). Its website will repay an early visit, as it goes much further than providing up-to-date answers to these particular questions. Many institutional websites give their own answers to similar questions.

Box 11.1 Common questions about study in the UK

Finance

- *What is the cost of living in the UK?*
- *How much cash should I bring?*
- *Will I pay the 'home' or 'overseas' fee?*
- *How much will the 'overseas' fee for my course be?*
- *How can I get details of scholarships that are available?*
- *Can I claim welfare benefits?*

Immigration

- *Do I need to get a visa (entry clearance) before I travel to the UK?*
- *What conditions must I meet to be a student in the UK?*
- *Can I bring my family with me to the UK?*
- *I have not yet finalised my arrangements; can I come to the UK to attend interviews for a place on a course?*

Working in the UK

- *Can I work while I am studying in the UK?*
- *Can my husband/wife/son/daughter work while I study in the UK?*

- *Can I stay in the UK to work after I have finished studying?*
- *Do I have to pay tax if I work while studying in the UK?*

General

- *Will my qualifications be recognized in the UK?*
- *How can I find out about different courses of study in the UK?*
- *What information should I check about the institution I want to study at?*
- *How can I tell which institutions offer UK degrees?*
- *How do I apply for a place on a course at an institution in the UK?*
- *How do I find somewhere to live in the UK?*
- *Can my children go to school in the UK while I study in the UK?*
- *Can I get free health care for myself and my family while I study in the UK?*
- *Can I use my driving licence from home to drive in England, Scotland or Wales?*

(Council for International Education (UKCOSA) undated)

Note: Answers to these questions are available on the UKCOSA website.

Box 11.2 Things for international students to do before the start of their research programmes

For starters, [international] students had better make themselves familiar with the universities and the countries they are going to spend some time in. Thus they should find out as much information about those countries as possible, in terms of, for example, government, religions, culture, languages, weather, and ways of life.

(Premkamolnetr 1999)

The extract in Box 11.2 makes additional suggestions about what to do before leaving home.

Selecting a suitable institution

Chapters 2 and 3 should be helpful for all prospective students looking for postgraduate programmes in the UK, irrespective of their country of origin, and Chapter 10 considers various personal circumstances, such as accommodation, which may affect some students, including international students.

If you are starting your search from within your own country, there is the problem of distance, in that you will probably not be able to visit to check things out before committing yourself. Fortunately certain institutions send out delegates to meet, advise and recruit students in their own countries. You will probably have to scan institutional websites for further information.

It is crucially important that you find an institution which is particularly caring towards its international students and which follows the guidelines of good practice, as documented on the institutional website. Check, in particular, that you will be supervised by a genuine team rather than, effectively, a single individual and, ideally, that there is also some sort of adviser on hand. Also check through your personal networks of current and past students.

Before finalizing on an institution, there is one matter which is pertinent if your family and friends are staying back home. You need to ask yourself whether there is already a community from your country nearby and, if not, whether this matters to you. Frequent or lengthy stays away in London or other centres of social activity will not be acceptable to an institution which will require its full-time students to fulfil certain obligations of residence. Students who flout this lay themselves open to having their registration terminated.

Finally a word of caution: the financial benefit that international students bring to institutions is very considerable indeed, and there can be the temptation for some to give such students the benefit of any doubt when it comes to accepting their language qualifications. If you think that this may be applying to you, think carefully before proceeding, as your interests may be better served by spending time at home to improve your English before moving away for postgraduate work.

Funding issues and their implications

Of all the differences between postgraduate research students from the UK/EU and elsewhere, the one with the highest profile is that of fees. Although fees differ across institutions and across departments, it is always the case that 'overseas' students pay very much more. The UKCOSA website (www.ukcosa.org.uk) elaborates, as do various institutional websites.

If your funding comes from your own country, you need to be aware that it can be cripplingly expensive for your funding body. Not only are the fees so much higher for overseas students, the exchange rate may not be favourable. Consequently funding bodies require and demand value for money. Funding for three or (in some cases) four years may seem a comfortable deal at the outset, but students will need to hit the ground running to be sure that all aspects of the work are completed before the money runs out. Only in very special circumstances and with a great deal of paperwork will funding be extended. Furthermore the people back home will expect anyone who has studied away for so long to be returning as a success. This can 'hang over' international research students as a source of unremitting strain and worry. If this applies to you, you would be well advised to familiarize yourself with the rest of this book as soon as possible, so that you can understand and manage what lies ahead. In particular, do make sure that the project you undertake will not be too ambitious in terms of data collection and analyses. Aiming for 'quantity' is not necessarily the best way of achieving the quality, originality and significance appropriate for work at PhD level. You will need to think independently and take advice from supervisors while not following instructions blindly. Chapters 19 and 20 elaborate.

Timing the application

Ideally students should apply for admission well before the date they wish to start. UK institutions normally advise prospective students from overseas to apply, if possible, a year in advance for full-time registration on the longer postgraduate programmes, and not to set out from their home countries until they have received and accepted a formal offer.

The challenge of working in another language

Language issues are likely to be the foremost of all the challenges which confront those international students whose first language is not English.

Their English for academic reading and writing tends to be good, sometimes better even than that of native English speakers – although they, like all students, will benefit from Chapters 16 and 23. Spoken English, however, is also important because of the benefits of being able to communicate freely and easily with supervisors and others. Obviously proficiency in English should improve over the course of the postgraduate programme. However, a problem can be that international students tend to conduct their social lives with others from their home country, so that they can relax in their own culture and interact without language difficulties. Whereas this is entirely understandable, it does nothing to develop spoken English. So, if English is not your mother tongue, you should orient yourself to taking up opportunities to include native English speakers in your social life. Some of the most successful international students improved their English dramatically by having an English girlfriend or boyfriend.

To end this section on the bright side, once an institution has accepted a student, it bears the responsibility to provide the resources necessary to complete the programme of work – which includes language support. Also at the level of a research degree, editorial help – if that is all it is – is not generally regarded as cheating. After all, authors who write for publication, even in their own language, always have someone nominated by the publisher to work through the manuscript in an editorial mode, and no-one argues that the work is consequently not theirs. It should be pointed out, however, that a reasonable grasp of English is expected from graduates of English-speaking universities who may be expected to interact and teach in English afterwards. (In the unusual event of a supervisor claiming that a student's command of English is beyond help, the institution should never have accepted that student in the first place.)

The challenge of thinking independently

International students may face another significant challenge. It applies where they come from cultures which expect a student never to stray from giving the outward appearance that a teacher is right in all respects all of the time. These cultures value deference, humility and compliance, without displays of emotion. Students from such cultures face a major readjustment when they first arrive in a Western educational system where independent thinking is valued and where students, particularly research students, are expected to demonstrate this in ways which may seem alien and uncomfortable.

Some supervisors are sensitive to the issues and help their students to handle them, but supervisors who have never worked outside their own country may not be. This puts the onus on the international students. The issues will not go away. Remedies are matters for individual preference, often worked out with guidance from more experienced members of the same culture. Often all that is needed is a form of 'permission' from supervisors that academic argument and creative thinking are acceptable within the framework of the research; that this is what will please supervisors; and that it will not be regarded as lack of respect. Pages 47–54 of Chapter 6 consider the move towards independence in more detail and suggests ways of taking initiatives with supervisors on this and various other matters.

A related matter is that students from these cultures tend to think that their written work should include chunks copied verbatim from the publications of experts, because this shows that they honour those experts. Whatever the intentions and rationales of the students doing the copying, it is nevertheless an attempt to pass off the work of others as one's own. This is known as 'plagiarism' and the temptation to do it must be overcome. Plagiarism is considered more fully in Chapter 9, along with some techniques for avoiding it.

> ## Suggestions and points to ponder
>
> - As an 'international' research student, do you recognize yourself in the description of the last few paragraphs?
> - If so, turn to Chapter 6 and work carefully through the parts on the developing nature of supervision.
> - Then turn to Chapter 9 and work carefully through the sections on plagiarism and how to avoid it.

Whatever the culture at home, postgraduate research students in a Western culture are expected to work things out for themselves. At the level of postgraduate research no supervisor or teacher will tell students what to do – at least not after a relatively short induction period. General training will be given but, after that, supervisors are there to advise, warn and encourage. It will be a good idea to watch how British students interact with supervisors and take that as a rough model. It is also important to realize that, because supervisors are not all-knowing, they can, just like everyone else, be sufficiently insecure to feel threatened in certain situations. Some ways of handling this are suggested in Chapter 6.

In contrast there are students from some cultures who may give the impression that, having paid their fees to the institution, it is obliged to give them the corresponding award, regardless of anything else. Such students need to appreciate that their fees are buying opportunity, i.e. the opportunity to develop themselves, and that it is up to them how they use this opportunity. In particular no academic with any professionalism will sign certificates of attendance at training where the student has not participated.

Other possible challenges

Most of the challenges that international students have to face are not unique to international students. Many students, and by no means all international ones, have to face up to such challenges as leaving family and friends, finding suitable living accommodation, having to make up for a missed 'IT way of life', taking time out for prayer, having limited finances, and – for agreed periods – working away from the institution. All these challenges, and more, are considered throughout the book. See in particular Chapter 10 on adapting to personal circumstances. Whatever challenges arise for international research students, there are always people to advise. International students do succeed in postgraduate research and they are invariably happy to pass on tips and techniques. The extract in Box 11.3 gives an example.

Hopefully this chapter has succeeded in stressing that differences between postgraduate research students due to their country of origin are tiny in comparison with what all postgraduate research students have in common in undertaking research degrees. Although this chapter has attempted to tease out the main challenges so that they can be considered and addressed, what is far more important is in the rest of the book. It deals with matters that are as applicable to international research students as to all research students.

Points to ponder

- As an 'international' research student, what do you think are the greatest challenges you have had to face, over and above those which 'home' students have had to face?
- How have these challenges changed as the research has progressed?
- What is the best advice you could give to other research students from your home background?

Box 11.3 A suggestion for improving communication between international students and their supervisors

The language barriers also contribute to some difficulties in communication between students and their supervisors. . . . Overseas students may feel uneasy talking to them or asking about some academic problems because of this barrier. To deal with this, students should write their entire questions on paper and show this to the supervisors at the same time as they are trying to communicate with them. Students may need to ask the supervisors to write down any important points the supervisors have suggested as well. This strategy worked perfectly well with me.

(Premkamolnetr 1999)

12

Managing your skills development

What is the use of transmitting knowledge if the individual's total development lags behind?

(Maria Montessori at www.annabelle.net)

The importance of skills • The characteristics of a skill • The process of becoming skilled • The transferability of skills • Ways of thinking about the skills developed in postgraduate research • Recognizing the skills that you will develop in your own research • A do-it-yourself training needs analysis/ skills audit • The joint statement on skills by the UK Research Councils • Collecting and using evidence to demonstrate skills proficiency • Locating suitable training • 'Personal development planning' (PDP) • The place of PDP in formal assessment processes

The importance of skills

Nowadays most people take on a variety of employments during their working lives, as existing jobs become obsolete following new technological developments and the changing requirements of society. Even qualified professionals have to change their career directions, and this trend is growing. So students, whether they are already in a career or not, need to prepare themselves, by thinking not so much about what they 'know' but more about what they will be able to 'do' with adequate competence in the employment market – i.e. what their *skills* are. The terms 'competencies' and 'attributes' tend to be used as loosely equivalent.

Various high level dictates have imposed on institutions of higher education the requirement that all the training elements of a PhD need to be strengthened, particularly those in transferable skills. Box 12.1 shows a frequently quoted extract from one of them.

All institutions have taken the call very much to heart, but interpretations and practices vary considerably. Irrespective of the type of scheme available to you, this chapter should support it. The chapter can also be used on a self-help basis.

The rewards of attending to your skills development will be both immediate and long term. They will support the successful completion of your research as well as your career progression.

The characteristics of a skill

Being skilled carries with it a sense of a job well done. Broadly speaking, a skill is the ability to do something well within minimal time and with minimal effort. A skilled typist, for example, can type a report quickly and accurately, probably without even looking at the keyboard, whereas an unskilled person would have to keep looking for keys and would probably press the wrong ones by mistake. The typing would be awkward, would require excessive concentration and would take an excessive time. It might still get done eventually, but the final product would almost certainly have an amateur look about it. Typing is an example of a skill which is largely manual, but skills can also be interpersonal and intellectual. For example a skilled speaker can comparatively effortlessly hold an audience spellbound; an unskilled speaker might have a go, but the task would consume a great deal of preparation time and emotional energy and would probably not be received particularly well by the audience anyway.

The straight division of 'skilled' and 'unskilled' is of course an oversimplification, as there are varying degrees of skills-proficiency. However, knowing what is involved in a skill is never the same as being skilled.

Box 12.1 A recommendation on skills from a recent review

. . . The Review therefore believes that the training elements of a PhD – particularly training in transferable skills – need to be strengthened considerably . . .

(Roberts 2002)

The process of becoming skilled

The importance of elapsed time and good feedback cannot be overestimated. The development of a skill requires cyclic repetition of 'receiving feedback on performance', 'reflecting on that feedback' and 'practising the skill again'. As Figure 12.1 shows, the more times the cycle is repeated, the greater the eventual proficiency. This is why the process of becoming skilled cannot be hurried, and why it is important to start early. However, without informed and constructive feedback, the repetition merely reinforces bad habits.

The transferability of skills

Some skills are more 'transferable' than others, in that they can be used in a range of different situations, i.e. they can be acquired in one situation and 'transferred' to another. How much so depends on the situation. It is easy to see how the skill of, say, 'being able to spell well' can transfer from one situation to a whole range of other situations. So it is reasonable to describe it as 'transferable'. The skill of being able to use a complex piece of laboratory equipment, on the other hand, would not readily transfer to situations outside the laboratory. It would, however, more readily transfer from one laboratory to another, and aspects might transfer more widely. So all skills are transferable to some extent, and it is important for research students to keep asking themselves what is 'transferable' about what they are doing, and whether it is something that they can claim as a skill, rather than just a completed task or information acquired.

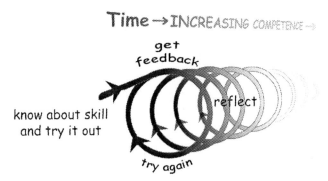

Figure 12.1 The cycle of skills development that leads to ever greater proficiency.

Points to ponder

- Think back to what you have been doing recently in your research programme. Do you think you been sufficiently round the cycle of Figure 12.1 to claim it as a skill? If so, how transferable do you think it is to other situations?

Ways of thinking about the skills developed in postgraduate research

In order to develop understanding of skills, they need to be thought about and discussed. This is often best achieved by considering them in categories. Several category systems are in common use, and there is nothing definitively 'right' about any one of them, i.e. none is any more valid than any other. The issue is only how helpful they are for furthering thinking. This section will use a category system that works well for thinking about skills in connection with postgraduate research and employment. It is in four categories and is due to the Association of Graduate Recruiters (AGR) (1995):

- Specialist skills
- Generalist skills
- Self-reliant skills and
- Group/team skills.

The 'complete graduate' is regarded as having competence in all the categories. Figure 12.2 is an adaptation for postgraduates. The skill-set of the 'complete postgraduate' is skewed towards specialist skills, because graduates of research degrees ought to be able to claim superb skills in their specialisms.

'Specialist' skills are the skills of 'being an expert at something'. For students on research programmes, these are the skills associated with doing research, teasing out knowledge, and being able to use understanding and scholarship in their subjects. For students on other programmes the same is true to varying extents which could be debated at length.

The AGR defines 'generalist' skills as 'general business skills and knowledge, e.g. finance/basic accounting, written communication, problem solving and use of information technology'. There may, in some circumstances, be an over-lap between generalist skills and specialist skills, as for example with the skills of foreign language proficiency, using certain computer packages or having expertise with use of the Internet. An example which many postgraduates

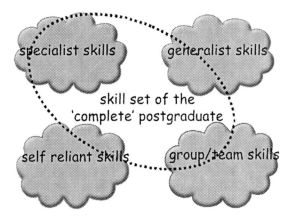

Figure 12.2   Skills of the 'complete postgraduate'.

develop to a high standard is that of teaching, as in tutoring individuals and groups, demonstrating in the laboratory and even lecturing.

The AGR defines 'group/team' skills as those skills associated with 'team players, e.g. management skills, meetings skills, networking skills, and presentation skills'.

The AGR defines 'self-reliant' skills in terms of being 'able to manage [one's] own career and personal development', e.g. self-awareness, self-promotion, exploring and creating opportunities, action planning, networking, decision making, negotiation, political awareness, coping with uncertainty, having a developmental focus, being able to transfer flexibly from one situation to another, and self-confidence.

There are clear links between the notion of 'emotional intelligence' of the extract in Box 12.2 and the AGR's 'group/team' skills and 'self-reliant' skills.

Recognizing the skills that you will develop in your own research

In order to extend and develop your skill-set, it is important to recognize the skills which you already have. To some extent all students develop skills as a natural part of progressing through their studies and receiving guidance and feedback from their supervisors. However, unless students are specifically alerted to the fact, few seem to appreciate the richness of what they acquire this way. Once alerted, the skills can be built on and readily developed further.

Box 12.3 suggests a framework for the sorts of skills that are most likely to be developed during an extended research programme. The word 'framework' is used advisedly, because all the skills could be described differently, summar-

---

Box 12.2 Emotional intelligence

*When Goleman's book, Emotional Intelligence came out, it was an instant hit
. . . The main message [is that] IQ* is less important to how you do in life than
what he calls 'emotional intelligence', a set of skills unrelated to academic
ability . . . Goleman identifies five 'domains' of emotional intelligence. The
first is 'self-awareness', the ability to recognise your own emotions, to know
your strengths and weaknesses and to generate a sense of self-worth. The
second is 'self-regulation', the ability to control your emotions rather than
allowing them to control you. The third is 'motivation', the strength of will
needed to achieve your goals and to pick yourself up after a fall. While these
first three concern your own emotions, the last two, 'empathy' and 'social
skills', relate to other people's emotions, the ability to recognise them and to
nurture relationships or inspire others.*

(Ochert 1999: 20)

Note: * Intelligence quotient, arguably regarded as a measure of intellectual ability.

---

ized, elaborated or sub-divided. It is important to make adaptations yourself in order to make the terminology more relevant to you and your field of study. All the skills are more advanced and have a wider scope than those which first degree graduates can normally claim.

Suggestions and points to ponder

- Modify the framework of Box 12.3 and fill it out to make it applicable to your own field of study.

A do-it-yourself training needs analysis/skills audit

Some institutions offer sophisticated schemes to support the skills development of their research students, and these include techniques for identifying the skills that students have, the extent to which they have them, and where further development is called for. The techniques go by a variety of names, such as 'training needs analysis', 'learning needs analysis', 'skills audit', etc. Figure 12.3 shows a tool which students can use by themselves. It is not a quantitative measuring device. 'Measurements' are subjective, with the

Box 12.3 A digest of a framework for a transferable skill-set for MPhil/PhD students

All MPhil/PhD graduates who are adequately able and have been properly supervised should be able to claim skills in the specialist research-related aspects of their MPhil/PhD topic. The extent to which these skills are 'transferable' to employment will depend on the individual concerned, nature of the MPhil/PhD work and the requirements of the employment.

In addition, there are numerous skills which are more 'transferable', which employers would understand and value, and which it is reasonable to expect from PhD and possibly MPhil graduates, over and above those transferable skills which have received so much attention at undergraduate level:

1   *All MPhil/PhD students will, by the time they complete, have spent two, three or more years on a research programme, taking it from first inception through its many and various highs and lows. This is no mean feat and should develop the transferable skill of being able to see any prolonged task or project through to completion. It should include to varying extents which depend on the discipline and the research topic the abilities: to plan, to allocate resources of time and money, to trouble-shoot, to keep up with one's subject, to be flexible and able to change direction where necessary, and to be able to think laterally and creatively to develop alternative approaches. The skill of being able to accommodate to change is highly valued by employers who need people who can anticipate and lead change in a changing world, yet resist it where it is only for its own sake.*

2   *All MPhil/PhD students should have learned to set their work in a wider field of knowledge. The process requires extensive study of literature and should develop the transferable skills of being able to sift through large quantities of information, to take on board the points of view of others, challenge premises, question procedures and interpret meaning.*

3   *All MPhil/PhD students have to be able to present their work to the academic community, minimally through seminars, progress reports and the thesis. Seminars should develop the oral communication skills of being effective and confident in making formal presentations, in intervening in meetings, participating in group discussions, dealing with criticism and presenting cases. Report and thesis-writing should develop the transferable written communication skills needed for composing effective reports, manuals and press releases and for summarizing bulky documents. These communication skills should go far beyond the level acquired during a first degree.*

> 4 *The road to completion of an MPhil/PhD can be a lonely one, particularly in the humanities and social sciences. Yet the skills of coping with isolation are 'transferable' and can be highly valued by employers. They include self-direction, self-discipline, self-motivation, resilience, tenacity and the abilities to prioritize and juggle a number of tasks at once.*
> 5 *MPhil/PhD students working on group projects, which is most common in the sciences, should be able to claim advanced team-working skills.*
>
> *Further examples of transferable skills are many and various and depend on the interests of the student and the nature of the research programme. Possibilities include advanced computer literacy, facility with use of the Internet, the skills of being able to teach effectively, to negotiate access and resources, to network with others, to use project management techniques, and to find one's way around specialist libraries or archives.*
>
> (Extracted with minor modifications from Cryer 1997: i)

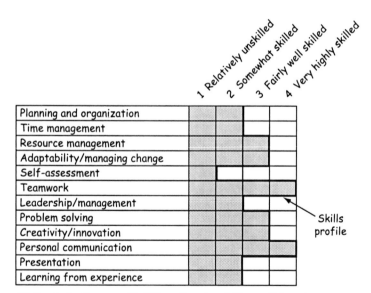

Figure 12.3 A do-it-yourself skills rating (or skills audit) tool.

purposes of aiding understanding and suggesting future action. The grid has been completed for a hypothetical student and its outline is known as a 'skills profile'. The change in shape of the skills profile over time is an indication of the student's skills development.

The joint statement on skills by the UK Research Councils

The Appendix reproduces a list of skills which students ought to find a way of developing during a PhD programme. It is a joint statement by the UK Research Councils, and should consequently be taken very seriously indeed by everyone involved in postgraduate research across all disciplines.

Suggestions and points to ponder

- Make a grid similar to the one in Figure 12.3 using the main headings of the UK Research Councils' list of skills (shown in the extract in Box 12.4).
- What evidence (or what description of what you did) would you supply to support your claim of being very highly skilled, fairly well skilled, somewhat skilled or relatively unskilled?
- Try to tell someone about this, so as to develop the skill of 'being able to sell' yourself verbally.
- In what areas, do you think that you need particular help or training?
- Date your skills profile and keep it safely. Then see how it changes over time.
- Repeat the exercise using the full list of skills, as shown in the Appendix on page 256.

Box 12.4 The UK Research Councils' joint statement on skills training requirements, as embedded in the QAA Code of Practice (2004)

The UK Research Councils identified the following categories of skills in which research students should receive training:

- *Research Skills and Techniques*
- *Research Environment*
- *Research Management*
- *Personal Effectiveness*
- *Communication Skills*
- *Networking and Teamworking*
- *Career Management*

The Appendix shows the complete list of the skills.

(QAA 2004: Appendix 3)

Collecting and using evidence to demonstrate skills proficiency

A common way of justifying claims for skills proficiency is through a personalized collection of documentary evidence to show to interested parties. It could include records of supervisions, copies of progress reports, evidence of training undertaken, etc. Also useful are photographs and newspaper cuttings showing involvement in certain activities; products or outcomes generated during the research (or plans, photographs or sketches representing them); and any special awards or commendations. The collections need to be built up over time and some students like to keep them in a purpose-designed box, called a 'portfolio'.

Box 12.5 E-portfolios (ePortfolios) and Internet blogs for postgraduate research students

What is an ePortfolio?

An ePortfolio is a website that showcases the research, experience and professional development of a graduate research student. It is owned by the student, and its development is their responsibility.

The e-lab and Graduate School Programme teams at Warwick have designed an easy-to-use template, which will enable you to produce an ePortfolio that is world-wide accessible, professionally designed and simple to use and update.

Why should I have one?

- *Established presence. As a researcher, it is important that you have a presence within the online academic community. You represent some of the intellectual resources of the University and your work is also – by definition – an original contribution to your area.*
- *Academic career. Increasingly, academic researchers at all stages of their career set up and maintain their own website; we are now offering this to all PhD students right from the beginning of their career.*
- *Networking. Your ePortfolio can provide a powerful means for presenting your work and making contacts, both within and beyond the University.*
- *Personal development. You can also use it as a focus for your personal development, say by recording courses attended.*

(University of Warwick 2005)

An alternative and excellent way of taking the portfolio idea a stage further is by publishing a personal home page on the Internet, with photos and newspaper cuttings, etc. embedded in the text of a curriculum vitae (CV). Web space is free via any of the free Internet service providers, and expertise to set up the site should not be difficult to find. Alternatively the institution may facilitate the site, as described in Box 12.5. The website address (URL) can be quoted along with the other personal details on letterheads, in email signatures and anywhere else that seems appropriate. A personal home page has the added advantage that it sends a clear message that the individual concerned is computer-aware and reasonably computer literate. Web pages used in this way may be known as e-portfolios or Internet blogs.

Locating suitable training

Skills audits invariably show up the need for further development and training. Institutions offer much of the training that students are likely to need anyway. For example, students are usually required to give presentations on their work, and – assuming that they have bothered to find out what is involved in presenting, receive feedback and gain practice – this is training in the skill of presentation.

Opportunities to develop skills of leadership, teamwork and ingenuity may be offered by a graduate school or other central support unit. Examples could be peer mentoring schemes; off-campus army-style training courses; and simulations of the world of business and finance. There may also be workshop-style activities on-campus to develop advanced presentation skills, perhaps with the opportunity of video for in-depth analysis. Students may be guided to produce action plans and to keep journals logging their skills development.

Outside the institution, the first place to look for training events, information and advice is UK GRAD. The extracts in Box 12.6 give more information.

Remember to take a long-term view of meeting your training needs and don't overlook training associated with future employment as described in Chapter 22.

Suggestions and points to ponder

- What aspects of your research programme serve as skills training? Are you aware of where else you could go for additional skills training?

Box 12.6 Support on skills development from UK GRAD

The UK GRAD Programme is constantly developing support tools for post-graduate researchers, supervisors, universities, training providers and employers, to achieve its vision to increase awareness of postgraduate talent. A number of online resources are available.

Events for research students mounted by UK Grad: GRADschools.

What is a GRADschool?

A GRADschool is a 3–5 day experiential learning course, aiming to raise parti-cipants' awareness of their personal and professional transferable skills: the majority of skills addressed will be from those outlined in sections D-G of the Joint Research Skills Statement of the UK Research Councils, ie. personal effectiveness, communication skills, networking and teamworking and career management. GRADschools are individually-designed courses for doctoral researchers and use small facilitated groups to enable individuals to review their experiences at intervals as the GRADschool progresses.

There are three main types of GRAD courses:

- *National GRADschools are residential and vary between three and five days in length. Participants attend from all institutions, disciplines, age ranges and experience.*
- *Local GRADschools complement existing course provision. They vary in length between one and four days, and there are residential and non-residential courses.*
- *UK GRAD also runs shorter sessions at universities and at conferences, which may be anything from one hour to two days long. These interactive sessions are designed individually to meet the individual needs of the institution.*

(UK GRAD Programme undated)

There are two useful booklets on skills development which, although in a series produced for supervisors, may also be of interest to students. They are in the References section under Cryer (1998) and Coe and Keeling (2000).

'Personal development planning' (PDP)

The chapter has now provided enough background to be able to elaborate on some of the comprehensive skills-related schemes that have been adopted by institutions. Although they differ in detail from one institution to another and possibly from one field of study to another, they all provide some sort of framework by which students can monitor, build on and reflect on their personal development. The schemes are generally known as 'personal development planning' or PDP.

> [PDP is] a structured and supported process undertaken by an individual to reflect upon their own learning, performance and/or achievement and to plan for their personal, educational and career development
>
> (QAA 2004: para. 27)

The words 'structured', 'supported' and 'process' are not included lightly. PDP is not a one-off activity. It is a process because it takes place over time. It is supported in that advice and training activities are on hand during the process. It is structured in that it is tied to phases of the research programme or registration and is rigorously documented. If the structure and support are not there, the procedure is not genuine PDP. So no student can sign up to PDP without being in a group, department or institution which supports it.

Students will probably be introduced to PDP at their induction where they will be provided with templates of some sort for documenting the process. These may be paper based, online or in the form of text files or logbooks, and they will facilitate looking backwards in a reflective mode and forwards in a planning mode as well as recording achievement. Each student is expected to take the initiative for keeping the documentation up-to-date, although some records will be kept by the professionals who are overseeing the PDP. In some cases these are the individual supervisors, and in other cases they are dedicated PDP staff. There will be regular meetings with professionals, training needs analyses and opportunities for reflection and training.

Out of the training needs analyses will emerge lists of requirements for particular training. In theory students only have to make a good case for attending a training event (like for example a UK GRAD event as described in Box 12.6) and it will be funded. In practice limits on financial grounds do not seem to present any major obstacles because institutions receive dedicated pots of money for students who are funded by the UK Research Councils, and they try not to be divisive for their other students. In practice, too, the funds are not taken up as they might be due to the constraints of students' time. Part-time students seem particularly loathe to take time out for training.

PDP generates various documents. Because schemes differ in detail across institutions, it is impossible to generalize about what these documents may be. The following are offered as a broad outline and for guidance only, and are not necessarily comprehensive. If you are participating in a PDP scheme and find a lack of correlation between your documents and these, it is probably because of different terminology or because some documents are part of others.

- Personal information such as name, registration and contact information
- Previous qualifications and experience, where relevant

- Lists, with dates of, for example, supervisions, courses or conferences attended; presentations delivered; reports written; publications; etc.
- Documents such as reports of supervisions; training needs analyses; action plans; work plans; laboratory notebooks or logbooks; reports; records of achievement; etc.

There is always scope for innovative documentation, like the e-portfolios of Box 12.5.

The preparation of PDP documents should aid students' reflections on their personal and professional development; prepare them for lifelong learning generally and their ongoing personal and professional development in the world of work; and form a basis for eventual job applications. With respect to job applications, evidence of willingness and ability to learn and records of achievement are particularly important, and you may like to look forwards at Chapter 22 where these are discussed more fully.

The extracts in Box 12.7 illustrate the allotted responsibilities for research students' personal development planning (PDP), as interpreted by one institution.

Box 12.7 Responsibilities for research students' personal development planning (PDP), as interpreted by one institution

Responsibilities of the faculty/school

- *All postgraduate research applicants to the University should be informed of the Institution's PDP policy for postgraduate research programmes.*
- *All postgraduate research students should be introduced to the opportunities for PDP within their faculty/school induction programme and should be provided with the opportunity to undertake PDP and be able to plan, record and reflect upon their development.*
- *PDP should be embedded at appropriate stages throughout the research student experience in order that students have the opportunity to undertake and be supported in the process in a meaningful way which clearly relates to the research objectives.*
- *Written guidelines for research students should be provided for all research programmes in relation to the purpose and content of PDP and the opportunity to undertake it through the course of their study. Adequate information about PDP should be provided within research handbooks with clear indication of how a student can expect to encounter PDP.*
- *All research programmes should provide students with a record by which to plan, record and reflect upon their academic, career and personal development.*
- *Research supervisors should provide advise and guidance to students engaged in the PDP process.*

- *Support and guidance opportunities should be provided for supervisors in order that they may participate in the PDP process in informed and effective ways.*
- *The operation of PDP should be monitored and evaluated offering opportunities to supervisors and students to reflect upon the process and its contribution to the learning experience.*
- *PDP should adopt a holistic approach encompassing academic, career and personal reflection and planning and should enable students to draw on all areas of their life including academic, work and extra curricular activities.*
- *Customised PDP processes should be developed at Faculty, School or Programme level to reflect the particular needs of their research students and they will be embedded within the distinctive learning experiences offered by individual research programmes.*

Responsibilities of students

- *Research students should meet with their supervisor on a regular basis (at least once every six months) to discuss their PDP.*
- *Research students have the primary responsibility for driving the PDP process, ensuring the plan is developed, updated and maintained, with supervisor guidance to support progression.*
- *Research students should ensure they know how to effectively access their PDP.*

(University of Manchester 2005)

The place of PDP in formal assessment processes

PDP documents should form part of students' regular (normally annual) progress assessments. At the moment, though, PDP is not formally assessed in the final examination, although examiners may well ask about it in the viva/oral examination to probe students' personal development as a researcher and scholar. Students who have engaged meaningfully with PDP during other research programmes will undoubtedly be able to impress the examiners by responding confidently, and so ease the way into natural conversation and debate.

13

Planning out the work

Those who fail to plan, plan to fail.

(Proverb)

The value of working to a plan • Planning in the long/short term • The project management approach to planning • The critical path approach to planning • Developing a style of plan for your own use • Identifying what is to go into a plan • Planning extended work on location • Coping with things not going according to plan • Abandoning a plan

The value of working to a plan

Since time is of the essence in research programmes, research students need to plan out what they have to do along with projected dates. A good plan has considerable advantages. It should:

- Ease anxiety by externalizing what has to be done so that it need not be constantly occupying one's mind
- Provide a focus in discussion with supervisors and others
- Generate training needs
- Provide a sense of security that one is on track
- Prevent too much time from being spent on long, only vaguely relevant activities just because they are the most enjoyable
- Allow one to relax and to take a certain amount of time off with a clear conscience
- Provide a basis for reflection so that future planning can be more realistic
- Form part of the records on skills development and Personal Development Planning (PDP) – see Chapter 12.

The responsibility for planning out the research lies with research students, although supervisors will offer advice and support and will almost certainly want to check the plans over. This chapter should help.

Planning in the long/short term

Where the objectives of the research remain unchanged over an extended period, a fairly concrete and extended plan of work is feasible. It is indeed a necessity where a team is working on a single large project, and individuals have to tie their work in together.

In contrast plans can normally be made only on fairly short time-scales where the direction of any one stage of the work is based on recognizing and grasping opportunities which present themselves as the work progresses and which cannot be foreseen. This may be where understanding grows holistically or where changes of direction are frequent, normal or imposed through circumstances.

For most research students, the maxim is to plan in outline in the long term and in detail in the short term. As things seldom go entirely according to plan in research or development, detailed plans inevitably need regular amendment. How much and how often tend to depend on the nature of the work.

The project management approach to planning

Project management is a formalized approach to planning which can be as simple or as sophisticated as users care to make it.

A basic technique, which would repay the time and effort of any student in any field of study, would be a bar chart of activities marked on a time-scale, as shown in Figure 13.1. Different colours could be used to indicate:

- Tasks expected to occupy all of the allocated time. In Figure 13.1 this might be scanning the journals and writing the report.
- Short tasks to be done at some stage during the allocated time. In Figure 13.1 this would be meeting the visiting professor.
- Tasks which must fit the allocated time-slot if they are to be done at all, because they interlink with arrangements which are firmly fixed. In Figure 13.1 this would be attending the conference.

Symbols indicate when something has to be completed. The symbols are known as milestones and the 'something' as a 'deliverable'. In Figure 13.1, the deliverable is the report and the milestone is the date it is to be handed

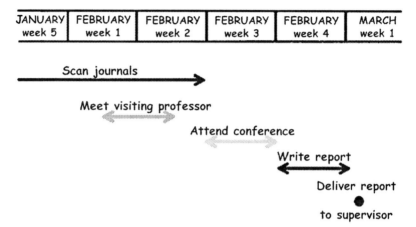

Figure 13.1 An example of a bar chart as a planning tool.

in. Other common milestones could be formal meetings with supervisors, submission of progress reports and training events.

Bar charts, also known as Gantt charts, are snapshots which capture how things are or are expected to be at a moment in time. They will rapidly become out of date and need revision, because the unanticipated is in the very nature of research.

All students, working alone, could sketch out a simple bar chart such as that in Figure 13.1. However, sophisticated project management software is available. It can manage the interlinking work of individuals in a team and the anticipated use of resources, and it has the advantage that plans can be simply and easily updated. You will probably want to involve yourself seriously with computerized project management only if your supervisor already operates it and is concerned that everyone in a team should be able to see the progress of everyone else at a glance, together with the usage of resources. If, however, you have ready access to software such as Microsoft Project, you may like to check out what it can offer. Further information is readily available via the web.

Suggestions and points to ponder

- Draw a rough bar chart for the next stage of your work, basing it on the style of Figure 13.1. Include:

  1 Key tasks, their start dates and periods over which they have to be done.
  2 Milestones and deliverables – your own or any that may be imposed.

- Annotate the bar chart with:
  1 The resources you want or need at each stage, together with their availability and costs.
  2 When and how your work links with and depends on inputs from other people.
- How far ahead did you feel it reasonable to plan and how realistic or helpful did you find the planning?

It should be enlightening to reflect on the start date that you gave your plan. There is a tendency to make this sometime in the future rather than today or tomorrow. Students undertaking research as part of an otherwise taught course are particularly prone to taking time off between the taught modules and the research. Then the research may never get started or be so rushed that it is below standard.

The critical path approach to planning

There is another technique, known as 'critical path analysis', which may be useful for the widespread problem of not knowing where to start among a sea of activities. It provides an overview for sequencing purposes, so that no work is held up while waiting for another on which it relies. In its simplest form, it involves labelling each task on a sheet of paper and then drawing arrows between them, linking them together in the order in which one relies on another. This may involve a certain amount of trial and error and possibly also, if one cares about aesthetic appearance, redrawing with tasks positioned differently on the page. Where there is considerable interrelationship between tasks, critical path diagrams look more like networks than linear paths. Figure 13.2 is an example for illustrative purposes only. There is no intention of suggesting that it necessarily shows a safe or comprehensive list of tasks in preparation for a holiday. It does, though, clearly indicate that some cannot realistically be started until others are completed. As with bar charts, project management software exists to take the chore out of the presentation and to highlight the critical path through the labyrinth of tasks.

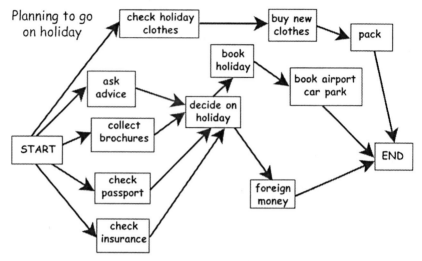

Figure 13.2   An example of critical path analysis as a tool for sequencing activities.

Suggestions and points to ponder

- If you feel uncertain about where to start any part of your work, see if developing a critical path diagram might help.

Developing a style of plan for your own use

The ways in which most people develop and document their workplans are highly personal, guided by the ideas and norms of others in similar fields and refined through personal experience. Planning is an ongoing activity and you may never feel that you have it quite right for your sort of work. This hardly matters because the act of progressively refining plans should markedly improve your work, your related skills and your general attitude.

Suggestions and points to ponder

- Discuss planning techniques with other students and your supervisor(s) and develop a style that seems to suit you.
- Practise and refine this through use.

Identifying what is to go into a plan

If you are working alone in an area where others are not closely involved, you may find it difficult to identify the activities that need to go into your plan. Any of the creative thinking techniques of Chapter 20 can help.

Suggestions and points to ponder

- Look at Chapter 20 and note the various techniques for creative thinking. Try some of them to develop ideas for the activities that ought to go into your plan. With the mind map technique of pages 28–30, suitable spokes might be 'required outcomes', 'deadlines', 'resources' and 'other people', but there are many possibilities.

Planning extended work on location

Planning for extended work away from your institutional or work base requires special attention because, if not done carefully, lack of finance and lack of opportunity may mean that there can be no second chances to have another go. This can be extremely serious. So check and double check everything before you go, and make fall-back arrangements where possible. It may be too late to do so once you have left base. It will be helpful to identify someone local who can act as a mentor while you are away. Some knowledge of the subject is desirable, but it is not as important as sound, logical and creative thinking, a commitment to being supportive and time to be so. Provided that you can find such a person, your own creative thinking and academic training should help you cope with the unexpected, at least until you can get in touch with your supervisor.

Email is the obvious cheap, fast and reliable way of keeping in touch with supervisors. For this and for general record keeping, a laptop computer will be extremely useful, if not essential. So take your own if you can, but do try to organize communication mechanisms before departure. The value of your own computer will be much reduced if it can't use the Internet to log on to emails and search the web. Also ensure that you will be able to back up your computer files while away. Attention to this is particularly important if you have got used to relying on the institution for automatic daily backups.

Institutional regulations invariably state the proportion of time that has to be spent 'on campus' for various awards. Application for study leave must normally be formally supported by a supervisor and approval must be given before departure.

There will, of course, be other administrative issues relating to your particular subject area and to the location of the work, and there will certainly be methodological issues. These need to be considered in advance by you and your supervisors together.

Points to ponder

- If your anticipated work is at some considerable distance from your normal base, particularly if it is in another country, what plans do you intend to make, or have you made, for the following?

  1 Financing your travel, accommodation and living expenses while away. How far in advance ought you to start organizing this?
  2 Arranging meetings with individuals or access to buildings or resources at the new location. How far in advance ought you to start organizing this? Who needs to be contacted?
  3 Identifying someone to talk things over with while you are away. When should you contact them to get their agreement?
  4 Using a computer and printer, and accessing the Internet (for web work and email).
  5 Keeping in touch with your supervisor.
  6 Fall-back arrangements for data collection (where relevant) if the intended source of data becomes unavailable.
  7 Resources to take with you, such as money, stationery and equipment.
  8 Anything else.

- Have you checked that the time you wish to spend away from the institution is allowed within institutional regulations?

Coping with things not going according to plan

Quite generally all research students seem to report that they had unusually bad luck somewhere along the way that played havoc with their plans. In fact it was probably not bad luck, or at least not in the way that bad luck is usually understood. Instead it was and is a normal feature of research: perhaps equipment is not delivered on time or breaks down; perhaps people are not available when wanted; perhaps crucial information centres are closed for refurbishment; perhaps an essential book takes weeks to filter through the inter-library loan system. Then there is always illness. The list could be endless.

The way of coping with unpredictable delays is in two parts. Firstly, build in 40% more time than you expect for everything, without getting lulled into the sense of security that this allows a more laid-back approach. Secondly, have a list to hand of all the other related tasks that you always meant to get round to, but never had time for or that you mean to do at some stage in the future. Examples might be:

- Getting to grips with the more sophisticated features of a software tool
- Tidying up your store of references from the literature
- Checking on websites that have come to your attention or have proved helpful in the past
- Surfing the web
- Acquiring any important keyboard skills which you don't already have, such as learning to touch-type using all fingers
- Getting to grips with computer-aided projection for making presentations (such as PowerPoint)
- Producing neat diagrams or tables for reports or the thesis
- Visiting a library some distance away that specializes in something that might be relevant
- Writing a draft chapter of a thesis
- Going to see someone
- A treat of some sort in the way of leisure activities or a short holiday

---

Suggestions and points to ponder

- Make your own list of things that are non-urgent and somewhat peripheral to your main work, but which nevertheless would support it.
- Beside each one, jot down a reasonable estimate of the time-slot that it would require.

Abandoning a plan

Things not going according to plan is not the only reason for changing a plan. It can be that something original pops up during the research that would be much more worthwhile pursuing, so that the thesis can be rounded off more quickly and effectively. Or perhaps the creative thinking techniques of Chapter 20 show up alternative, original and significant new directions (see Chapter 19). In such cases initial plans should not constrain, and new plans need to be made. The extract in Box 13.1 puts this well.

Box 13.1 Planning does not mean blueprinting

Here, then, is perhaps the first lesson of research; it can, in a very general way, be planned, but not blueprinted. One simply does not know what one is going to discover. These discoveries may lead to a complete change of direction.

(Berry 1986: 5)

14

Getting into a productive routine

Plans are only good intentions unless they immediately degenerate into hard work.

(Peter Drucker at www.quotationspage.com)

The importance of a productive routine • Maintaining a sense of direction: roles in which researchers need to operate • Keeping records of ongoing work • Finding out where your time goes • Using time efficiently when supervisions and seminars are cancelled • Matching the task to the time-slot • Handling interruptions • Coping with information overload • Managing time at home with partners and family • Managing time at the computer and on the Internet • Attending training • Using departmental research seminars • Networking and serendipity • Keeping 'office hours' versus using the 'psychological moment' • Keeping 'office hours' versus keeping going for hours at a time • Matching your approach to your preferred learning style • Using music to manage yourself • Directing your research to suit your personal needs and preferences • Maintaining a healthy lifestyle • Being realistic with yourself

The importance of a productive routine

It has been said that research is 1% inspiration and 99% perspiration. The 1% inspiration relies on creativity and is discussed in Chapter 20. The 99%

perspiration is the routine work, like attending meetings, reading around the subject, gathering data, keeping records, writing drafts and then rewriting in the light of feedback, etc. Although opinions differ about the relative magnitudes of the inspiration and the perspiration, the adage does stress that both are important and that the routine work is always likely to be much the greater in terms of outlay of time. This chapter considers some ideas which may be new to you for making routine work more efficient.

Maintaining a sense of direction: roles in which researchers need to operate

It is all too easy to work hard, in terms of putting in time and effort, while achieving next to nothing. One very useful way of overcoming this problem and making sure that your work is always on-target is to stop and check that you are always in one of the roles outlined in the workshop handout of Box 14.1. If you can appreciate which one you are in, or should be in, at any particular time, you will work much more productively.

Points to ponder

- When you put this book down and go back to your 'routine' of research, which role should you be in and how soon do you expect this to change for another role?

Keeping records of ongoing work

Of the variety of possible ways of keeping records of ongoing work, the most obvious is logbooks or diaries. Records of supervisions were considered on page 52 of Chapter 6 and page 124 of Chapter 12.

In some fields of study, it is usual for records of ongoing work to be in pre-bound form so that every mistake and doodle is recorded and dated in sequence alongside the more formalized records. The idea is that such apparently extraneous material meant something when originally made, and even though its significance may not have been obvious at the time, it can turn out to be important later. In other fields of study, it may be considered appropriate to keep a more formalized diary, either using the day-to-a-page

Box 14.1 Roles in which research students need to operate

There are four main roles in which research students need to operate, and they are presented below roughly in the order in which research students need to occupy them. There will, however, inevitably be a certain amount of to-ing and fro-ing between them and cycling around them.

1 **An explorer to discover a gap in knowledge around which to form the research problem or problems etc.** *(Students may of course be using a different terminology, e.g. 'research questions', 'hypothesis', 'focus', 'topic'. However, no-one should be gathering data for the sake of it, so research students should always be able to couch what they are doing in terms of a problem to solve, even if different terminology appears in the thesis.) For those students who know their research problems from the outset, the time spent in this role can be very short, although not non-existent because the problem still needs some refinement. Other students can spent a considerable time in the role. Most of the time this is likely to involve reading round the subject, but research can be such a variable undertaking, that students may need to drop into the role at any stage.*

2 **A detective and/or inventor to find solution(s) to the research problem(s).** *The role is that of a detective where the problem is about something unknown and an inventor where the problem is to develop or produce something.*

3 **A visionary or creative thinker to develop an original twist or perspective on the work and a fall-back strategy if things don't go according to plan.** *Also, if necessary, to find a way of ring-fencing nebulous or discrete investigations into a self-contained piece of work appropriate for the award concerned.*

4 **A barrister to make a case in the thesis for the solutions to the research problem or problems** *(rephrased if necessary in terms of terminology appropriate for the work and field of study).*

Research students may, of course, occupy other roles at times, such as fire-fighter, manager, negotiator, editor, journalist, etc., but these reflect the sorts of task which everyone, research student or not, has to handle on occasions, and do not generate any sense of overall direction in the research.

(Cryer undated)

sort available from stationers or loose-leaf word-processed printouts, filed in sequence.

Records of ongoing work, such as logbooks and diaries, should include such things as:

• What you do, and where, how and why you do it, with dates, possibly with an indication of time spent

- Notes on what you read (possibly in conjunction with bibliographic management files)
- What data you collect, how you process it and what the outcomes are (possibly including a purpose-designed spreadsheet or database)
- Particular achievements, dead-ends and surprises
- What you think or feel about what is happening
- Any thoughts that come into your mind that may be relevant for your research
- What your supervisor's reactions are, possibly in note form or as appended audio-cassette tapes
- Anything else that is influencing you.

Depending on the field of study, it may be sensible to keep records in the form of drafts for the next report or for the thesis. Although at the outset the thesis outline will contain only a few major landmarks, it can provide a basic shape to your work. Even though it is likely to change considerably as the work progresses, it facilitates thinking about what you are doing: why you are doing it, what you ought to do next and what the outcomes are likely to be. All are powerful motivators.

With computerized records, it is essential to keep backups. Most experienced researchers can tell horrific stories of how days or even months of work were lost when a computer crashed and they had not bothered to keep backups. Box 5.2 on page 37 in Chapter 5 tells one such typical story, and pages 37–38 make some suggestions.

Before deciding on the best way to keep records of your ongoing work, talk to several people, including your supervisor and a sample of other research students who keep their records in different ways.

Suggestions and points to ponder

- How do other workers in the field keep records of ongoing work?
- How well do they think that various methods help them to:

  1 Retrieve data later?
  2 Reflect on their time and resource management?
  3 Get ideas for future work?
  4 Set targets for future work?

- What advantages and disadvantages do they see in their forms of record keeping, and what general advice do they give?

Finding out where your time goes

It is common experience that time seems to disappear and one wonders where it has gone and what has been achieved. Whereas this probably does no harm when it happens occasionally, something must be done if it becomes a regular occurrence. The first step lies with finding out where the time goes, to provide a basis for re-evaluating activities. Some people like to do this by keeping a detailed diary over a period of time, and noting down the various activities in each day. The task can be amusing and even essential, but it does itself take considerable time which may not be worth the benefit. Nevertheless, you may like to try it for a short period or for certain days.

Suggestions and points to ponder

- If you feel that time is disappearing without any noticeable achievements, try keeping a detailed note of what you do. This can be as accurate or as rough as you please or think you need.
- Does the exercise show up any surprisingly large usages of time?
- Do you think you need to make any major changes in your use of time?

There are no hard and fast rules on how to spend time while on a research programme. What matters is that you should be content with your own use of time. Do realize that time spent on leisure activities or talking to people is not necessarily time wasted. Everyone needs them to maintain physical and mental health (see later in this chapter), and they can, as Chapters 15 and 20 explain, also help the work.

Using time efficiently when supervisions and seminars are cancelled

Supervisions and seminars do sometimes have to be cancelled at short notice and it is worth taking all possible steps to ensure that you are informed in good time, so that you can use the time slot to good advantage. Normally the cancellation is through email, which you can all too easily miss if you aren't logged on at the time. This can be particularly annoying if you have to travel from a distance and if you use dial-up Internet access once or twice a day.

Suggestions and points to ponder

- Whose responsibility is it to let you know if a supervision or seminar has to be cancelled at short notice?
- Liaise with them, particularly if you are part-time, to ensure that they have your most reliable contact details.

When free time-slots arrive unexpectedly, it is worth making full use of them, as suggested on page 137 in Chapter 13.

Matching the task to the time-slot

Sometimes the urgency of certain tasks must dictate the order in which they have to be done. Although this may occasionally be unavoidable, it is seldom ideal. First, it may mean that an important task has to be rushed; and secondly, it may be an inefficient use of a time-slot. Try the following to get a feel for the benefits of taking the trouble to match tasks to time-slots.

Suggestions and points to ponder

- Imagine that you have the following tasks ahead of you. If you like, replace them with tasks which fit better into your own type of research.

  1 Sticking stamps on 100 envelopes.
  2 Making two five-minute personal telephone calls.
  3 Writing up notes of an interview you have conducted and analysing its ramifications.
  4 Arranging a meeting to help another student.

- Arrange these tasks into your personal timetable for the next week or month, ensuring that the use of time is as efficient as possible. Have you merely filled the next available blank slot? If not, what principles were you using, explicitly or implicitly?

Arranging tasks such as these efficiently is a personal matter, but here are some principles to consider. They may appear self-evident, but you may be surprised to see the extent to which you have or have not applied them.

Tasks which require considerable concentration need periods of uninterrupted time and they are also best done at a time of day which suits an individual's metabolism. This is one's prime time, and it may be early in the morning or late at night, depending on the individual. Tasks which rely significantly on what is in short-term memory need to be completed as soon as possible, and this is true irrespective of the detail of any notes taken at the time, because notes can never record everything and are often difficult to transcribe. Tasks which do not rely on concentration can be done in parallel with, for example, talking to people or watching television.

You may have felt that the most important aspect of writing up the interview was that the required concentration demanded no interruptions. If so, it would be sensible to schedule it into a lengthy period of uninterrupted time – perhaps at home when other people in the family have gone to bed or during a weekend when they are out, or perhaps when a room in the department is quiet. Alternatively or additionally, you may have felt that the concentration demanded your prime time. Or you may have felt that the most important aspect of writing up the interview was that it had to be dealt with immediately while still fresh in your mind. If so, you would have scheduled it for immediately and moved other tasks accordingly.

Least concentration would be needed for sticking on the stamps. So it would be efficient to do this at a time when interruption is likely, or when you are likely to be tired or watching television. Try not to waste precious prime time on such things.

Did you think of suggesting the meeting for a time which would least disrupt you? Perhaps in the middle of the day if you wanted to use it as a break; or at the beginning or end of the day if you wanted it to interfere as little as possible with an extended block of otherwise free time. Timetabling to suit yourself is not selfish or self-centred, provided that the other person's preferences are also allowed for, and it is one of the most important aspects of time management.

Handling interruptions

Some people can work with interruptions, but most people, particularly as they get older, prefer to work without them. The following Points to Ponder provide a stimulus for developing your own ways of dealing with interruptions.

> ## Points to ponder
>
> - Is there a place to work where you won't be interrupted, such as at home when everyone is out, or in a library?
> - Is it reasonable to put a notice on a door somewhere giving a time when you will be available and requesting not to be disturbed until then?
> - Can you let the phone ring when you are really busy or use an answerphone and call back at your convenience?
> - Can you turn off the 'new mail' alert on your computer, so that you are not interrupted by emails and can deal with them all together at a time of your choosing?

Coping with information overload

A problem with electronic communication is that it is so simple and easy that information tends to come in too fast for it to be properly dealt with. The advice in Box 7.1 on page 58 may be of some help. However, there are no complete solutions. This tends to worry some people more than others. For those who are not satisfied with any performance which is less than their best, it is particularly hard. Such individuals need to learn the very important lesson that for certain problems there are no ideal solutions, however hard one searches; there are only some solutions which are less bad than others. Applying this to information overload, one just has to have a strategy for prioritizing incoming information and be ruthless about disregarding whatever comes lowest down.

Managing time at home with partners and family

Particular difficulties arise when working at home and having to deal with interruptions from members of the family. It is natural for them to feel that the home is a place for being together; it is not that they are unsympathetic or insensitive. Some people find the following tactics useful:

- At the outset of the research, negotiate an informal contract with partners, older children and other relatives about time commitments; their implications; and how long a period of time you expect the contract to have to last. (If you didn't do this at the time, it's probably not too late to do it now.)

- Every weekend, or at some other convenient time, go through your diary with your family, to agree what periods you can spend with them and when you ought to be alone working. Work periods are likely to increase considerably while writing up or finalizing the thesis, and sensitivity is needed on how and when to let the family know this.

- When you start a period of work at home, consider role-playing the 'joke' of saying a formal 'Goodbye, I'm going off to the office now' and a formal 'Hello, I've come back' when you are ready again for disturbances.

Points to ponder

- Can you adapt any of the above suggestions to fit your own circumstances?

Managing time at the computer and on the Internet

It is a waste of time to do tasks 'manually' which the right IT tools can do very much faster and more efficiently. In the long run, for example, it certainly saves time to learn how to consult a library catalogue on the Internet rather than having to visit the library for it. Furthermore, web skills and other IT skills are important in their own right and are expected of today's professionals. So it is crucially important to take time to find out about the right tools for a job and to learn how to use them. Unfortunately, though, computers and the Internet can run away with time.

Although some of the information on the web is the most up-to-date and pertinent available, which is reason enough for accessing it, much of what also seems, on the face of it, to be fascinating and useful, often turns out to be trivial, peripheral, frustrating and even wrong. The web can all too easily consume time to little or no advantage, and this is made worse if access is via a slow modem. So it is important to be firm with yourself, and decide in advance what precisely you are going to use the web for, and stick to it; or to allow yourself a specific small amount of surfing as a treat or a break from work.

Chatting via email can similarly run away with time. So you again need to be firm with yourself. You certainly don't normally need to respond to an email instantly. Essential aspects of email apart, you need to establish a balance between wasting time chatting electronically and invigorating yourself through interaction with others. You also need to learn to recognize junk mail quickly and not spend time on it. Spam filters are not always up to the task.

Playing games on the computer can obviously run away with time, but perhaps the worst time-waster is 'playing' which masquerades as work, because it carries a spurious acceptability. Creating a 'PowerPoint' presentation that you don't need, ostensibly to 'learn how to use the most sophisticated aspects of the package', is just one of many possible examples. You can almost certainly think of others.

When you find yourself spending more time at a computer than you originally anticipated, think of it as 'spending' time which ought to be 'buying' something worthwhile. Try a cost-benefit analysis to see whether you ought to move on to another task or take a break to do something else.

Attending training

It is difficult to identify the boundaries between training which is essential for the research and training which might come in useful. This is particularly so as there is currently so much emphasis on general skills development (see Chapter 12). However, time is of the essence for research students; so they have to find a balance between, on the one hand, ensuring that their basic training is adequate and, on the other hand, not wasting time on things that are too peripheral.

In establishing the balance, there is also the issue that the meaning and scope of research training are interpreted differently from one field of study to another. In the arts, humanities and social sciences, it is widely assumed that once students are trained in how to go about research, they can find out about various methods or techniques for themselves, should this become necessary. In the natural sciences, each research method tends to require a unique competence with specialized equipment; and students often feel justified in demanding experience of the different methods, irrespective of their relevance to any research in hand, so that they can bolster their job applications.

Using departmental research seminars

Most departments run regular research seminars. The discussion that takes place afterwards can often be as important as the seminar content. Although your first thought may be to doubt the value of attending where the topic is far removed from your own, your further thoughts should be very different unless you are very near the end of your work. There are several reasons:

- Research seminars may be your only access to academic staff other than your supervisor. Not that these individuals will be objectively in any way superior to a supervisor, but they will have different ranges of experience to call on and different ways of expressing themselves. You can learn a lot about what does and does not constitute good research by listening to their contributions to the discussion and then testing out the quality of your own work against their inputs.
- Research seminars provide easy access to what is going on in different and related areas, in case you may need or wish to link it to your own work.
- Research seminars provide excellent opportunities for developing an appreciation of the research culture of your discipline.
- Research seminars provide excellent opportunities to learn about how to give a seminar yourself.
- Research seminars are good occasions for picking up useful bits of information (see the next section on serendipity).

A valid reason for not attending research seminars is that they are so badly attended by others that it is not possible to gain the benefits outlined above. It may be possible, though, if you choose the right time and place so as not to cause offence, to have a word with the seminar organizer to suggest ways of boosting attendance, for example by moving the seminars to a different time of day.

Networking and serendipity

As your work develops, there may be the need for research tools and techniques that you know nothing about. Then the only way forward is to make a point of going out and meeting other researchers, talking to them and letting them know what you are doing. This is variously known as networking or keeping your eyes and ears open and giving serendipity a chance. The story in Box 14.2 gives one example of its many uses.

If you are part-time in the institution or working at a distance from it, you will have to find your own means of networking, guided by the time and resources at your disposal. Colleagues in the workplace may help. So will support groups, particularly electronic ones.

Box 14.2 The value of serendipity in research

Lewis Elton tells the story – which he admits dates him! – of how he first learned about computers at a time when they were very new. He was giving a conference presentation in which he regretted that he could not follow up a particular approach because the calculations would be impossibly onerous. One of the participants came up to him afterwards and suggested that the mathematics would not be at all onerous if he used a computer with a suitable program. Between them they did indeed use a suitably programmed computer, and the work was completed successfully.

Keeping 'office hours' versus using the 'psychological moment'

As the adage about research being 99% perspiration suggests, research certainly does involve long periods of routine work. Some students recommend keeping to 'office hours' during these periods, to ensure a balance between work and social and leisure activities.

Often, however, the routine work needs to be sparked off by an idea. Indeed, many students say that they can go for days without producing seemingly productive work; then an idea occurs to them, together with immense enthusiasm for pursuing it. If they can work on it then, they produce a great deal of high-quality work very quickly. If, on the other hand, other commitments force them to delay, the moment seems to have gone, and the work, when it is eventually started, is slow and hard going. It is worth trying to recognize these 'psychological moments', and, if at all possible, to let them take over, even at the expense of other commitments and office hours.

Keeping 'office hours' versus keeping going for hours at a time

During some parts of the research, particularly while writing reports or finalizing the thesis, it is not unusual for students to keep working for 13 or more hours at a time. This may be due to the pressures of deadlines or it may be due to pure delight and fascination. Do realize the dangers of sitting in front of a computer screen for long periods: eye strain, excessive tiredness, unknown effects on pregnant women, repetitive strain injury (see the extract in Box 14.3), and much more. Humans need to take regular breaks. Cups of coffee

---

Box 14.3 Repetitive strain injury

*Repetitive Strain Injury (RSI) is an acute inflammation of the muscles, liga-
ments and tendons and it's caused by performing the same physical task over
and over again . . . Poor posture, sitting in a fixed position for too long, even
stress and a tense body, can all combine to form RSI . . . The warning signs of
RSI are aches or tingling in the fingers, wrists, elbows or shoulders. At the first
sign of discomfort you should act. If you continue typing without improving
your work habits, just hoping that the ache will go away, it may well develop
into the shooting, burning pain that real sufferers know so well. In severe
cases, they are hardly able to use their hands at all and a few end up disabled
for life. Why some people and not others fall victim is all a bit of a mystery. But
if RSI really gets you in its agonising grip, your doctor's first order will be to
stop typing and possibly stop using your hands altogether for a time. Physio-
therapy, ultrasound and even osteopathy can all help the sufferer. But it may
take as long as six months before any activity is pain free . . . Prevention, as
always, is easier than cure. For more advice contact The RSI Association, 152
High Street, Yiewsley, West Drayton, Middlesex, UB7 7BE.*

(Prima Magazine 1994)

---

and biscuits or chocolate bars often seem the obvious ways of justifying and
filling them, but what generally works better is some form of physical activity
for five to ten minutes. It can be exercise or it can simply be one of the essential
chores, like washing up. It can be a good idea to use such chores to fill breaks,
rather than rushing to get them all done before starting work.

Not infrequently, students work far into the night. Only you can decide
the extent to which it is advisable for you to go without sleep. It is not
advisable as normal procedure, although it may be appropriate in certain
circumstances.

Matching your approach to your preferred learning style

Managing yourself can be made much more efficient if you get to know your
own personal preferred learning style and then try to match your approach
to it.

You may already know your preferred learning style. However, many stu-
dents have never realized that there are alternative ways of setting about work.
Consequently, they have never consciously analysed how they prefer to do it.
Try the following task to see for yourself.

Points to ponder

- When faced with a deadline for a task, do you tend to finish it with time to spare, to fill the time available with it, or not to get properly started until the deadline is upon you?

- When faced with a large task, do you find yourself breaking it down into small parts and then starting just with one small, well-defined part, and only after completing it going on to another part? Or do you find yourself spending time trying to understand the full context of the large task before attempting any part of it? (If you are unsure, try to think of a concrete example, which need not be to do with work, like designing a dinner party or a touring holiday.)

- Do you find yourself starting with the easiest parts of a large task to get them out of the way, before concentrating on the harder ones, or do you prefer starting with the harder parts to 'break the back' of the large task?

- When faced with new information, do you consciously consider whether your aim is simply to reproduce parts of it; to understand certain parts of it; or to understand as many implications and ramifications as possible?

There is no right or wrong learning style. It is a matter of personal preference, dictated by the purpose behind the task. However, everyone's work could be made much more efficient by using a repertoire of learning styles which could be called on according to the situation.

In particular starting a task only when the deadline approaches may be ideal where crucial aspects are changing by the moment, but for postgraduate research a better approach is likely to be to allow oneself time to mull things over, and develop and improve on one's thinking. Some students, though, take this to extremes. For them it may be sensible to aim to do several good jobs rather than one excellent one. Be guided on this by your supervisor, once he or she has had the opportunity to get to know you.

Letting a context emerge gradually by completing one part at a time is described as 'serialist' thinking. Needing to see the whole context before studying any part of it is described as 'holistic' thinking. The adage about 'not seeing the wood for the trees' is relevant here. It is normally used disparagingly to imply that someone cannot see clearly what they ought to be doing and where they ought to be going, and there is a lesson in this for research students, for whom it is important to be able to see the wood as well as the trees. Doing so requires holistic thinking, which will probably have to be cultivated, because early education tends to train children into serialist thinking at the expense of holistic thinking, because high-priority subjects such as languages and mathematics require a step-by-step approach. Subjects which foster holistic thinking tend to have a lower priority in the school system. Art appreciation is an example because it can require the complete picture to be taken in at a glance before the detail is considered. A technique to foster holistic thinking is the use of the mind maps, introduced on pages 28–30.

The intention to reproduce material without understanding it involves what is called a 'surface approach' to learning, and the intention to develop understanding involves what is called a 'deep approach'. It is not true that students should always use the deep approach, although of course no academic work could progress with an entirely surface approach. Both approaches have their places, and what is important is to decide which approach to use in which circumstances and why.

Using music to manage yourself

Some people work best with complete quiet. Others find that music can increase their efficiency. Most people know their musical preferences by the time they become students. What they may not appreciate is that different types of music can be better for different types of work.

Points to ponder

- If you like to work with background music, what pieces or styles are your preferences for the following?

  1 Reading
  2 Writing
  3 Creative thought
  4 Routine administrative work

- How would the people around you respond to these questions?

Some people find that certain routine administrative work, such as the sticking of stamps on envelopes mentioned earlier, can wind them up because it is occupying only part of their mind. Music can occupy the other part, and hence make the work more relaxing. But the music has to be the right sort.

Directing your research to suit your personal needs and preferences

There is usually some flexibility in designing a research programme, particularly where the precise formulation of the research problem grows out of choices made at the various stages of the research. So it makes sense to build in personal preferences, because doing what one likes aids efficiency.

Points to ponder

- Give an approximate rating for how much the following modes of working appeal to you personally. Then see how far people who know you well agree.

  1　Working alone
  2　Work involving being with or talking to people generally
  3　Work involving being with or talking to specific types of people
  4　Work involving long hours of private study
  5　Work involving using the Internet
  6　Work involving making or using equipment
  7　Work which is primarily out of doors
  8　Work which is primarily of use to others
  9　Work which is primarily of personal fascination
  10　Work which involves travelling

Some or all of the above modes of working, and other modes as well, are required to some extent in all research, but students usually have more freedom than they realize in terms of designing their work around the modes of working that are most enjoyable or fascinating to them personally. The freedom is greatest where the research students are working individually in a mode in which decisions about the direction of the work at any stage grow out of the findings of previous stages. The freedom is least where the research involves a closely predefined research problem or working as part of a team, particularly in laboratory-based subjects.

As an example of flexibility, if you happen to prefer working away from other people, it should be perfectly possible to define or redefine the direction of your research to involve reinterpreting data which is entirely secondary (that is, already collected by other researchers and probably already published). Then contact with others will be kept to a minimum. If you happen to prefer working with people, out of doors or in any other particular situation, you should be able to define or redefine the direction of your research to maximize this. Much depends on 'personality type' which is worth checking out sooner rather than later, as suggested on page 227 of Chapter 22.

Maintaining a healthy lifestyle

Part of managing oneself must be to maintain a healthy lifestyle, by giving attention to adequate and appropriate exercise and to healthy eating. This is particularly important for students who feel that things are getting on top of them. Dealing with this includes maintaining a balanced outlook by keeping physically fit.

According to a television documentary (*The Lady Killers*, ITV, 16 August 1995, 10.40pm), long-term, serious depression is readily avoidable and is treatable on three levels, according to its severity: physical exercise, which releases natural therapeutic chemicals into the body; talking things over; and then – if these fail – taking drugs prescribed by a doctor. The dangers of taking drugs which are not prescribed by a doctor are well-known.

Being realistic with yourself

It is all too easy to be unrealistic about what it is reasonable or possible for you or anyone else to do in a given time. If you aim at too much, you will get fraught and disappointed when you fail to achieve. If you aim at too little, you will never complete the research programme. You have to get to know yourself, and then be firm with yourself while at the same time treating yourself with generosity and understanding. The extract in Box 14.4 encapsulates what is realistic.

Box 14.4 A maxim for realism

A doctoral thesis is a piece of work which a capable, well-qualified [full-time] student, who is properly supported and supervised, can produce in three years.

(British Academy 1992: para 12)

15

Cooperating with others for mutual support

No man is an island.

(John Donne at www.bartleby.com)

The importance of mutual help and support • Receiving advice, feedback and criticism • Accepting or rejecting advice, feedback and criticism • The rights and wrongs of using help from other people • Looking after one's intellectual property when helping other people • Supporting and getting support from other students • Getting advice from academics in the department • Soliciting help from experts in other institutions • Getting support from family and friends • Getting support from colleagues in the workplace • Giving advice, feedback and criticism

The importance of mutual help and support

Although doing research can mean a great deal of working in isolation, students who are successful invariably rely heavily on the support of others – to suggest leads, to give informed judgements, to provide constructive criticism and to boost motivation. This chapter is about giving and receiving help and support from other students, other academics, partners, family, friends and other professionals in the department, institution, workplace or elsewhere.

Receiving advice, feedback and criticism

When people offer advice, feedback or criticism, they will almost certainly be hoping that the recipient is taking the trouble to try to understand what they are saying, will seriously weigh up the implications and will show a certain amount of appreciation. So the best thing to do as a recipient is simply to thank the person, to seek clarification if necessary, and then to say that one will go away and do some thinking. It is seldom worth launching into a justification of why what they say may be inappropriate. It may irritate them and probably prevent them from giving further help in future. Take time to think over advice, feedback or criticism. Then it is quite in order not to accept it as it stands, although often, to one's surprise, there may turn out to be gems of truth there which can be adapted to advantage.

Accepting or rejecting advice, feedback and criticism

It is important to recognize suggestions which could be seriously detrimental to one's progress. Their tell-tale signs are that they would involve any of the following:

- Undertaking major changes of direction which are unnecessary for the purposes of the award
- Not fitting comfortably within the boundaries of a consolidated piece of research
- Not being of a suitable academic standard
- Unreasonably extending the period of the research
- Not fitting within your area of interest
- An unappealing change in ideology or methodology, particularly when the existing one is valid
- Unduly expensive.

Such suggestions are usually well-meant, but they tend to come from people who do not know the ins and outs of a student's work, or are making invalid assumptions about it, or have vested interest in a different slant on the research, or have different ideological or methodological predilections. There is no single right way of undertaking research into a general area or of teasing out a research problem or theme or focus, and if suggestions make one feel uncomfortable, even after due consideration, it is almost certainly best to reject them. Supervisors should guide decisions. Normally, though, it is only when one has taken time to consider advice, feedback and criticism that one can decide how much to accept, reject or adapt. If the advice is substantial and it is accepted, then formal acknowledgement is warranted.

Occasionally people give feedback which seems designed only to make themselves feel superior by denigrating others. This can be because the individuals concerned have been caught at a bad moment, in which case they usually apologize later. People who give destructive feedback as a norm invariably lose the respect of those around them. If you find that you are receiving destructive criticism on a regular basis, stay polite and take whatever steps are necessary to steer clear of the source.

The rights and wrongs of using help from other people

In an academic community, there is no shortage of ideas, and there is nothing inherently wrong in finding out about them and using them. If you turn someone else's ideas into a significant part of your research, it is you and you alone who deserve the credit for recognizing its significance and developing it into something forceful and academically convincing. This is neither cheating nor any other form of misconduct, provided that sources are acknowledged. To be on the safe side, though, and to keep one's friends, it is sensible to keep the originator of the idea informed about how you are developing it.

Published sources should be fully referenced, so that other people can, if they wish, go back to the originals to check. Individuals who provide substantial help should be acknowledged by name.

Looking after one's intellectual property when helping other people

There can be a fine line between giving others help and giving away something that could be of financial, commercial or academic value. You may need to think sensitively about this. It is entirely reasonable to bat around ideas freely in informal discussion, but it is also reasonable to be alerted if others want to develop an idea of yours into something significant. You may want to take steps to protect your intellectual property, although the chances are that you would be happy merely to wish good luck to the individuals concerned. Be advised by your supervisor. It is reasonable that you are kept informed of progress if you request it, and that, depending on the significance of your input, you are given due acknowledgement for it.

Supporting and getting support from other students

Students in the same department or research group may be able to give and receive advice and support from one another which relates specifically to the subject of their research. Students from other departments and other institutions can give and receive help of a more general nature, and often, being rather more distant from any piece of research, they have a clearer perspective on it. If you can build up a mutual support group with one or more students, all of you will benefit. Such groups can be large or small; formal or informal; ongoing or transient. In any form, they can serve their members well. As mentioned at various points already in this book, some of the most useful support groups are email discussion groups.

Getting advice from academics in the department

Other academics in the department may be able to suggest useful references, information or leads to explore. However, academics are busy people and will not welcome being expected to spend time solving the problems of students who are registered with other supervisors. Also they have a professional duty towards their colleagues. So it is unreasonable to put them in the position of having to listen to what could be construed as criticism of how a supervisor supervises a student. If you do want a formal consultation, it should be cleared, with due sensitivity, with your own supervisor in advance.

Soliciting help from experts in other institutions

Most academics have stories to tell of receiving requests from students they have never met, asking for information. Academics seldom look favourably on this. First, they smack of the students apparently trying to get someone else to do their work for them; and second, they show a lack of understanding of what students' research work ought to be about. General leads can, after all, be gathered from institutional libraries and websites, and research for a degree ought to be about students processing ideas themselves and then following through the themes that develop.

Unfavourable reactions do not extend to requests for specific unpublished pieces of information in an academic's own published research area, where these are phrased in such a way as to show that students have already

---

Box 15.1 A definition of an expert

[An expert is] someone who knows some of the worst mistakes that can be made in his [or her] subject, and how to avoid them. *

(Heisenberg 1971: 210)

Note: * Or someone who answers questions you didn't know were important to ask.

---

done sufficient groundwork themselves to recognize the significance of their requests. Then academics usually do what they can to help and their advice can be very valuable – see the extract in Box 15.1.

Suggestions and points to ponder

- On the basis of your reading, name a few national and international experts in your field.
- Develop a few questions that you would ask each of them if you were to meet them. These should be questions that would further your work while not causing them irritation.
- If this activity stimulates questions that would really seem worth following up, mull them over for a few days, to see if they 'answer themselves' or if you can answer them from your own resources. If you and your supervisor both agree that it is reasonable to contact the expert, then think about doing so.

Getting support from family and friends

If you are a mature student living with a partner or family, you will realize that they will have much to put up with while you are working on your research. You may work late into the night, or over weekends, or at other times that might be considered as 'belonging' to them. You may be short of money and they may have to go without. You may be preoccupied for much of the time. Tell them what to expect from the outset, negotiate ways of meeting their needs as well as yours, and get their support.

If family members have also studied for a qualification involving research, you may be able to enlist their help in the same way as with academics and fellow students. They do not need to have a background in your subject. If you talk about your work, they can come to know it almost as well as you do. They can react by pointing out logical inconsistencies and they can suggest ideas and new directions.

Getting support from colleagues in the workplace

If you are working on contract or collaborative research, colleagues in a workplace can provide valuable support in various ways. However, if your research topic is intended to be of value to your place of employment, you need to watch out for colleagues there who are not familiar with what you are doing, have misunderstood its point and have vested interests in a somewhat different piece of research. Worst of all, they may not appreciate the requirements of the award for which you are registered. Their advice can be depressing and destructive, and should be politely 'forgotten'.

Giving advice, feedback and criticism

Helping others often involves giving them advice, feedback and criticism. Before going ahead with this, do make sure that they actually want it, and don't proceed otherwise. Try to understand their insecurity and put them at ease by starting with a comment about something you like. You will always be able to find something if you set your mind to it. Before moving to anything critical, it is a good idea to suggest extenuating circumstances where this seems appropriate, and to ask how they would do it differently another time. Propose realistic ways forward. Make your suggestions for consideration, not as unequivocal statements of what must be done. Take the attitude that you can comment constructively because you are not so close to the work, not because you are in any way superior. Close with good wishes and offers of future help if they so wish.

If you don't have time to prepare feedback properly, it is usually safest not to give it at all. It is unfair to give weak, ill-considered platitudes which are of no help, or to upset people by giving feedback destructively. Being able to give constructive, acceptable feedback takes time, but is a skill worth working at. It is a hallmark of academic ability and will serve you well along any career path which involves working with people.

16

Producing progress reports

Woolly writing is frequently a reflection of woolly thinking, and students who have trained themselves to write clearly will soon discover that problems of expression often arise from a lack of understanding, whereas students who write poor English can write rubbish without even realising it.

(Science and Engineering Research Council 1992: 16 (modified for sexist language))

The importance of reports during the research programme • Developing the content of a report • Structuring the report • Using basic word processing features to aid structuring • Constructing the introductory paragraph as an orientation to the report • Constructing the final paragraph for effective closure of the report • Citing literature • Adding figures and tables • Adding appendices • Developing an academic writing style • Making the writing process more effective and efficient • Capitalizing on all the features of word processing software • Using reports to get feedback and advice • Towards writing the thesis

The importance of reports during the research programme

Reports may have to be produced for various reasons during a research programme. At one extreme are the informal and private reports that students may choose to write for their own records. At the other extreme are formal reports which are required by the department or funding agency at specified stages of a research programme. Between these extremes are less formal reports required by supervisors as part of good supervisory practice.

Report-writing should benefit research students in any of the following ways, although the relative importance of each will change as the programme of work progresses:

- To see whether the work is on target, so that any problems can be spotted in time to be attended to
- To provide an opportunity to reflect on progress, consolidate arguments and identify any gaps in knowledge, data or methodology
- To develop an appreciation of standards, hence to learn to monitor one's own progress
- To provide practice in academic writing and academic discourse, so that any additional training which may be necessary in this respect can be supplied at an early stage
- To include with PDP documentation, as introduced in Chapter 12
- To form a basis, in due course, for the thesis and possibly a journal article.

This chapter aims to help with the sorts of interim report that have to be written at various stages in a research programme. If your interest is in making a claim for a transfer from MPhil to PhD, you should also read Chapter 18; and if it is in a final report to a funding body, there is material on writing the thesis in Chapter 23 that may need to be included.

Developing the content of a report

The content of a report must depend on its purpose. For most fields of study, the content of early reports probably ought to be such as to review progress to date and to identify a plan of action for the next phase of the work. Reviewing progress is not merely a matter of cataloguing what tasks one has done, although this will come into it. Rather, it should make a case that what one has done has been thoughtful, directed and competent.

Students should probably include the following in the report, presented where possible as a substantiated argument rather than as a straight description:

- How one has defined or developed the research question(s), topic(s) or theme(s), etc. with which the report is concerned – possibly with reference to the original research proposal
- How one is developing the research methodology, stressing how it is appropriate

- How one expects to ensure that appropriate data will be collected which is convincing for its purpose
- How the literature is being used
- How any constraints are being handled
- How subjectivity, where relevant, is being handled
- Progress to date
- Problems or potential problems to be flagged up
- General reflections. These should be relevant, not just padding, and the nature of what is required is likely to vary considerably from one discipline to another
- A plan for the next phase of the work.

Interim reports should build on previous ones and, where appropriate, refer to them. Thus there should be no need for repetition of previously reported material that remains unchanged.

With a formal report such as that to a funding agency, certain headings or sections may be obligatory. They may also seem bureaucratic or irrelevant, and if so, they may be there to provide the institution or funding agency with data for other purposes. So it is probably a good idea to start the report by drafting brief notes along the lines indicated by the above bullet points first, and then, in negotiation with supervisors, to edit these together to fit under the required headings. If the headings seem particularly bureaucratic or irrelevant, the help of supervisors will be essential for handling them.

If you liked the 'mind map' technique introduced on pages 28–30 you may also like it for developing the content of reports. As a starting position, possible spoke labels might be 'purpose of report', 'links with previous knowledge', 'work to be reported', 'constraints on work' and 'outcomes'. Once the mind map has produced the ideas for content, these still have to be structured into a meaningful order, but that is a separate activity.

Structuring the report

A report should be structured to make a case for something, such as the validity of a conclusion to a piece of work or the design for the next stage of the work. If this means writing little or nothing about something which occupied a great deal of time and writing a lot about something which occupied little time, so be it.

To achieve a clear structure when developing a report, it is worth making the title and headings sufficiently detailed that a list of them summarizes the case that the report is making. This means making the 'contents list' show the 'storyline'. The technique can be extremely powerful because shortcomings in structure are immediately obvious from the contents list and can be attended to immediately, before time is wasted on detailed writing which might later have to be rejected. If, of course, your discipline is one where standard practice is to write discursively in continuous prose, the storyline technique is not for you.

Points to ponder

- Look at some reports or journal articles in your own field. If there are headings, turn them into contents lists.
- The chances are that the storylines could be clearer, either by differently worded headings or by having more or fewer headings. Make some suggestions.

A good way to make contents lists communicate storylines can be to prefix headings with '. . . ing' words, such words as 'identifying', 'preparing', 'using', 'analysing'. The mere act of establishing the best '. . . ing' word to use can shed considerable clarity on what one should be writing about, and as a result, the next draft will be much sharper and to-the-point.

Using basic word processing features to aid structuring

Word processing software, such as Microsoft Word, can display and update a form of 'contents list' – and hence the storyline – while a document is being prepared. It can only do so, though, if the writer specifies what headings are to be at what level. This is done by assigning headings a 'style', via a pull-down menu, as in the top screen-shot of Figure 16.1. Merely emboldening or enlarging headings is not enough. Once a style is assigned to every heading, the current contents list can be made to appear on the left of the screen when the 'document map' button is selected – as in the centre screen shot of Figure 16.1.

A contents list can also be produced at the cursor position via the *Insert* button. Choose *Index and Tables* and then *Table of Contents*. Unlike the *Document Map* form of contents list, this one does not get updated as one writes, but it does have the advantage of being neat and printable. So it is most useful at the later stages of the writing. The bottom screen shot of Figure 16.1 shows one of the options for how it can be made to appear.

Another advantage of using 'styles' is that any document which uses them can be quickly and easily reformatted later to another specification, for example

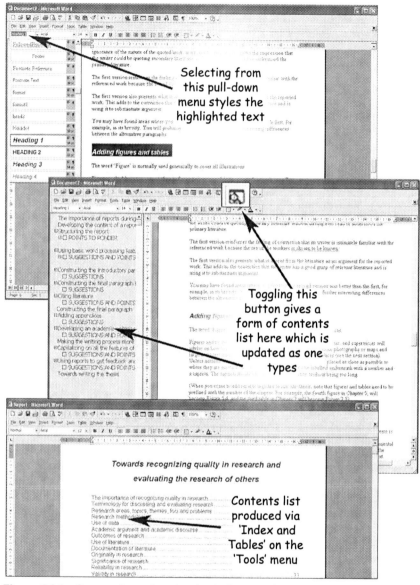

Figure 16.1 Screen shots showing basic features from Microsoft Word to aid structuring (*Office 2000* version).

to satisfy journal requirements or requirements for thesis presentation. So it is well worth getting to grips with 'styles' sooner rather than later. If you are not already comfortable with them or if formal training is not scheduled for the near future, it will be worth taking a couple of hours out to work on them, if necessary with help from a more experienced user.

Suggestions and points to ponder

- If you are not familiar with your word processor's use of styles, the outline and document map views and contents lists, see what you can learn about them using the built-in 'help' facility.
- If necessary, ask around for someone to advise you informally, or request some formal training.
- Try to get into the habit of dropping into 'outline' mode at intervals as your prepare documents to check their structure.

Constructing the introductory paragraph as an orientation to the report

Readers of reports need to be orientated to what the report is about and how it is structured. Since it is not unusual for writers to change their minds somewhat during writing, it is common practice to finalize the introductory paragraph once the bulk of the report is complete. There is a useful technique for this. The first step is to write a few keywords or some notes under each of the following headings:

- Setting the scene for the report, i.e. the general area(s) that the report considers
- The gap in knowledge or understanding which the report addresses
- How the report fills the gap
- A brief overview of what is in the report.

Then turn the notes into the introductory paragraph by editing them together. Figure 16.2 illustrates the idea, although the resulting text is somewhat brief because of the constraints of space. The figure uses a report on a conference as an example, although the method is suitable for any kind of report.

Write notes under each of the following

1 Setting the scene for the report, i.e. the general area(s) that the report considers, e.g.:

Annual conference, location, dates, keynotes, seminars, workshops, accommodation.

2 The gap in knowledge or understanding which the report addresses, e.g.:

Other members of department unable to participate, so lack information.

3 How the report fills the gap, e.g.:

My experiences of conference

4 A brief overview of what is in the report, e.g.:

Full programme as appendix. Appraisal of events. Recommendations of AGM.

Edit the notes together to form an introductory paragraph, e.g.:

The Annual Conference (July 14 15) was hosted by the University of Poppleton this year. For the benefit of members of the department who were unable to attend, this report documents my personal appraisal of the keynotes, seminars, workshops and accommodation, and it provides appendices showing the entire programme (Appendix I) and the recommendations of the AGM (Appendix II).

Figure 16.2   An example of the use of a technique for developing an introductory paragraph for a report.

Suggestions

• To try out the advice on writing the introduction to a report, imagine that you have to produce a report on a recent piece of work. Write a few keywords or some notes under each of the headings indicated by the above points, and then edit them together into an introductory paragraph.

Constructing the final paragraph for effective closure of the report

The concluding paragraph of a report should serve as an effective closure. The technique for doing this is similar to that for the introductory paragraph. Start with writing a few keywords or some notes under each of the following headings:

- What the report has done
- What new questions the reported work has identified
- How, in broad terms, you will deal with these new questions or how you hope that others might do so.

Then edit the notes together to form the concluding paragraph.

Suggestions

- To try out the advice on writing the concluding paragraph of a report, write a few keywords or some notes under each of the headings indicated by the above bullet points, and then edit them together into a concluding paragraph.

Citing literature

Citing literature is made a great deal easier with bibliographic management software. However, there is much more to citing literature than using helpful software tools. As Chapter 7 pointed out, literature should be used to substantiate and carry forward an argument. It should never be a catalogue of everything you could find that might seem remotely relevant. However, where seminal works in the general area are not directly relevant, it would be unwise to omit them. Try instead to find a way of bringing them in, possibly in terms of what they do not do, thus making a case for work that you will be doing or have done or that still needs to be done by someone at some future time.

Suggestions and points to ponder

- Imagine that the following are two alternative versions of a paragraph in a report by a postgraduate research student. (The subject area is probably not your own, but the example makes some valuable points which are valid across all subject areas.) Comment on the convincing, unconvincing and interesting aspects of each.

1 Brown (1991) reports on a study based on questionnaires to explore the feelings of teachers in Poppleton School about using self-study materials to teach schoolchildren, but she does not tease out mathematics from the other subjects taught in the school. Smith (1992) uses interview techniques to elicit how a sample of mathematics lecturers in several universities feel about using self-study materials. No studies appear to be reported in the literature about the reactions from schoolteachers to using self-instructional materials for teaching mathematics to schoolchildren, although Jones (1939) argues strongly for the need for such studies if the teaching of mathematics in schools is to be made more efficient . . .

2 Questionnaires have been used to explore the reactions of teachers to using self-study materials to teach schoolchildren (Brown 1991). Interviews have been used with mathematics lecturers in several universities (Smith 1992). There is a need for studies with mathematics schoolteachers if the teaching of mathematics in schools is to be made more efficient (Jones 1939) . . .

There are many issues that you may have considered, and it would probably be worthwhile to explore them further with supervisors. The following relate particularly to the last few paragraphs of this chapter:

Words such as 'reported' and 'argued', as used in the first version, inspire confidence that the writer has read and understood the literature. In contrast, the second version leaves the reader in ignorance of the nature of the quoted work or its conclusions, and so gives the impression that the writer could be quoting secondary literature without having ever read or understood the primary literature.

The first version reinforces the feeling of conviction that its writer is intimately familiar with the referenced work because the sex of the workers is shown to be known.

The first version also presents what is absent from the literature as an argument for the reported work. This adds to the conviction that the writer has a good grasp of relevant literature and is using it to substantiate argument.

You may have found areas where you felt that the second version was better than the first, for example, in its brevity. You will probably also have identified further interesting differences between the alternative versions.

Adding figures and tables

The word 'Figure' is normally used generically to cover all illustrations.

Figures and tables are an essential part of reports in many subject areas, and supervisors will advise on how to incorporate any specialized ones, such as oversize photographs or maps and large computer printouts. These may need to be placed as appendices, as outlined in the next section. Unless advised otherwise, however, figures and tables should be placed as close as possible to where they are mentioned in the text and each should be labelled underneath with a number and a caption. The caption should be sufficiently descriptive without being too long.

(When you come to edit reports together into the thesis, note that figures and tables need to be prefixed with the number of the chapter. For example, the fourth figure in Chapter 5, will become Figure 5.4, and the third table in Chapter 7 will become Figure 7.3.)

Adding appendices

Different disciplines have different norms about the use of appendices. A view at one extreme is that the main text of a report should be for making a substantiated case for something and anything that interrupts the flow of the argument, such as tables of data or copies of instrumental documents, should be placed in an appendix and merely referred to in the text. A view at the other extreme is that if material is worthy of a place in a report, it should be in the main text.

Suggestions

- Ask around in the department or look at some reports, journal articles and theses to find out normal practices in your field of study for the use of appendices.

Developing an academic writing style

By the time students come to write a report, they will probably be thoroughly familiar with the accepted style of academic writing and academic argument in the discipline. However, they may not. If you feel ill-prepared for academic writing, you must work on it.

It is not necessarily the job of supervisors to tutor students directly in writing, but they should be able to direct to where help is available, possibly to the institutional language centre if one exists. Alternatively you may like to enlist the help of a more linguistically able friend. Remember, though, that a reasonable grasp of English is expected from anyone once they achieve the postgraduate qualification.

Quite generally, academic writing relies on coherence, argument and precise meanings of terms. Other issues are whether it is normal in a discipline to:

- Write discursively or to use section headings and bullet points to break up the text and orientate the reader
- Use the active or the passive voice for reporting your own involvement, e.g. 'I did something' or 'something was done'; (the workshop handout of Box 16.1 illustrates some pros and cons)
- Use the past tense or the timeless present; (the first version of the paragraph in the last but one 'Suggestions and points to ponder' is written in the 'timeless' present to imply that the work is as valid now as when it was done)
- Use complex sentence structure.

Box 16.1 Use of active and passive voices in academic writing

In some subject areas, the use of the active voice in academic writing is regarded as unacceptable because it would indicate subjectivity and lack of modesty. Yet consider the following:

'The liquid was evaporated.'

Which of the following might it mean?

- I heated the liquid as part of my work.
- Someone else did this part of the work for me.
- The liquid evaporated naturally over time without anyone doing anything to make it happen.

How far do you think it reasonable that academic writing which is supposed to be unambiguous should not permit clarification through use of the active voice?

(Cryer undated)

Suggestions and points to ponder

- Check on the written style of academic writing in your subject area. If you are at all uncertain on any aspects of style, raise the matter with your supervisor in advance of doing much in the way of your own writing.
- Check out the complexity of your own writing by using the fog-factor technique, as explained in the extract in Box 16.2. (Or play around with the 'grammar' tool in Microsoft Word and see how helpful the various options are for your writing.)

Box 16.2 The fog factor – a guide to clear writing

We are often told to use short words and write clearly. A helpful device here is the 'fog factor'.

For this, we count the words of three or more syllables and the number of sentences on about half a page of writing. (I count the long words in my head and the sentences on my fingers.) We then divide the number of long words by the number of sentences.

A piece with a fog factor of 2 or 3 remains easy to read. If the count goes up to 4 or 5, it becomes heavy going. Yet academic and technical writing often averages 6 to 8 long words per sentence and sometimes more than 10. Long words strain our short-term memory. They make it difficult to remember how a sentence started by the time we reach the end.

Good novelists cope with basics like life and death on a fog factor of less than 1. But in technical writing, we are handicapped. We need long jargon words like statistics, regression or correlation coefficient – they can be a useful shorthand if used often enough to be worth learning . . .

The definition of the fog factor is not watertight. Are there two syllables in 'ratio' or three? What about names, numbers and abbreviations? . . . Splitting a sentence in two will halve its fog factor . . . Not all sentences should however be short. That would make for too abrupt a style. But long sentences should be there for a reason, such as giving a qualification or illustration before the reader is allowed to stop and think.

(Ehrenberg 1982)

Making the writing process more effective and efficient

Writing a report, or indeed any academic writing, can seldom be done in a single attempt. It is generally a matter of progressively refining some parts in the light of the others. This cannot be done quickly if it is to be done well. People who are new to academic writing usually underestimate the time required.

The early emphasis should be on producing a reasonably coherent whole. It is a waste of time and effort spending hours refining style, if what is written is likely to have to be discarded later. There is of course a balance to be struck, as no-one can develop coherence in meaning if the style is too rough. It can be helpful to write at a time and in a place where you feel relatively relaxed. How and where are personal choices – perhaps with a laptop computer so that you can put your feet up, or at a desk, or somewhere where no-one else is around. Then write, imagining that you are writing to and for yourself alone. Keep on writing until you feel intuitively that you have run out of what you have to say for the moment. Don't worry too much about style or typing/spelling errors at this stage. Word processing software should take care of them later anyway, and no-one else is going to see what you are writing. With this approach, you will invariably find that you create a piece of writing which serves well as a framework for refining later.

All writing is improved by the 'drawer treatment', i.e. putting it away in a drawer (or on the computer) and coming back to it after an intervening time in which you have been concentrating on something else, preferably after at least a few days. Then, arriving fresh to what you have written, you can act on your second thoughts, and go into an editorial mode to tidy up the arguments and general writing. Several cycles of putting aside and editing and re-editing will probably be required.

Throughout the writing, be meticulous about keeping backups! Keep and label all versions by date. Don't just assume that the last version has been overtaken by time. You may want to refer to what you wrote some time ago; and it is all too easy to overwrite a file on hard disk and then copy it on to a backup disk before realizing that you have lost your backup as well as the current file. Having backups of previous versions can be a life-saver. (For advice on the logistics of backing up, see pages 37–38.)

Capitalizing on all the features of word processing software

Most people know that word-processing software like Microsoft Word have spell-checkers. It is important, though, to realize early on that there are other features which can be extremely helpful, especially for working with longer documents. They include: automatic dating of documents; automatic numbering; automatic cross referencing; coloured highlights for emphasis; bookmarks for marking places to return to later; embedded messages or comments for on-screen readers; track changing features which enable others to make amendments for consideration; templates; tools for producing tables, charts and pictures; production of contents lists, etc.

It would certainly be worth your while to find out about them, and it may be worth your while to use them. That, though, is a highly personal matter. Some people regard them as burdensome, and many excellent writers do not bother with much beyond simple spell-checkers.

Suggestions and points to ponder

- What features in word processing software do your supervisors and other students in your field of study find useful? (Talk to experienced as well as new computer users!)
- If any of the features are unfamiliar to you, try to get someone to demonstrate them.

Using reports to get feedback and advice

If you are to get maximum benefit from your reports, it is important to receive feedback on them. This may be done informally during the process of refining them with your supervisor, or more formally on the basis of the completed report. Either way, it needs to be done. You will recall from Chapter 12 that without feedback, followed by appropriate action, there is no improvement in skills proficiency, just a reinforcement of bad habits.

Suggestions and points to ponder

- Make sure that, either formally or informally, you receive feedback on your report and that it minimally answers the following questions:

  1 Am I on target as far as expected progress is concerned, or are there any problems that ought to be addressed now?

> 2 Am I reading adequately?
> 3 Am I demonstrating acceptable standards in my work?
> 4 Am I reflecting sufficiently thoughtfully on my work?
> 5 Is my writing style acceptable?

You should discuss with supervisors how 'reflecting sufficiently thoughtfully' could be interpreted in your field of study, and what your particular needs are in this respect. For example, you may need to spot more effectively where, how and why others might argue differently from you, and you may need to modify your own case accordingly. You may need to identify how and why it would be better to do things differently if certain constraints were not operating, or how it might have been possible to have done things better anyway with the benefit of hindsight. You may need to consider the implications of your work more deeply. You may need to give your writing more of a 'drawer treatment' so that others – including supervisors – do not have to spend unnecessary time and effort trying to understand it. Maybe some other form of thoughtful reflection is what you need.

Towards writing the thesis

It is usual for reports or parts of reports to be edited together at some stage to contribute substantially to the thesis. There is no simple answer to the frequently-asked question of when to start the process. The best advice is to start on the shape of your thesis as early as possible, but to appreciate that it will change considerably as the research progresses. It is never too early to consult Chapter 23, which is about producing the thesis.

17

Giving presentations on your work

The communication of the results of research is an integral part of the research process, which is incomplete and ineffective if findings are not made available to others.

(Engineering and Physical Sciences Research Council 1995: 9/1)

The value of giving presentations • Identifying the purposes of a presentation • Developing the content of a presentation • Developing the structure of a presentation • Developing visual aids/using computer-aided presentation • Things to think about at the rehearsal stage • Drumming up attendance for a departmental seminar • Giving a conference presentation • Giving other types of presentation

The value of giving presentations

It is important for students to be able to give confident and effective presentations on their work. Some departments require it as part of formal progress monitoring; some offer it as part of their training for personal and professional development (see PDP on pages 126–129) and some request it to support interactions with outsiders such as funding bodies and prospective students. Having to present in formal situations has considerable benefits for students. The preparation forces them to look at what they are doing from different perspectives, which tend to reveal any flaws in argument which might otherwise have been missed. It also stimulates ideas for new ways forward. The presentation itself invariably generates useful feedback and suggestions.

Giving presentations is a large subject, and this chapter can only touch on those aspects that seem to be of particular concern to students working on research. If you would like further information, there is no shortage of advice. If you are already a fairly experienced presenter, you may choose only to scan this chapter for revision purposes.

Good preparation for a presentation can never be a matter of working through certain steps in sequence, even though this chapter has to present its suggestions sequentially. Good preparation must be more of a cyclic activity, because decisions on one aspect of a presentation affect decisions on another. So it is best to start by planning each aspect in outline only and then progressively to develop them as the whole presentation takes shape.

Identifying the purposes of a presentation

A presentation may have a variety of purposes, and in advance of any serious preparation, students should identify their purposes and prioritize them. Some possibilities include to:

- Show what one or one's group or department has achieved so far
- Get advice and feedback from the audience
- Provide a forum where everyone can learn and mutually support one another
- Contribute to assessment or monitoring procedures, such as the MPhil/PhD transfer
- Make a case for something, such as the need for a continuation in funding
- Impress, for example, a funding agency, prospective future students or a prospective employer
- Develop the skill of making presentations.

For formal monitoring purposes or for an information-giving presentation near to or after completion of the research, the priorities should be to show what has been achieved and to provide a forum where everyone can learn from the speaker and from each other. Even at this stage, though, where one might be forgiven for regarding the work as entirely complete, it would be inappropriate not to solicit advice and feedback from the audience. After all, further work can always still be done, even if not by the student concerned or for this particular piece of research, and it is advisable to show that one appreciates this.

For a departmental seminar/presentation that is not part of a formal monitoring process, the emphasis ought probably to be on getting advice and feedback, but this is a matter for discussion with supervisors or the seminar organizer.

Points to ponder

- Imagine that you are some way into your research and that you are to give a 20 minute presentation on it to the other students and academics in the department. Rate the relative importance of each of the following purposes for the seminar:

  1 To show what you have achieved so far
  2 To get help, advice and feedback
  3 To provide a forum for mutual help and support
  4 To contribute to assessment or monitoring processes

- List several areas where you would like help, advice or feedback.

- How would you change your responses for a full departmental seminar where you would be expected to speak for about 45 minutes and facilitate discussion for a further 45 minutes?

Twenty minutes is a very short time for a presentation, and it is very unlikely indeed that you can present in any depth on what you have achieved so far. A longer departmental seminar is the place for that. So be selective and concentrate on one or maybe two purposes.

As far as help, advice and feedback are concerned, you will not impress if the areas where you want help are such that you could help yourself given a few hours in the library, or a few minutes on the Internet or with a supervisor. You may even alienate people if you seem to be putting supervisors down because they could or should have helped if only you had asked, without having to call on the rest of the department. The areas where you want help should link in some way to soliciting fresh ideas, but you should clear such things in advance with supervisors.

Developing the content of a presentation

For all but the most experienced presenters, a presentation usually passes much more quickly than expected. The difficulty is compounded because enough time may have to be left for audience participation afterwards. For some types of presentation, this time ought to be as long as the actual presentation. So, when you come to prepare a presentation, you have to overcome the natural tendency to prepare too much material – although it is understandable that you may feel more confident knowing that some additional material is in reserve.

You should think carefully about how much of your work needs to be described and explained for your particular purposes. Sound advice is to present no more than a minimum of background material and not to give details that the audience has a right to expect that you can be trusted to have handled competently on your own. This will inevitably vary from one type of audience to another.

The following are helpful starting points for thinking about what to put into a presentation:

- The purposes of the presentation
- The purpose of the work on which the presentation will report
- What has been achieved so far – for which the pointers for reports in Chapter 16 may be useful
- Options for ways forward, and their apparent advantages and disadvantages as you perceive them at the moment
- What is likely to interest the audience.

It is probably sensible to start developing content in terms of topics. The mind map technique (see pages 28–30) may help, but it equally may not, depending on your personal inclinations. It is a good idea to mark some topics as less important than others, so that you can be set to leave them out if you find yourself short of time on the day. Similarly it is worth making sure that you have some 'filler' material in reserve, to use if you find time on your hands.

Suggestions and points to ponder

- Identify some topics for inclusion in a 20 minute presentation on your work, assuming that the audience will be other research students and academics in the department. If you like, use the above bullet points to stimulate your thinking.
- Mark some of the topics as suitable for leaving out, if time should catch up with you during the seminar.
- Add a few additional topics that you could present if you should find yourself with spare time.
- How would you change your responses for a full departmental seminar where you would be expected to speak for about 45 minutes and facilitate discussion for a further 45 minutes?

Developing the structure of a presentation

Once the topics for the presentation have been identified, they have to be put into a meaningful order. It will save you a great deal of heartache if you accept that there is no single 'right' way of doing this. The most immediately obvious way is likely to be the order in which you did things, but this may not be as interesting or illuminating as, say, a problem-solving approach or an opportunistic approach. You will need to play around with a few possibilities to see what you feel comfortable with.

Box 17.1 gives a maxim on structuring presentations. Although it is somewhat flippant, it does make the point that presenters need to top-and-tail their presentations to orientate the audience for what is to follow and to summarize the message afterwards.

Bear in mind that the audience needs to understand at every point where the presenter has reached in the structure.

Box 17.1 How to structure a presentation

Here is a maxim to help presenters to get their message across:

Say what you are going to say, say it, then say what you've said.

(Anon.)

Suggestions and points to ponder

- Play around with ways of putting the topics that you identified into a logical sequence with which you feel comfortable.
- How would you describe the logical arrangement of this sequence? Chronological? Problem-solving? Opportunistic? . . .?

Developing visual aids/using computer-aided presentation

Fleshing out the presentation and producing visual aids are often most easily done in parallel with one another, because each influences the other. The process tends to be a matter of starting out with a rough idea of content and sequence, giving a rough test-presentation to yourself with draft or imaginary visual aids, noting where modifications are necessary, making the modifications and going through the whole process again.

Confident use of computer-aided presentation, such as PowerPoint, is a skill that is expected of today's professionals. So it is well worth developing it as a student. Training in its use will probably be provided and you can practise in your own time on your own computer. If you like, you can probably take your own laptop to use in the presentation. However, be prepared for the possibility, however slight, that the system may fail on the day. So prepare a few transparencies or handouts as a back-stop. PowerPoint can produce them automatically ahead of time.

There is a balance to be struck between too many and too few visual aids and handouts. Too many can be perceived as patronizing to a mature and intelligent audience. A commonly quoted guideline is one visual aid for every few minutes of talk, but it is ignored successfully by most experienced presenters. Short presentations can, to advantage, be based on a single visual aid. Too many visual aids encourage the feeling that one 'has to get through all this'. Also, it is generally true that presentations appear most professional when the talking/lecturing/presenting leads the visuals rather than the other way round.

Computer-aided presentation can produce animations and transitions which are very impressive as fancy visuals. Yet they seldom improve presentations. More often they are annoying for an audience, and it is usually counterproductive for students to attempt them in short presentations. Whatever the length of the presentation, it is inadvisable to use more than one type of transition or animation.

Suggestions and points to ponder

- Think back to some presentations that you have attended and which you found (i) stimulating, (ii) boring. Below are some of the features which may have characterized the stimulating ones. Can you add any more?

  1 The visual aids illustrated something worth illustrating, rather providing props for the presenter to talk from.
  2 The presenter faced the audience and treated them in a friendly and polite manner, with good eye contact, varying the rate of talking as in normal conversation, but loud enough to hear at the back of the room.
  3 The presenter did not read directly from notes.
  4 The presenter's enthusiasm seemed to electrify the whole room.

Try to emulate these in your own presentations. In particular presenters can get away with a lot in the way of less than adequate technique if they enthuse the audience. This starts with a genuine belief that what one has to say is fascinating.

Things to think about at the rehearsal stage

Rehearse the presentation in private to check that the timing is about right. Some people find it helpful to keep a clock or watch on the table in front of them while rehearsing. PowerPoint has its own timing facility.

The actual presentation is likely to go more slowly or more quickly than during rehearsal, for all sorts of reasons. If you should find that you are over-running, never speed up to cram everything in and do not shorten discussion time. Instead, simply be prepared to say what, if time had permitted, you would have spoken about. Make this sound as if the time constraints have been imposed on you rather than that you have mismanaged your own time. If you should find that you are seriously under-running, use the extra material that you planned for just such a contingency. If you are only marginally under-running, simply finish early. No-one will mind extra discussion time or an early end.

Practise sounding enthusiastic. If you are not interested in your work, no-one else is likely to be. You may find it helpful to practise the seminar in front of someone who can provide constructive help, such as a member of your family or another student. Do be open to their advice. If they spot a lack of consistency or an error, the chances are that they will be right and that the reason why you did not spot it yourself was not that it was unimportant, but that you are too close to your own work.

It seldom gives a good impression to read directly from a script. No-one bubbling with enthusiasm would ever do that. So you need to experiment with whatever form of notes enables you to feel most comfortable. Some people like to make notes on cards or annotations on copies of the visuals or handouts. Using the visual aids themselves as prompts tends to interrupt the natural flow of the presentation. If you have prepared carefully on a topic that is 'your' research, you shouldn't need a detailed script. If you feel nervous, it can help to learn the opening couple of sentences by rote and then ad lib from there on.

It may also be helpful to plan answers to likely questions. Also think about how to respond to questions that you will not be able to answer or questions that seem designed primarily to show the expertise of questioners. For the former, it is probably best to admit that you don't know and ask if anyone in the audience can help. For the latter, one response could be to invite questioners to share their expertise with the audience.

Another could be that it would be rather too time-consuming to follow up that particular area then and there and to suggest speaking together afterwards.

Other things to consider when you rehearse include whether you can be heard properly; whether to stand or sit; what clothes suggest the right degree of professionalism while also preventing you getting too hot; and body language to suggest relaxed confidence. A balance needs to be struck between walking up and down, hopping from one foot to another and standing bolt upright.

It may be useful to set up someone to take notes on the comments and advice from the audience, as it will be difficult for you to concentrate fully on these while also attending to the process of the presentation.

In your own interests, find out at what stage supervisors wish to be involved in the preparation of your presentation. Never present it without giving them the opportunity to comment or advise first.

Finally, if you get the chance, visit the room where the presentation is to take place to get a feel for what it will be like standing in front and addressing people. In addition to an overhead projector or PowerPoint projection, there may be the options of a microphone, a slide projector, video playback equipment, and lighting and blind controls. If you decide to use any of these, you need to find out, in advance, how to manage them yourself, or how to signal directions to a technician. Audiences are likely to be irritated if you waste time finding out how to use such facilities during the presentation.

Drumming up attendance for a departmental seminar

If a major purpose of giving a departmental seminar is to get advice and feedback, it is important that the audience should contain people who have the background and experience to give informed reactions. This usually means other academic staff. They are inevitably busy people, so it may be worth making a point of personally and individually asking them to attend. Even if they do not make particularly helpful comments at the time, they will get to know your work, and may therefore be able to pass on any useful tips which come their way later.

If you have to rely on an abstract on a notice board to drum up attendance, you may find it helpful to look at Box 17.2 now. Although designed for presentations at conferences, there is much there that is worth adapting for other situations.

Giving a conference presentation

Your supervisor will suggest that you give a presentation at a conference only when you are far enough into your work to have some meaningful results, and he or she will almost certainly tutor you to make sure that you are a credit to the department. So only a few words are in order here. A conference presentation is not the same as an internal seminar presentation. The purpose is different. Also time will be a much greater constraint.

The purpose of a conference presentation varies from one field of study to another, so check with your supervisor. It may be to put down a marker in the national or international academic community that it is you who are doing a specific piece of work, and to show that you are making good progress with it. A journal is the place for presenting completed work.

Ideally, the conference presentation will result in publishers or other workers in related fields speaking or writing to you later to follow up on your work – but the first step must be to encourage them to attend the presentation. This is the function of the abstract, and Box 17.2 gives excellent guidance for constructing it.

For the presentation itself, you need to give an overview of what you are doing, why it is so important or interesting, how far you have got, what your results are so far, what they mean to you, and where you intend to go next. Describe your research methods briefly, but do not delve into the difficulties unless they are likely to be of particular interest to others. It is important that visual aids and handouts be very professional-looking because you will want to convince your audience that you are someone to be taken seriously. Many a conference participant has been put off by slides that could not be read from the back of the room and by the presentation of too much material.

Since work is often publicized at conferences before it is formally published, conferences are good places to get information to keep ahead of the field and to find out who is heading what work in your general area. You may even meet your future external examiner.

Giving other types of presentation

Students may find themselves giving presentations other than seminars or conference papers. Most likely are presentations to prospective employers or funding agents and to prospective students on departmental open days. The advice in this chapter can readily be adapted for such alternative presentations.

Box 17.2 Guidelines for writing effective abstracts for conference presentations

Form and Content

'in this paper I explore "x" in order to suggest "y" '

An abstract submitted for a conference paper should do two things – tell conference participants what you are going to say and interest them in coming to hear you say it.

Telling them what you will say

- *Identify the topic/subject of your paper – the question/problem it raises*
- *Locate the topic/subject in terms of a field of scholarship – who/what provides the intellectual context for the problem/question the paper raises*
- *Emphasise your position/argument – your proposition/thesis regarding the question/problem*
- *Indicate – this is optional – your reasons for undertaking this investigation (i.e., a part of your thesis research, a political motive, an intellectual motive, etc.)*

Interesting them in hearing you say it

- *Devise a title that is descriptive and inviting*
- *Find words that are accessible to both specialists and non-specialists; if it is a crossdisciplinary conference (disciplinary terms sometimes seem like jargon to those not in the field)*

Presenting the abstract

- *Plan the abstract as a single paragraph that is unified (i.e. one topic) and coherent (i.e., ideas flow continuously) – two (maybe even three) paragraphs are OK so long as the abstract as a whole is unified/coherent*
- *Ensure it conforms to the 'house style' of the conference*
- *Edit it for grammar, punctuation, typos, etc.*

Of course, often you have not fully written the presentation before you write the abstract, and so the abstract is often something of a fiction. Still it should be much more than an ambit claim – it should be a clear statement of your central hypothesis – the central idea that the paper will explain and argue for.

(Deakin University undated)

18

Transferring registration from MPhil to PhD

> ...decisions about transferring the student's registration to a doctoral qualification should take place when there is sufficient evidence to assess the student's performance.
>
> (Quality Assurance Agency 2004: 19)

Why the MPhil/PhD transfer is such a significant landmark • The mechanisms for the transfer • When to apply for the transfer • Preparing the case for the transfer • Writing the transfer document • Handling the outcome • Towards producing a journal article

Why the MPhil/PhD transfer is such a significant landmark

Most postgraduate research students who wish to take a PhD are required to register first for an MPhil award, and then, in time, if the work is deemed worthy, they may transfer or upgrade their registration to a PhD, backdated to the start of the MPhil. Most students try for this route rather than being satisfied with an MPhil. Fortunately the transfer should be fairly routine for competent and well supervised students who work responsibly, but it is nevertheless, a boost to morale to have it over and done with. This chapter offers suggestions to ease the process.

The mechanisms for the transfer

The mechanisms for the transfer are not uniform across institutions, and they also – for good reason – vary from one field of study to another. They will certainly require the student to make a sound case and to produce a report that is more detailed and rigorous than any previous one, possibly meriting the title of a 'mini-thesis'. They may also require the student to make an oral presentation and/or be examined orally, to enable assessors to clarify any ambiguities and to satisfy themselves that the work is the student's own.

The requirements of your own institution will be readily accessible in the student handbook or on its website. There may be appendices for your department.

Suggestions and points to ponder

- Find out what is involved in your institution in order to transfer registration from MPhil to PhD:

    1 A substantial report or mini-thesis (of which the case for transfer may form part)? What length and against what criteria?
    2 An oral presentation? How long and to whom?
    3 An oral examination? Who will be the examiners?
    4 A satisfactory report and recommendation from supervisors?
    5 What else?

- When are the earliest and the latest dates that you can apply for transfer? (i.e. how soon after registration for the MPhil and how near to the anticipated completion date of the PhD?)
- When do your supervisors suggest that you put in your application?

When to apply for the transfer

Subject to the institution's regulations, the application for transfer may be made at any time after one year of the programme. However the right time for you may not be the same as the right time for someone else. As frequently pointed out, research is different in different subject areas, and this has implications for when to make the transfer application.

In subject areas where the research questions and research design are laid out in advance in the research proposal, it is relatively straightforward to discern whether the work is on track and whether it looks likely to meet the criteria for transfer. This occurs most often in the natural sciences. Then there are advantages to applying for the transfer earlier rather than later. These go further than merely boosting students' morale. As the external scrutiny covers all aspects of the work, any problems can be picked up and addressed before they escalate.

The position is different in subject areas where the next stage of the research grows out of the results of the previous stage. It may well be possible, after just one or two stages, to see that a student's work is on track as far as general approach and progress are concerned, but it is not really reasonable to expect it to show the required significance and originality so soon. Students involved in such exploratory research will probably be advised to wait longer before submitting their applications, and it will be helpful for them to read and reflect on Chapters 19 and 20 first.

Preparing the case for the transfer

Whatever the precise format required for your transfer, you will certainly need to:

(i)   Review progress to date in the light of the original research proposal.
(ii) Identify one or more aspects in the work to date which are suitable for developing further, to a PhD standard.
(iii) Produce a plan of action to complete the work.

With regard to (i), reviewing progress to date is not primarily a matter of how you have spent your time. The emphasis should be on showing that what you have done has been thoughtful and competent. The following should probably be included, presented as far as possible as a substantiated argument rather than as a straight description, with literature referenced fully according to the norms for the discipline:

- How you defined the research topic or problem, taking your original proposal as the starting point
- How you have developed your research methodology so far, from the originally defined research topic or problem
- How you have ensured that you have collected data which is appropriate and convincing for its purpose
- How you have used literature
- How you have dealt with any problems and constraints
- How far you have got.

Most of this should come out of previous reports and records.

The scope and depth of (ii) and (iii) must depend on the stage in the programme. Normally the next stage of the work has to be a significant contribution to knowledge and be sufficiently challenging to demonstrate independent, critical and original scholarly work to a PhD standard. Also it must be such that it can be realistically achieved in the remaining time. All these invariably require narrowing the scope and focusing down. (The adage in Box 18.1, although intentionally flippant, does carry more than an element of truth.) With some work, the identification of a suitable next stage is obvious. Yet, this is by no means always so, and Chapters 19 and 20 offer advice.

The plan of action for completing the work (i.e. (iii) above) should normally be in the form of a fully argued research design with attached timescales.

Box 18.1 A definition of a PhD

Here is a flippant adage which carries more than an element of truth.

A PhD is about finding out more and more about less and less until one eventually knows everything about nothing.

(Anon.)

Suggestions

- Check out the advice of this section with your supervisor and develop an action plan for your own MPhil/PhD transfer.

Writing the transfer document

In order to produce a sound transfer document efficiently, you will need to brush up on your writing skills. Chapter 16 on report-writing should be helpful, and it will also be worth your while to look ahead to Chapter 23 on preparing the thesis.

Handling the outcome

If your work has been competent and you have made a sound claim, there is no reason to assume anything but a positive outcome. However, if you feel that you have a case for appeal, the procedures will be detailed in the student handbook or on the institutional website.

Towards producing a journal article

As the documentation in support of the MPhil/PhD transfer must be the most elaborate in the entire research process, bar the thesis itself, there is an ideal opportunity to have a go at editing it into one or more articles to submit to refereed journals. Supervisors should be able to identify parts that are suitable and they will advise on journals and the writing process.

It is becoming increasingly important for students to publish their research this way, particularly if they aspire to academic careers. Furthermore it serves them in good stead when the oral examination (or thesis defence) comes round, as it is difficult for examiners to make any serious criticisms of work that has already passed external peer review.

Some supervisors of the four-year (1 + 3) PhDs unofficially admit to encouraging their students to finish at the three-year point so that they can spend the last year writing and submitting journal articles. However, students should never feel pressurized to publish if they think that it would distract them from their research programmes.

19

Coming to terms with originality in research

All good things which exist are the fruits of originality.
(John Stuart Mill at www.quoteworld.org)

The need for originality in research • Originality in tools, techniques and procedures • Originality in exploring the unknown/unexplored • Originality in exploring the unanticipated • Originality in data • Originality in transfer of mode or place of use • Originality in byproducts • Originality in the experience • Originality as 'potentially publishable' • The variety of interpretations and configurations of originality • The balance between originality and conformity • Protecting the ownership of original work • Putting originality into perspective

The need for originality in research

'Originality' is an essential and widely stated requirement for research at PhD level, although it should also exist to some extent in research at all levels. Some students are fortunate enough to have it already built into their research proposal in some way – more of which later. More often, though, it needs special attention at later stages. This is a threefold process of:

- Appreciating the fullness and richness of what 'originality' is and can be
- Learning and using creative skills to recognize and/or develop originality
- Allowing a considerable incubation period for the creative skills to function effectively.

This chapter is concerned with the first of these, and Chapter 20 addresses the second and third.

A useful way to appreciate the scope of originality is through an analogy, where the research programme can be likened to an exploration into a wilderness at a time in history when the world was still largely unexplored and when explorers still had considerable personal autonomy. In the analogy, the explorer may have certain visions in mind concerning what he or she hopes the expedition will achieve, but appreciates that these may not materialize and is open to alternatives. To avoid cumbersome repetition, the explorer and student will be taken as having different sexes, arbitrarily male and female respectively.

Originality in tools, techniques and procedures

In the analogy the explorer uses all the information he can to firm up on why he wants to explore the wilderness and how he might do so within the resources at his command and within any constraints that may exist. He uses this information to plan and organize what background knowledge, procedures, tools, equipment and personnel he will need, tailored to the available resources and constraints. Some procedures may have to be specially designed, some tools and equipment may have to be specially made and some personnel may have to be specially trained or brought in.

Similarly, the student studies the literature, talks to experts and attends relevant training to get background knowledge and to develop an appropriate research methodology. The latter must include decisions about the procedures, tools and techniques, and possibly also the people to be involved. These may be fairly standard in the field of study, but if she uses them in new untested ways, this would justify a claim for originality. Or if she develops new procedures, tools and techniques for a specific purpose, this, too would justify a claim for originality. If neither is the case, her claim for originality must lie in later stages of the work, as suggested in the next few sections.

Originality in exploring the unknown/unexplored

In the analogy the expedition begins along the pre-planned route. If this is previously unexplored, the mere exploration is original work.

Similarly, if the student is conducting a major investigation on something which has never been investigated before, such as a recently discovered insect, star, poem, etc., the work will necessarily be original. This was what was meant in the second sentence of the chapter by originality being 'built into' the research.

Although 'originality' in some types of research is built in, in many fields of study it is not, and its pre-existence should never be taken entirely for granted. The extract in Box 19.1 puts this well. So students undertaking research have to learn to live with a certain amount of uncertainty, which Box 19.2 also puts well. Living with uncertainty may be difficult, but it is a fact of life for researchers, and can be ameliorated to some extent by welcoming the uncertainty as a precursor of creativity; thinking of the uncertainty as fascination with the unknown; and realizing that committed students do normally manage to complete their programmes of research and earn the award for which they are registered.

Box 19.1 Originality is unpredictable

A view from a Nobel laureate:

In real life . . . the truth is not in nature waiting to declare itself and we cannot know a priori which observations are relevant and which are not; every discovery, every enlargement of the understanding begins as an imaginative preconception of what the truth might be. This imaginative preconception – a hypothesis – arises by a process as easy or as difficult to understand as any other creative act of mind; it is a brainwave, an inspired guess, the product of a blaze of light. It comes, anyway, from within and cannot be arrived at by the exercise of any known calculus of discovery.

(Medawar 1981: 84)

Box 19.2 Uncertainty is a fact of life in research

A view from a President of Ireland:

Research is like putting your foot out at the edge of a precipice and hoping that there's territory underneath.

(MacAleese 1998)

Originality in exploring the unanticipated

In the analogy the main route may already have been broadly explored. However, the explorer will, from time to time, come across unexpected and unexplored sidetracks. He may not notice them; or he may continue on the planned route anyway, in which case nothing original is involved. If, however, he does notice the sidetracks, he has to make decisions about whether to explore any of them, and if so, which ones. These decisions may be difficult, because he cannot know whether anything of interest will turn out to lie along them without at least partially exploring them, and doing so will use resources of time and equipment which will delay the expedition on its main route. Yet, one or more of the sidetracks could contain something of such great interest and importance that it would be worth abandoning the expedition as first planned and putting all the resources into exploring the sidetrack.

Similarly, in fairly mundane research, one phase of the work can open up alternative ways forward which have never previously been researched, and it is often these that can provide 'originality', as well as the fascination with the unknown that ought to accompany research. They can, on the other hand, equally turn out to be dead-ends which consume time and effort fruitlessly. Researchers cannot know without devoting some time to looking, and even if nothing worthwhile results, a research student can at least claim to have searched for something original.

Originality in data

In the analogy the explorer may make notes and observations along the way which cannot be processed at the time. So he packs them up for carrying back home where they can be examined properly.

Similarly, the student may find herself collecting much unprocessed data which she hopes may provide something usefully 'original' later when processed or analysed. This is a perfectly possible way of incorporating originality into work, but it is not at all safe. To do it successfully, students need either good hunches about how the data might be used to advantage or considerable creative abilities.

Originality in transfer of mode or place of use

The explorer may collect all manner of goodies along the way, ranging from what he hoped for when planning the expedition to the entirely unanticipated. These goodies may have an obvious uniqueness, beauty or value, like gold or precious stones. More likely, though, the goodies are commonplace where they were found, but unknown back home, like the potato which Sir Walter Raleigh brought to England from America.

Similarly, originality in research need not be new in absolute terms. It can merely be new to the situation or the discipline. The example in the extract of Box 19.3 shows that even data need not be new, in that it is both feasible and acceptable for researchers to make something original and significant with secondary data, i.e. data that they did not gather themselves. This is a route to originality that is often overlooked by research students.

Box 19.3 Originality and significance in the use of secondary data

In 1980, Jack Sepkoski compiled a detailed database showing the dates when all the biological families lived on Earth. On the face of it, the database appeared to be rather uninteresting, but when David Raup carefully analysed the information, he found that the major extinctions of life on Earth occurred in cycles of roughly 26 million years.

(Mathews and Taylor 1998: 17)

Originality in byproducts

Things may go so badly wrong on the expedition that it has to be abandoned with seemingly nothing achieved. Yet, the illnesses of the team could be used to testify to the diseases that are rampant in the area. Or the torrential storms that washed away the collections of specimens could be monitored for interpretation in terms of what is already known about storms in that type of terrain. Neither of these would have been the purpose of the expedition, but they would be none the less valuable and count as original work.

Similarly, the student may be able to capitalize on things that seem to go wrong. Important equipment may not work; crucial resources may not be available; people may not agree to be interviewed; funding may be withdrawn; or there may be other serious and unforeseen obstacles. Just as in the analogy, a little creative thinking can rescue the situation, which is the primary reason for the third point in Box 14.1 on page 141 about roles in which students need to operate. There are almost always byproducts during any research, perhaps the development of a certain piece of equipment or some interesting secondary findings in the literature. These can be moved into the mainstream, focused on or developed further. When the thesis is written, the research problem, theme or focus merely needs to be reformulated to reflect the new nature of the work.

Originality in the experience

Whatever happens on the expedition, the explorer should, provided that he did not give up and return home early, have some interesting stories to tell.

Similarly students who stay the course with their research should be able to tease out something worthwhile from an academic or scholarly standpoint. The creative thinking techniques of Chapter 20 should help.

Originality as 'potentially publishable'

Departing from the analogy, another useful way to stimulate thinking about originality is through the concept of 'potentially publishable' in a peer-reviewed journal. This is increasingly being equated to 'originality' for students' research. The work does not necessarily have to be published, only to be worthy of publication, in principle, if suitably written up at a later stage. 'Potentially publishable' is a useful notion, because most research, particularly at PhD level, ought to be able to generate at least one, and probably several, journal articles. The focus of any such article would provide an acceptable claim for originality. If, by the time of the examination, the work has already been accepted for publication in a peer reviewed journal, that is a considerable plus.

The variety of interpretations and configurations of originality

It is not very difficult to develop new and original twists to research, and Box 21.1 in Chapter 21 gives some examples of how real students have done so. You should be able to do it too.

Suggestions and points to ponder

- Use the examples in the workshop handout of Box 19.4 as a checklist of possible solutions to research problems or of other outcomes of research. Now, within your own general field of study, think of something which you could argue to be 'original' for each item. It could be something that was original when it was first developed or something that would be original if it were developed in the future. It could even be something that you could develop yourself out of your own work. The emphasis is not on 'right answers', or even on your own research, but on realizing that there really are a host of possibilities for originality in research, in all discipline areas, including your own.

The balance between originality and conformity

Since the research components of all higher degrees are expected to show a certain amount of originality, the question is 'how much?' On the face of it, the more stunning and original a new development is, i.e. the more it is a significant contribution to knowledge, a seminal work in the field, or a beneficial technological achievement, then the more highly it ought to be acclaimed. Unfortunately things do not always work like this, because it is a tendency of human nature for people to be slow to appreciate what is outside their understanding. Box 19.5 gives some examples.

Highly original research is all too often slow to be accepted. To understand why, imagine overworked examiners faced with a thesis that is so original and significant that, if borne out, it would shake the very foundations of the subject. The first reaction of the examiners would be to wonder whether such a thesis really is valid – and to be fair, the chances are high that it would not be. However, it just might be. If so, the examiners might argue with themselves, then it would surely have come out of one of the major research centres, not from a mere research student. The examiners would realize that they would have to work through this thesis very carefully indeed, weighing every step of the argument and considering the reasonableness or otherwise of every piece of data, in order not to miss something that might invalidate the whole work. Even then, the examiners would fear that they might still overlook that crucial something. They know that if they ratify the thesis, its contents will spread like wildfire through the academic community; then someone else might find that 'something' that actually invalidates everything. Then they, the examiners, would be seriously discredited.

So examiners' own reputations are at stake when they ratify a thesis. Consequently, before spending very much time on the details of a highly original and possibly controversial thesis, there would be the temptation to check first on more mundane matters and put the problem off. This might result in their returning the thesis for clarification on a few issues or for rewriting or re-punctuating some of the references. Where examiners are faced with a highly original thesis that relies on bringing different academic disciplines together,

Box 19.4 Examples of originality

The following are examples from a wide range of possibilities:

- *A new or improved product.* There are many examples in all fields of study, e.g. a book, a synthetic fabric, a synthetic food. There is a hazy borderline between a new product and an improvement on an existing one. For example, a design for a five-bedroom house could be regarded as new in itself or as a development of a design for a two-bedroom house. For the purpose of developing a research problem, the distinction is unimportant.
- *A new theory or a reinterpretation of an existing theory.* The best known examples of what were once new theories happen to be in the natural sciences, e.g. Darwin's Theory of Evolution and Einstein's Theory of Relativity. The research problems of research students are most likely to involve reinterpretations of existing theories, rather than the development of new theories, e.g. how far an existing theory is valid in a new context or how far it needs to be re-appraised in the light of new evidence.
- *A new or improved research tool or technique.* An example could be a measuring device; a computer package to undertake certain tasks; a piece of equipment to identify disease; or a set of questionnaires to identify problem areas in certain sections of the community.
- *A new or improved model or perspective.* In all fields of study, knowledge can be interpreted or looked at in a fresh way. An example from science fiction would be the perspective of thinking about time as a fourth dimension, which can be travelled through, like the other dimensions of length, breadth and height.
- *An in-depth study.* In all fields of study there can be the opportunity to study something that has never been studied before, such as, the moons of Jupiter, following the enormous amount of data collected by the Galileo probe, or the Van Gogh painting which was thought to be lost and has recently been rediscovered.
- *An exploration of a topic, area or field.* This is a particularly useful starting point where the main features of the work are not known at the outset.
- *A critical analysis.* Examples might be an analysis or re-analysis of a novel or of the effects of a government or economic policy.
- *A portfolio of work based on research.* Professionals in many fields can produce these.
- *A fact or conclusion or a collection of facts or conclusions.* This is a particularly common outcome of research in all fields. Examples might be the determination of a scientific constant or factors which favour or militate against crime on housing estates.

(Cryer undated)

Box 19.5 The highly original may be the unappreciated

These are examples of three different kinds of innovative work which are now highly acclaimed and respected but which were not accepted or appreciated at the time, almost certainly because others could not grasp what was outside their present understanding:

Example 1. Charlotte Brontë, who in the nineteenth century wrote the novel *Jane Eyre*, submitted some of her work to Robert Southey. At the time she was the unknown daughter of a Yorkshire parson and he was the poet laureate. He counselled her that her vivid imagination could give her brainfever and 'a distempered state of mind' and that 'literature cannot be the business of a woman's life'; he described her work to his friends as 'flighty'. Yet her work was soon to become much more famous and widely read than his. The *Guardian* (15 July 1995: 8) described the episode as 'one of the most notorious put-downs in the history of English literature'.

Example 2. Nowadays few people would deny the significance of the cheap production of the hormone progesterone, a constituent of the contraceptive pill. Yet when Russell Marker of Pennsylvania State College tried to interest drug companies in a cheap way to produce it in quantity, they were not interested. He could have given up, but instead he rented a small laboratory in Mexico City and began production himself. Several years later he arrived at a drug company with two jars, about 2 kg, of progesterone, equal to most of the world's supply at the time. When the company had recovered from the shock, they invited him to join them.

Example 3. The painter Van Gogh is reputed to have been so frustrated at his work, that he cut off his own ear in a fit of frenzy! Although there are various versions of this story, the fact remains that his works were not recognized in his lifetime and only remain today because his brother collected them. Now they hang in prestigious galleries all over the world.

---

one of which is not their own, and which they do not really understand, their immediate reactions would be the same. The story in Box 19.6 is an example. The extract in Box 19.7 documents similar experiences with regard to original and significant journal articles.

Although not all examiners would behave in this way, it has to be said that students with highly original PhD theses do seem to have them referred (returned for alteration) much more often than students with more commonplace ones. Many such students never bother to complete after a referral and become totally disillusioned with academia.

Box 19.6 Risks of highly original research in terms of examiners' reactions

I once knew a student whose research was in a field on the border between two fields and so he had two examiners, one in each field. Each said that he would pass the candidate, if the other passed him, and so the student failed. He is now a professor and eminent researcher in his field.

(Elton 1999)

Box 19.7 Highly original articles and reactions of journal referees

There is much evidence that the best papers are more likely to be rejected [when submitted for publication in journals]. Current Contents *ran some articles by the authors of the most cited papers in the physical and biological sciences – those that were cited more than 1000 times in ten years. The authors complained: 'I had more difficulty in getting this published than anything else I have written.' Some of the more prolific authors in economics and statistics have found the same: it is easy to place a routine paper but it is difficult to place an original, important or controversial paper. I know a case where one journal rejected a paper as rubbish, but another, of higher status, accepted it as being 'the most important paper ever published in this journal'.*

(Bowrick 1995: 11)

The lesson is that students whose work seems to be showing extreme originality must be guided by their supervisors. The supervisor may warn against pursuing a highly original theme, not because it is inherently bad, but because it is unsafe. The supervisor may feel with some justification that the research student ought to be more established in the field before risking taking a novel idea further. On the other hand, a supervisor may see the original work as lying entirely within his or her own competence and expertise. If such a supervisor belongs to an internationally renowned research group and publicly endorses the work, then it is well worth pursuing. The supervisor's backing should ensure that the thesis is safe.

One of the safest and most common outcomes of a research degree is a set of findings or conclusions which are well substantiated through investigation and argument and which are generalizable from one situation to another. An example might be 'factors which facilitate crime on housing estates'. These might not set the academic world afire, but they could certainly claim to be original if the work had never been done before. Properly substantiated, the

PhD would be safe because examiners would have no difficulty in recognizing some value in the work.

Protecting the ownership of original work

Original work may have implications for the career advancement of the students and supervisors concerned. Or it may have commercial implications. So ownership needs protecting. This is considered on pages 88–90 of Chapter 9.

Putting originality into perspective

Although originality is a crucial requirement for research at postgraduate level; it must be put into perspective. Also crucial is that the research is well conceived and competently handled according to the scholarly norms and practices of the discipline(s) concerned.

20

Developing ideas through creative thinking

> I envisage a dialogue between two voices, the one imaginative and the other critical.
>
> (Medawar 1981: 85)

The importance of creative thinking in research • Recognizing how intellectual creativity works • Techniques to facilitate creative thinking • Talking things over • Keeping an open mind • Brainstorming • Negative brainstorming • Viewing a problem from imaginative perspectives • Concentrating on anomalies • Focusing on byproducts • Interrogating imaginary experts • Viewing the problem from the perspective of another discipline • Using 'the solution looking for the problem': serendipity • Using mind maps • Creativity and free time • Testing out the techniques • Creativity and routine work • Creativity and planning

The importance of creative thinking in research

Research and scholarship tend to be regarded as systematic, analytical and logical. Yet that is not the whole story. The extract in Box 20.1 explains.

The need for creativity turns up at various stages in postgraduate research, whenever one faces a 'mind block' of any sort. Teasing out 'originality' is one

---

Box 20.1 Logical analysis and creative thinking in research

If we look carefully at how creative, eminent scientists describe their own work, we find [a world] which uses logical analysis as a critical tool in the refinement of ideas, but which often begins in a very different place, where imagery, metaphor and analogy, intuitive hunches, kinesthetic feeling states, and even dreams or dream-like states are prepotent.

(Bargar and Duncan 1982: 3)

---

example, as considered in the previous chapter. Another example is the need to find new ways forward when one feels like giving up, of which there is more in the next chapter.

Creativity can be encouraged through the use of certain techniques. This chapter presents some which have proved particularly useful for researchers.

Recognizing how intellectual creativity works

Creative thinking works differently for different people, so, to prepare for it, you first have to recognize how it works for you.

Suggestions and points to ponder

- Think back to a number of difficult problems that you have had to solve – ones that needed creative, i.e. novel or unusual, solutions, not just the application of some standard procedure or formula. The examples need not be to do with research or even with your field of study. In fact, for this purpose, it is probably better if they are personal, family or financial. In each case note down some characteristics of the process by which you eventually arrived at the solutions. (What the solutions were is irrelevant.)

- Now see if there is anything in common in the ways in which you developed solutions to these problems.

Most people find that some or all of the following are usually involved in arriving at a creative solution:

- There is a considerable mulling-over period before arriving at a solution, and there is no way of predicting how long this might be.
- The idea for a solution just pops into one's mind, usually when not consciously thinking about it and when not thinking particularly hard about anything else either.
- Once the creative part of the problem-solving is over, hard groundwork still needs to be done to make a solution viable.

Most lists also include the use of one or more creative thinking techniques, although these may go by different names, such as 'talking things over with other people'.

Techniques to facilitate creative thinking

Some techniques which facilitate creative thinking are well known and well practised because they are common sense, second nature or fundamental to good research. Others are not widely known, which is a pity because students who do know about them usually find them very useful. The next few sections present a selection of techniques which are likely to be particularly useful in research. The first three are included for completeness although they will already be familiar to most researchers. The same is unlikely to be true for the others.

You will probably feel that some of the following techniques may suit you but that some will not. However, it is best not to dismiss any of them immediately. Practise them from time to time, and see which ones prove their worth. You only need one really good idea to set your research off in a new and viable direction.

Talking things over

Talking things over with other people does more than provide the benefit of their views and ideas. The very act of talking seems to stimulate one's own thinking. Whether or not the other person needs to be an expert in the field must depend on the nature of the problem. Although one would, for example, go to an expert for expert information, that is not at all the same as going to someone in order to facilitate one's own creativity. This merely requires someone of sound judgement who can supply time and commitment. You might choose other students or members of your family, particularly if they have the time and inclination to help.

Keeping an open mind

Keeping an open mind should be fundamental to all research. So you may not appreciate that it can be a technique for creative thinking. It involves identifying all the unlikely or seemingly implausible interpretations and then considering them carefully to see if they might have any validity. Keeping an open mind is particularly important when talking to others; without it, one is liable to 'hear', i.e. 'take in' only what one already knows.

Brainstorming

Brainstorming is a well-known problem-solving technique, particularly in groups. It is mentioned here for completeness, although it seems to be the least useful technique for the sorts of problem and issue that students have to address in research. It consists of listing as many ways forward as possible, however improbable, without pausing to evaluate them. Only when the list is complete may the value and feasibility of the possibilities be considered.

Negative brainstorming

Negative brainstorming is a technique that can be of considerable use for the sorts of problems and issues that students have to address in research, and it is suitable for individual as well as group use. It consists of listing as many ways as one can think of about how not to achieve a purpose, and then, when the list is complete, considering whether reversing any of them might be productive.

The idea of negative brainstorming may seem rather trite, and most of the reversed ideas usually turn out to be meaningless. Nevertheless, negative brainstorming really does have a proven worth, in that it can produce ideas that would never have been thought of via more direct methods – and only one needs to be worthwhile.

Viewing a problem from imaginative perspectives

Viewing the problem from imaginative perspectives is a technique that frees the mind from constraints which may have handicapped its creativity and which may in practice not be as binding as convention and normal expectations have led one to expect. The technique consists of giving the imagination free rein on the problem or issue in ways that may seem preposterous, to see if they generate any ideas that could be turned into something worthwhile. One asks oneself how one would feel about the problem or issue if one was, say, in outer space, or 200 years into the future, or living the sort of lifestyle that one has always dreamed of.

This technique is particularly valuable for generating originality in research and development – see for example Box 20.2.

Box 20.2 Creativity and imaginative perspectives

Einstein is reputed to have begun working on his theory of relativity by giving his imagination free rein to wonder what it would be like to ride on a light ray.

Concentrating on anomalies

Many researchers tend to concentrate on what they believe to be the main theme or central issue of their research, and when they come across some aspect that does not fit, they ignore it. The technique of concentrating on anomalies involves focusing on these anomalies and making a feature of them to see if they offer anything worth exploring or investigating. The anecdote in Box 20.3 is an example.

Box 20.3 Creativity and focusing on anomalies

When Joscelyn Bell Burnell, then an astronomy research student at Cambridge, noticed unexpected scuffs on her photographic plates while she was routinely surveying the night sky, she could have ignored them or assumed they were dirt. However, she chose to investigate the scuffs, which resulted in the major discovery of pulsars, i.e. stars which send out pulses of radio waves.

Focusing on byproducts

Research students can be so committed to the main theme of their research that they do not recognize the significance of something that may have happened or that they may have developed along the way. Box 20.4 gives an example of how focusing on byproducts can be really helpful in research and development.

Some students may have to make a particularly conscious effort to focus on byproducts because so much of their formal education has been modular. This is a comparatively recent move, which has resulted in the common complaint among academics that students seem less able than they once did to make connections across boundaries.

Box 20.4 Creativity and byproducts

It is said that the antibiotic penicillin would never have been discovered if Sir Alexander Fleming had not been interested enough to bother to investigate a stray contamination of mould.

Interrogating imaginary experts

The technique of interrogating imaginary experts consists of imagining that one is able to interview and interrogate a real or imaginary expert in one's field. The interview doesn't have to take place. One just prepares some suitable questions. These often turn out to be surprisingly perceptive; and they may open up some unexpectedly original and valuable ways forward for the research.

Viewing the problem from the perspective of another discipline

Pushing back the frontiers of knowledge in a single discipline can be a rather formidable way of achieving original and significant work. Often a simpler alternative is to see what can be done by bringing different disciplines together. A technique is to talk the problem or issue over with people from other disciplines to see how they would approach it. If you happen to have a sound grounding in another discipline yourself, perhaps from your undergraduate work, or if you would feel stimulated to learn more about that discipline, you could try viewing the problem yourself from the perspective of that discipline. You may not need to have any great expertise in it. The anecdotes in Box 20.5 give examples.

There is currently a considerable emphasis on multidisciplinary research and funding bodies look on it particularly favourably.

Box 20.5 Creativity and linking with other disciplines

Example 1: Sir Alexander Graham Bell had a deaf wife and therefore was interested in developing a device that would amplify sound. He was a biologist by training, and he applied what he knew about the form of the human ear to develop the telephone. It is said that if he had just been a physicist, the idea of developing a telephone would have appeared too daunting ever to attempt.

Example 2: Crick and Watson were not molecular biologists. If they had been, it is said that they might not have dared to propose their model for DNA.

Using 'the solution looking for the problem': serendipity

A good creative technique is to keep one's eyes and ears constantly open, to question anything and everything to see if it might be used to provide a creative leap forward. The anecdotes in Box 20.6 are examples.

Box 20.6 Creativity and serendipity

Example 1: It is unlikely that anyone looking for a way of speeding customers through supermarket checkouts would have thought of developing the laser as a means of solving the problem. The fact was that the laser was there, already developed, and someone was bright enough to spot a new use for it. Other bright people have of course spotted other practical uses for it in a wide variety of different areas – replacing torn eye retinas, for example.

Example 2: George de Mestral had no intention of inventing the Velcro fastener when he looked to see why burs stuck tightly to his clothing.

Using mind maps

The mind map technique of pages 28–30 can free the mind from the constrained and ordered viewpoint from which it has been seeing a problem or issue. It provides an overview, which shows at a glance all the components of the problem or issue and the links between them. This tends to stimulate new and creative ideas.

Suggestions and points to ponder

- To illustrate creative thinking using a mind map, think of a problem or issue which is currently concerning you. In order to illustrate the method, it may be best to make this fairly trivial, like what to have for supper or where to go next weekend, although if you prefer a research problem, feel free to choose one.
- Figure 20.1 shows a mind map with six spokes labelled with what are often called 'the six children's questions' because they are so fundamental. A seventh spoke is labelled as 'costs' because financial matters influence most decisions, and two spokes are left blank. Copy the figure onto a separate sheet of paper, then:

  1 Write down what the problem or issue is inside the central blank box.
  2 Either label the remaining two spokes coming out of the title box with any other questions that may seem appropriate to the problem or issue, or simply ignore them. Add more spokes if you think they would be useful.
  3 Let your mind wander over the questions on each spoke and label keywords for your thoughts – any thoughts – on the new spokes, so that, apart from the labelling, the figure looks somewhat like that of Figure 4.2 on page 30.
  4 Continue drawing more spokes and labelling them until you run out of ideas.
  5 Finally link any ideas that appear on more than one spoke, as shown in Figure 4.2.

- You may feel that a viable solution has already occurred to you. If not, put the paper aside and wait to see if a solution pops into your head later. If it does, how much later?

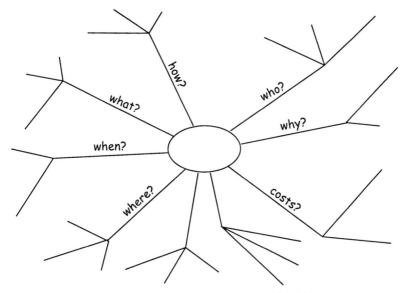

Figure 20.1   The mind map technique for creative thinking.

Creativity and free time

Solutions only pop into one's mind if it is not already occupied, i.e. if it is thinking about nothing in particular. The anecdotes in Box 20.7 are examples. So, although it is important for students to study hard, doing it all the time is counter-productive.

Box 20.7 Creativity and letting the mind wander freely

Example 1: The mathematician Poincaré claimed to have thought of his most profound idea quite suddenly while boarding a bus.

Example 2: In the middle of the nineteenth century the constituent atoms of a molecule of benzene were known, but no stable molecular structure could be visualized. The problem was solved by Kekulé, who, while musing in a semi-dozing state, visualized snakes coiling round eating their own tails. This gave him the idea, which has since come to be accepted, that the benzene molecule could be in the form of a ring.

Suggestions

- List activities which you enjoy and are practical for you to indulge in, and which free your mind from purposeful thinking.

You have probably identified some form of sport, or something like gardening, listening to music or yoga. Perhaps you should force yourself to spend more time on these mind-freeing activities. Television and reading may seem relaxing but they are unlikely to be appropriate for freeing the mind for creativity.

Many people find that creative ideas just pop into their mind when they wake up in the night, still half asleep. They recommend keeping a pen and paper beside the bed for jotting the ideas down, for full consideration later.

Testing out the techniques

It is worth knowing which techniques are most helpful for your own work.

Suggestions

- Assume that you want to develop your research in a new direction. Try each of the following creative techniques:

  1 Negative brainstorming
  2 Viewing the problem from imaginative perspectives
  3 Concentrating on anomalies
  4 Focusing on byproducts
  5 Interrogating imaginary experts
  6 Viewing the problem from the perspective of another discipline.

- Don't expect any dramatic ideas to emerge until some time in the future, when your mind has had time to mull things over.

You may like to look ahead to Box 21.1 on page 215, as it gives some examples of how creative thinking has helped research students.

Creativity and routine work

In research, having a good idea is not enough on its own. You will remember the adage about research being 1% inspiration and 99% perspiration. You must work on a good idea, to turn it into an approach, tool, model, theory, etc. that is convincingly tested and is justified according to the academic rigour of the subject. That is where all the other chapters of the book come in, particularly Chapter 14 on routine work.

Creativity and planning

Creativity cannot be done to command or to deadlines. Yet it is an essential part of good research. This can and will sabotage plans about where you would like your work to be by a particular time, and is one reason why planning has to be an ongoing process of revision. Plan in detail in the short term and in outline over the long term, as explained in Chapter 13.

21

Keeping going when you feel like giving up

Don't give up when the pace seems slow.
You might succeed with another blow.
Stick to the fight when you're hardest hit.
It's when things seem worst that you mustn't quit.

(Anon.)

Understanding and coping with loss of motivation • Lacking a sense of direction • Feeling overwhelmed by the quantity of work ahead • Aiming for perfection • Worrying about being pipped at the post • Feeling disorganized • Losing interest, becoming bored and getting depressed • Interacting ineffectually with associates • Everything seeming to go wrong • Frustrated at the difficulties of part-time study • Facing a time-consuming emergency • Feeling stressed and unable to cope • Wanting to get on with the next stage of life • Not wanting to get on with the next stage of life • Other possible reasons

Understanding and coping with loss of motivation

Research is a long undertaking, especially so at the level of PhD, and especially so for part-time students. It can be very difficult to maintain enthusiasm and commitment in the face of working independently to produce original and high quality work in an environment in which plans do not always work out as hoped or expected. In addition, there may be family matters, health matters, employment matters and financial matters which keep emerging to detract from the research. It is hardly surprising that students go through periods of doubting whether it is worth continuing. At their worst, these can lead to dropping out and at best to slowing down. The former is a sad waste of time, effort and opportunity and the latter is dangerous, because institutions can terminate registration after the stipulated official period.

The effects of lack of motivation can be minimized in three ways. The first is by talking things through with others – and Chapter 15 highlighted the need to put effort into finding suitable people as early as possible in a research programme. The second is by maintaining a balanced outlook through a healthy lifestyle of sensible eating and drinking, and appropriate exercise; and the third is to find out about common causes of wanting to give up and how best to deal with them. It is with the last of these that this chapter is primarily concerned. It is particularly directed towards students on long research programmes such as the PhD, although other students may also find it useful.

The examples in Box 21.1 illustrate how real students have managed to salvage work when they felt like giving up. All are practical manifestations of the archery analogy of Figures 8.1b on page 69.

Box 21.1 Creative ways in which research students have salvaged work that was not looking viable

The following examples are based on real anecdotes supplied by supervisors and students. They have been simplified and anonomized.

- Michael was some way into a project on wave power. Then the funding was unexpectedly cut off and all development work had to come to an abrupt halt. Michael was sure that this meant the end of his PhD. However, his supervisor advised him to look at what he had been doing so far and see whether any of it could be used as a basis for continued work with a different focus. Michael found that he could capitalize on the measurements that he had already made on winds, tides and grades of sand and pebbles at various points along a beach. He completed his PhD with little or no loss of time.
- Jill was exploring styles of teaching, for which she spent a considerable time developing a set of questionnaires. It then looked as if enough data to draw valid conclusions on teaching would take too long to collect. So she focused instead on the development and evaluation of the questionnaires, thus finishing her PhD much more quickly.
- Tara's PhD was on a particular author. Her intention was to work system- atically through all of his works and so arrive at his view of the purpose of literature. She worked very hard on this, but the answer eluded her. She read more and analysed more deeply, but still the answer eluded her. There seemed no alternative but to give up the search and abandon the PhD. When she eventually plucked up the courage to confide in her supervisor, he

pointed out that her work was indeed viable, and that all she needed to do was to justify a claim that the author did not have a particular view of what literature ought to be: that he wrote in different modes at different times, depending on the situation and how he was feeling. This is what Tara did, and she completed her PhD successfully.

- Abdul's research was to use established theory to calculate a parameter which would make it possible to predict what happens when subatomic particles of a particular energy are scattered in certain circumstances. He spent considerable time on this. Then he found that another student elsewhere had already calculated the parameter. Abdul's first reaction was that his own claim for original work had been snatched from under his nose. However he was able to extend his calculation to a range of energies, which enabled him to use what he had done so far, yet to claim that his work was, in fact, original.

- Angela was looking at a rather unpleasant historical episode. Her hunch was that money would turn out to be the root of all the evil. However her reading turned up contradictory findings. She just couldn't make a sound case, and she panicked. Her supervisor, however, pointed out that there is a great deal in research that 'won't go tidy'; that the model needed would have to be much more complex than originally envisaged; and that there is virtue in students recognizing such a fact. Angela went on to develop and justify a relatively complex model for the influences of money during the historical episode, incorporating the positive and energizing aspects as well as the negative ones. This earned her a PhD.

- Adam's research problem was to develop a conceptual software model and a prototype application for a particular type of electronic messaging library. After a year, he had identified the key-parameters of the problem and the weaknesses of related work. However computing moves on quickly and he found to his dismay that a software giant was producing its own application. This meant that his own envisaged development would no longer have any claim to be original. His supervisor advised him to focus instead on the techniques that he had identified (which had not been published by the software giant), to develop them further and to make them his focus for original work. Adam was greatly relieved at this advice and successfully followed it.

- Sarah was looking for the expression (non-dormancy) of a particular gene in a human tissue. However, the result came back negative. She refined her procedures and tried again, but still the result was negative. This kept happening and she became increasingly despondent that a substantial body of work had been wasted. Then it suddenly dawned on her that the negative result might be meaningful. She re-examined the literature in the light of the negative result and developed an alternative theory for the possible role of the tissue being examined. Her existing data thus provided the foundations of a new PhD.

- Judy, Anthea, Andreas and Peter were ecology students who went together on an extended field trip to gather specimens from a particular location. All four were full of enthusiasm and they each made large collections. However, back in the laboratory, they found themselves overwhelmed by the months of work ahead: to sort, count and identify what they had collected. Morale fell progressively lower, and they were on the point of giving up. However a new supervisor took a firm line. He stressed that they only had to do enough to get their PhDs and that the rest of the specimens could be shelved or discarded. He then worked with Judy, Anthea, Andreas and Peter, both individually and together, to help them to develop their own specific questions to guide their separate treatments of just a selection of their specimens. In consequence, morale picked up and the work progressed well. (In the normal way, supervisors would provide such guidance in advance of a field trip.)
- Melanie was an MPhil student developing a manual of training materials, for which she was collecting contributions from a number of experienced professionals. When she wanted to transfer her registration to PhD, her supervisor told her that the next stage of her work would need to be much more scholarly, with theoretical underpinning; and he advised her to complete the manual, run the training and then evaluate it in terms of learning theories. Melanie was appalled at how much extra time this would need. So she looked for an alternative and quicker way forward. What she eventually did was to use (and build on) the records that she had kept for administrative purposes to test theories about attitudes to change and innovation. She completed her PhD within her four-year period of part-time registration.

Lacking a sense of direction

Any piece of research can develop in a number of different ways, all of which could be viable. If you feel that you haven't got a firm direction, just look back on what you have done and see if you can consolidate your work around a focus of some sort. Read or reread Chapter 8 and think particularly about the message of Figures 8.1a and b. Then use Chapters 19 and 20 to take your thinking forward.

A related problem is that students who think they do have a sense of direction, suddenly find it undermined. Perhaps this is due to conflicting advice from different supervisors. Or a colleague or visitor may point out different expectations of what the research ought to be about, or who it ought to be helping, or how. The different approach may have some appeal, but your task is to complete just one programme of research – and the chances are that the one that you already have is entirely viable. If you like, in the final chapter of your thesis, you can always point out how you might have done things differently if starting again. This in no way detracts from the fact that you will already have produced a consolidated piece of research in its own right. In fact it shows your development as a scholar and researcher.

Students may feel that their lack of direction is due to lack of support from their supervisors, possibly because the supervisors lack interest or the necessary academic expertise. The truth may be very different. A supervisor's task is not to lead every step of the way. Postgraduates are expected to act independently, following their own ideas, under, of course, the watchful eyes of supervisors to advise and warn. If you think that the problem may be that you have not appreciated your supervisor's role, the answer is to start taking responsibility for yourself. If, after sufficient thought, you really do think that another supervisor would help, be resolute, and set about making it happen.

Feeling overwhelmed by the quantity of work ahead

Students can find themselves overwhelmed by what they see as the immensity of what lies before them. If this is your problem, glance back to Box 14.4 in Chapter 14. Essentially it is your task, in conjunction with your supervisor, to limit the scope of your work so that it can be fitted into the time available. The process may require some creative thinking to 'tweak' research problems, foci or themes, so that what can be achieved in the time, does, in fact address them and also forms a consolidated piece of research in its own right. Chapters 19 and 20 should provide some ideas.

Another aspect of feeling overwhelmed is the huge bulk of the literature. It isn't possible to read it all. For practical purposes you have to treat a literature survey in terms of diminishing returns on your time. When you find that whatever you read seems to reference works that you have already consulted, it is time to regard the survey as finished for all practical purposes. It can, after all, still be added to later if anything else relevant happens to come to light. If something crucial should come to your attention after the thesis is ready but before you are examined, few examiners would hold this against you.

It is always possible for every researcher to do more. If you have identified further work and are depressed that you don't have the time to do it (and your supervisor thinks that you have already done enough for the award for which you are registered), you can actually capitalize on the situation. Simply express your hopes in the final chapter of your thesis that other workers may undertake the work. Remember that you will be judged on the scholarly way in which you make your case in the thesis, not on quantity – provided of course that the quantity does reflect the nominal period of registration. So be ruthless about cutting down the scope of work that seems too large.

Aiming for perfection

Students ought to be vigilant to ensure that their work is good enough for the award for which they are registered. However, it is not necessary to aim for perfection, which is unattainable anyway.

Research at PhD level needs to be original, independent and significant. Chapter 19 considered the various manifestations and configurations of originality, and Chapter 20 suggested techniques to help develop it. Independence could be a problem where a team project is concerned, but with care and attention to the boundaries of individual contributions, and goodwill and professionalism all round, it seldom is. There is a view that all new knowledge must be significant, but the nature of acceptable significance does depend on the norms of the discipline. Discussion and reading are the means to identify these.

It is natural at times for students to feel that their work is rather trivial and to strive for a perfectionism that is not only time-consuming but also unobtainable. Be guided by your supervisor on this. If you would appreciate the reassurance of other people who are experienced in standards of research, you could give a departmental seminar so that other students and academic staff can give their opinions on your work. Bear in mind, too, that fine-tuning to your work, over and beyond what is required for the thesis, can always, later, go into a journal article or book.

Worrying about being pipped at the post

Students, particularly PhD students, can feel like giving up when they learn that someone, somewhere is working on the same problem and is likely to finish sooner. This is something that they must discuss with their supervisors, because supervisors know the work, the general field and the regulations of the institution.

In practice, the matter is probably not particularly serious. Even if the other work is identical, which is most likely to occur in natural science subjects, it normally takes some months for research findings to reach the market-place or be published in a journal, and most institutional regulations allow a breathing space for a thesis to go forward provided that this is sufficiently short to guarantee that the work is the student's own.

The chances are that the work is only broadly similar, particularly in the humanities and social sciences. Then the thing to do is to contact the other researchers to find out precisely what they have done. It is bound to be different in some way: perhaps in the research design, or the sample, or the precision of the result. You would merely need to build a new section into your thesis to compare and contrast the work with your own, drawing some meaningful conclusions. Have a look at some of the examples in Box 21.1.

Feeling disorganized

The independence which students have during lengthy research programmes can mean that it is all too easy to let time run away in talking to people, drinking coffee, spending time at the bar or popping out to the shops. Students need to plan their work and manage themselves and their time. If this is your problem, Chapters 13 and 14 should be helpful. Nevertheless, knowing what to do is not the same as doing it. Students have to learn self-discipline.

Your problem may be that you are working so hard that you cannot think straight. Then you must take a break or even a short holiday, so as to refresh yourself. Not only is there nothing at all wrong in doing this, it is probably essential if you are to continue the programme effectively and efficiently.

Losing interest, becoming bored and getting depressed

Research should be intellectually fascinating because it involves discovering or developing something new in an area that should have considerable personal appeal. Nevertheless, it is natural to lose interest or become bored at times. It is often helpful to have several themes on the go at once, so that there is more likely to be something tempting to work on.

You may be at a stage where your work really is excessively routine and monotonous. Some people find that it helps to listen to light music during tasks which do not require much concentration. Monotonous stages in research should pass. If they look unlikely to do so, a solution could be to take up an alternative direction or approach (see Chapter 19).

Some reasons for getting depressed and feeling unable to cope are intensely personal. This is where the support of others is so important, as they can often recognize and diagnose the cause of the problem before you can yourself. Listen to them and allow them to support you. Also, if it seems appropriate, make use of institutional counselling services. Most are excellent as well as confidential. There are few personal problems that professional counsellors have not seen before, and they can often point to sources of help.

For short-term depression, many people find that certain pieces of music can be mood-enhancing. For longer-term or more serious depression, do not make quick decisions about giving up. Find and use the support you need. Then you may feel differently before too long. If, after a time, you still feel like giving up, take a holiday. If, even then, you still feel like giving up, this may be the right decision for you. Before you do give up, though, talk with your supervisors. This may be difficult because you may feel that you are letting them down, but there is little that upsets good supervisors more than students just disappearing.

Interacting ineffectually with associates

It is self-evident that students need to be able to interact effectively with other people. Chapters 6 and 15 respectively consider the specifics of interacting with a supervisor and more generally with other people. Further advice and counselling on effective interaction need to come from someone who knows and cares about you or is a professional counsellor.

Everything seeming to go wrong

It is a fundamental feature of research that it seldom proceeds as one expects – see the extract in Box 21.2. No one is responsible, although it is the research student who has to find a way of compensating.

Also research invariably goes more slowly than anticipated. So the feeling of getting nowhere is to be expected, provided that it doesn't last too long. It is not that a jinx is on an individual; neither is it an indication that the individual is not up to the job. Small problems can normally be sorted out quite easily by keeping on good terms with others in the department: other students, academics, secretaries, technicians, etc. Then supervisors do not have to be disturbed unnecessarily.

Students' worries that they are getting nowhere can be simply because they

---

Box 21.2 The rational model of how research should operate

The rational model for the conduct of research is perhaps an idealised guide to how research ought to be conducted. [It] does not attempt to provide an accurate description of the process whereby research actually is conducted. At the present time, to my knowledge, a commonly accepted descriptive model of the research process is not available.

(Martin 1982: 19)

are so close to what they are doing that they cannot spot where a slight change of direction or emphasis could provide the security of a fall-back position. Spotting such changes in direction or emphasis requires creative thinking and an understanding of what would be acceptable at the level of the award concerned (see Chapters 19 and 20). Some of the examples in Box 21.1 illustrate the idea.

Frustrated at the difficulties of part-time study

Students register part-time because they have commitments elsewhere, and these invariably produce conflicting demands on their time and attention. It is particularly difficult having to do research work in the evenings, at weekends and on odd days. You are tired; you miss out on social activities with family and friends; and essential resources, such as specialist libraries or laboratories, may not be accessible at suitable times. Various parts of this book should help with your concerns. Remember that committed people in your situation do, in sizeable numbers, successfully complete their research programmes.

Facing a time-consuming emergency

If you are going through an emergency which needs a great deal of time and energy to handle, such as illness, you may find it helpful to take time out, rather than to try to cope ineffectively with too many things at the same time. Most institutions have a category of registration for students who are forced to interrupt their studies, but who intend to continue at a later date. A fee is seldom levied for this category, and the time out does not count towards the required period of registration. Funding bodies may not be as sympathetic as institutions; so the position does need to be explored with them.

A common alternative is to switch from full-time to part-time study. There are also other categories of registration, and it is important for your finances as well as your time management that you are registered in the most appropriate category. Changes of registration should, if possible, be discussed with supervisors well in advance of the term in which the change is to take place, and approval must then be given by the institution.

Feeling stressed and unable to cope

Everyone goes through phases of feeling emotionally wound up or drained and unable to cope. Students are no exception. If the reason is not one of those already mentioned, it is probably because they are overworked or need regular exercise, a break or a holiday. Or they may need to see a counsellor or doctor.

Box 21.3 gives some common and quite general reasons for feeling stressed. You may like to compare them with what you are experiencing.

Box 21.3 Causes of stress at work

Fontana (1993) lists general causes of stress under the following headings:

- *Organizational problems*
- *Insufficient backup*
- *Long or unsociable hours*
- *Poor status, pay and promotion prospects*
- *Unnecessary rituals and procedures*
- *Uncertainty and insecurity*

As for specific causes of stress at work, Fontana lists the following:

- *Unclear role specifications*
- *Role conflict*
- *Unrealistically high expectations (perfectionism)*
- *Inability to influence decision-making (powerlessness)*
- *Frequent clashes with supervisors*
- *Isolation from colleagues' support*
- *Overwork and time pressures*
- *Lack of variety*
- *Poor communication*
- *Inadequate leadership*
- *Conflicts with colleagues*
- *Inability to finish a job*
- *Fighting unnecessary battles*

(Fontana 1993)

Wanting to get on with the next stage of life

Wanting to get on with the next stage of one's life is a common cause, not just of flagging, but of dropping out completely.

A good job offer may come along, and it may seem a good idea to take it on the assumption that the thesis can be written up in the evenings and at weekends. In fact, this is an extremely difficult thing to do, and it is one of the most common reasons for not completing a PhD. So think carefully before taking any action in this respect that you may later regret.

In some fields of study, a reason for giving up may be that the qualification or research training seems unlikely to help employment prospects. This is by no means necessarily so (see Box 12.3 on page 121), and it is quite common, even for PhD graduates, to go into careers which are unrelated to their PhD topics. There are a range of skills which holders of research degrees can offer employers and which go far beyond those of graduates with first degrees. What matters is to be aware of them so as to be able to impress at interview. Pages 228–229 in the next chapter elaborates.

Not wanting to get on with the next stage of life

Being a student does offer a form of security: belonging to a community, being cared for by a professional, etc. This can make some students not want to get on with the next stage of their lives. The problem has to be recognized and faced up to. It cannot be allowed to go on, and the institution will not allow it to go on. The best solution is to talk it through with someone responsible and caring, perhaps the institutional counsellor.

Other possible reasons

There can be many reasons for a thesis being delayed or never completed. The extract in Box 21.4 lists some identified by a research council. Everyone needs to identify their own reasons, as only then can they be effectively handled.

Box 21.4 Reasons for delay in completion and non-completion

It is worth looking at some of the reasons for long completion times or failure to complete . . . One quite common reason for late completion [is] a slow start . . . If insufficient effort is put into the formulation of the problem, to making a literature survey where appropriate, or such other initial activities as are desirable, the result is that the remaining portion of . . . activities is always a scramble and the programme inevitably slips.

A second common cause of delay is the student who is never satisfied. He [or she] can always think of a way of improving his [or her] results. In short, he [or she] cannot bring anything to a conclusion. Perfectionism can be a virtue, but if only a student would write up what he [or she] had achieved, he [or she] would almost certainly see more clearly whether any improvement was actually necessary, the amount of effort required if it was desirable, or whether it was sensible to attempt that amount of work in the time available . . .

A third common cause of delay is distraction from the main line of enquiry. These days a common distraction is for a student to get 'hooked on' computing with the result that he [or she] over analyses his [or her] experimental data, largely because of the sheer pleasure he [or she] gets out of manipulating the computer; but with inevitable delays. leading to a delayed thesis . . .

When the work has gone well and opened up prospects for future research, the supervisor may in some subjects suggest that the student might like to consider a two or three year continuation as a post-doctoral research assistant. Experience shows that if the student accepts, and is appointed before handing in his [or her] thesis, in the vast majority of cases the progress on the thesis slows dramatically.

(Science and Engineering Research Council 1992)

Points to ponder

- If you feel yourself flagging, where, in view of this chapter, do you think the problem lies, and what can you do about it?
- From your experience or from the advice of others, what pieces of music are most likely to improve your mood?
- Should you take more exercise or eat more healthily?
- Should you take some time off as a break or to interact with others socially?

22

Job seeking

The people who get on in this world are the people who get up and look for the circumstances they want, and if they can't find them, make them.

(George Bernard Shaw at www.quotedb.com)

When to start looking for a job and when to start the job itself • Finding out the type of job you are suited to • The influence of the research topic on employment prospects • Where to look for vacancies • Making an application • Impressing at the interview

When to start looking for a job and when to start the job itself

This chapter is for students about to emerge from full-time research pro- grammes who need to find a job. It is also for those part-time students, who may already be in paid employment, but who are looking for a change in direction.

It is of course never too early to think about the sort of job that you will eventually want when the research programme is over. A word of warning is nevertheless in order. One of the main reasons for students not completing their theses is that they are, by the time of writing up, in a job which saps their time and creative energies. Delays to the thesis at this stage are disastrous. Writing (as distinct from editing) is most productively done when one can immerse oneself in it totally. With limited chunks of time available and with the passage of time, the intertwining threads of argument become increasingly difficult to hold onto and to present cogently. Furthermore institutions impose limits on registration; so if you don't complete within the designated time, your registration will be terminated, so that you never complete. The maxim has to be that if you can possibly manage it, don't start a new job until your thesis is complete.

Finding out the type of job you are suited to

Everyone belongs to a certain 'personality type' and some jobs are more suitable for some types than others. If you don't already know what sort of job you would enjoy, contact the staff in your institution's careers office. They will probably run self-awareness sessions based on Myers Briggs and Belbin assessments. The results may surprise you and may save you from many years in a job to which you are not basically suited. The results should be a worthy inclusion in the PDP records of Chapter 12.

Points to ponder

- Do you know what personality type you are and therefore the types of jobs to which you are most suited? If necessary ask for advice from the institution's careers office.

The influence of the research topic on employment prospects

In practice the topic of your research probably limits your employability much less than you might think, particularly if you have paid due attention to the transferable skills aspects, as considered in Chapter 12. Box 12.3 in that chapter reinforces this, as does the outcome of a study on PhD employability – see the extract in Box 22.1.

Where to look for vacancies

If you are looking for a job, the way forward is best regarded as a two-fold attack. One is to grasp every opportunity to raise the subject with people who may be able to help, such as supervisors, other students, friends of the family, etc.

Box 22.1 Employability of PhDs by field of study

The UK GRAD programme found that social science PhD graduates have the lowest unemployment rate – just 2 per cent. Those with PhDs in the physical sciences and engineering have an unemployment rate of 4.7 per cent, and those in the arts and humanities have a rate of 4.5 per cent.

Janet Metcalfe, director of UK GRAD, was quoted as saying 'It is good news for social scientists and, indeed, for those in arts and humanities – they are just as employable as scientists'.

The findings are part of the UK GRAD report 'what do PhDs do?', which was released on the 19th November [2004] and is available through the UK GRAD website.

Overall, the report found that more than half of UK PhD students quit academia for industry and that their qualifications make PhD students highly valued employees.

(University of Kent 2005)

The other is structured, by keeping a constant eye open for vacancies using newspapers and the Internet. Particularly useful should be the Prospects website, introduced in Box 2.1 on page 8 – but there are also various other websites which a web search should throw up reasonably quickly. Your institutional careers office should also be an excellent source of advice and help.

For the best possible sound-bites of advice on further career development, look ahead to the boxes in Chapter 25.

Making an application

The documents that grew out of the PDP described in Chapter 12 should serve in good stead for making job applications. Note that Prospects runs a CV checking service, as described in the extract of Box 22.2. For further information see its website. As the service is provided on a once-only basis, you may want to check the revised CV out with supervisors or friends, as well as with the institution's careers office.

Impressing at the interview

Following the preparation considered in Chapter 12 you should already have a sound understanding of the skills that you can offer an employer, and you will

---

Box 22.2 The CV checking service offered by Prospects

Graduate CV surgery

What is it?

A free CV checking service, which will assess the quality and marketability of your My Prospects CV form and provide you with constructive feedback by professional careers consultants.

Who is it for?

For graduates who are EEA nationals (i.e. residents of all EU states plus Norway, Iceland and Liechtenstein) and who have graduated within the last five years.

How can I use it?

Register with My Prospects, go to Your Online CV and complete the CV form. You will then be asked if you want to have your CV form checked by our team of careers consultants. If you click 'yes', your CV form will be stored in our CV Surgery database for our team of careers consultants to access, and you will receive feedback via an email within 5 working days.

Important Note: Graduate CV Surgery provides a once-only review service. Your My Prospects CV form will be reviewed once. If you decide not to have your application form reviewed when prompted, you cannot have it reviewed at a later stage.

(Prospects undated)

---

need to steer the interview in such a way that you can demonstrate your proficiency. The interview team may not use the same category system for skills that you are used to, so prepare to recognize and use alternative ways of talking about your skills. A limited portfolio, as described on page 124, can help. Particularly useful are photographs or newspaper cuttings showing your involvement in certain activities, products or outcomes generated during the research (or plans, photographs or sketches representing them), and any special awards or commendations. Photographs are particularly useful because they can so easily be carried around in a pocket or bag. You need to be able to talk about all of them in a fluent but not overbearing way, for which the preparation of Chapter 12 should serve you well.

Needless to say, you will need to dress appropriately and treat the interview panel with respect without being too deferential. Your aim should be to convince them that you will be pleasant to work with, and that you can, when the situation calls for it, fit into most of the roles expected in teamwork while also being able to act creatively and effectively as an independent individual.

23

Producing the thesis

Many research students believe that the quality of a thesis necessarily improves with the amount of time taken to prepare it and the number of words it contains. This is not true.

(Economic and Social Research Council 1986: 13)

The importance of the thesis • The need to recap on the writing and referencing techniques of previous chapters • Orientating yourself for the task ahead • Developing a framework of chapters • Developing the content of a chapter • Sequencing the content within a chapter • Linking chapters into one or more storylines • Cross-referencing in the thesis • The writing process • Producing the abstract • Presenting the thesis in accordance with institutional requirements

The importance of the thesis

The thesis is the culmination of a student's research programme, and it is on the thesis that he or she will be examined and judged, in conjunction, in the UK, with an oral examination or viva. So it is in your best interests to make your thesis good, and give it the preparation enough time to do yourself justice. The workshop handout of Box 23.1 summarises the points that most examiners will be looking for. It is on these that the book has concentrated so far, so this chapter should not be used in isolation from the previous chapters.

The chapter has to assume that you and your supervisor together believe that what you have done is of a scope and standard that it can be written up as a consolidated piece of work worthy of the award concerned. (The responsibility for the decision is of course yours.) This chapter therefore concentrates

---

Box 23.1 Some things that examiners may be looking for

- *The case for the research problem, focus or theme, etc. (or problems, foci or themes, etc.)*
- *Knowledge of the general field in which the work is being set*
- *The case for appropriateness of the research design (and all that this entails)*
- *The case for the appropriateness of the solutions to the research problem(s) (or conclusions, or outcomes, etc.)*
- *The originality of the work*
- *The significance of the work*
- *The independence of the work*
- *Critical ability and personal development on the part of the student*
- *The coherence of arguments*
- *The balance of quality to quantity*
- *General competence*

(Cryer undated)

---

solely on the tasks of writing and presenting the thesis. Most of the advice should be useful for producing theses for all awards, but the chapter is primarily designed for students registered for PhDs in the UK system where the examination is in two parts: a thesis and an oral examination or viva. If you will not be having an oral examination – which is the subject of Chapter 24 – your thesis needs to pay particular attention to the sorts of points that examiners normally probe in such examinations. So scan Chapter 24 before finalizing your thesis.

The suggestions in this chapter will not be totally appropriate for all fields of study, as there is no consistent view across disciplines about what constitutes an acceptable thesis, either for an award entirely by research or for one with just a research component. Nevertheless, the chapter should stimulate your thinking and indicate topics for discussion and clarification with your supervisor.

The need to recap on the writing and referencing techniques of previous chapters

As this chapter is solely about producing the thesis, it assumes that you are already well practised in the use of literature as outlined in Chapter 7; academic writing as introduced with report writing in Chapter 16: academic discourse; styles of referencing; use of software tools; and formats for figures and appendices, as introduced at various places in the book. As the thesis is the culmination of your writing, you should be approaching it as an experienced research student; and it should grow out of literature surveys and earlier reports. If necessary, go back to Chapters 7 and 16 before reading on.

Orientating yourself for the task ahead

As an orientation for producing a thesis, it is useful to return to the analogy of Chapter 19, where the research programme is a major expedition of discovery and the student is the explorer and leader of the team. (To ease cumbersome sentence structures, the leader/explorer was and is taken to be male.)

Knowing that he will be telling his story when he gets home from the expedition, the explorer will keep careful and detailed records while away. These are analogous to the students' records: logbooks, diaries, draft theses, etc. The explorer may start writing his story while still on the expedition – just as students may find that it aids their thinking to write draft thesis chapters and have a thesis outline as they go along. However, the explorer will appreciate that how he eventually tells the story will, with hindsight, be different in sequence, scope and emphasis, depending on who he tells it to and the time-slot available for telling it. So it is with a thesis. The crucially important audience for theses are the examiners, and in particular external examiners. In fact theses seldom reach wider audiences, which is why journal articles, conferences and books are the places for disseminating the research. Think of examiners as individuals who are exceptionally busy and grossly underpaid, and who therefore have to read theses quickly. They will expect a thesis to be well structured and to be argued coherently to make the case for the solutions, conclusions or outcomes, etc. Irrelevancies will irritate, as will having to cope with loose style and typing errors, and having to tease out meaning that students should have extracted themselves.

Returning to the analogy, there are a number of points that the explorer will bear in mind, when he comes to tell his story afterwards. He will certainly want to stress the novelty and value of the outcomes. Although he will probably include what he hoped at the outset that the general outcomes might be, he will give most attention to features of special importance that may or may not have been predicted in advance, such as finding hidden treasure, or special procedures developed for successfully tracking a certain animal, etc. So he will not necessarily tell the story in the order in which things happened, neither will he give every period of the expedition an equal slot of story time or length, although he may mention chronological development as a justification or explanation in connection with something else. Similarly, the final version of a thesis should be written with hindsight, to make best sense of what has happened. It should take the reader naturally and convincingly to the major outcomes, which may or may not have been anticipated at the outset. So, for your own thesis, although you should draft the introduction early for your own use, to orientate yourself for the writing to follow, you must finalize it much later to orientate the reader for how the thesis eventually turns out, after all the redrafts.

Examiners are very able and experienced in the general subject area, which means that background material should be as concise as is consistent with showing that it is known. However, no examiner can be an expert in a student's particular niche of work. By the time you finalize your thesis, you and you alone are the world's expert in what it contains. Otherwise it would not be original. Your task is to convince others of its value, by marshalling evidence and arguing with it, rather as a barrister makes a case in a court of law. The features that make your work significant, original and worthy of the PhD (or other award) need to be argued cogently: each step needs to be spelt out; the solutions, conclusions or outcomes must be stated unambiguously and all their implications identified and discussed in depth.

Suggestions and points to ponder

- Jot down at least one 'thing' that your thesis is to argue for.
- What others are there?

This is not a task to be skimmed over. If you don't know what you are trying to do in a thesis, you are setting out to waste an enormous amount of time. However, if you expect understanding to emerge as you argue with yourself in the writing, there is no reason why you shouldn't spend a short time playing around with possibilities.

Developing a framework of chapters

Once you know what case or cases the thesis is to make, the next step is to devise a framework of chapters. This needs to be treated as work-in-progress because, as the writing progresses, it will seem right to split some chapters and combine others. The following will need to be pegged somewhere onto the framework:

- The general research area and how the research problem, topic, theme or focus was identified and refined

- Discussion leading to statements of the research methodology
- Reports on work done
- The emerging data
- The analysis of the data
- The solutions, conclusions or outcomes to the work
- A discussion of their applicability and limitations, and the scope for further work.

Note that literature is not mentioned as a separate bullet point. This is because it is an integral part of the first two bullet points, and it may, depending on the nature of the research, also be part of the others. In fact the emphasis placed on a literature survey chapter in its own right depends largely on the field of study. Where it is usual to define a research problem early on and to keep it relatively unchanged, a separate and single literature survey chapter is the norm. In fields where it is usual for the direction of each stage of the research to rely on findings of an earlier stage, new literature will almost certainly need to be incorporated at each stage. Most theses will require some, if minimal, reference to literature to run throughout.

Running throughout should be the identification of difficulties and constraints, and how they were handled.

Suggestions and points to ponder

- Use the above ideas to develop a draft framework of chapters for your thesis.
- In your field of study, how normal is it for almost all the literature survey material to be in a single chapter?

Irrespective of whether or not a literature survey is considered worthy of a chapter in its own right, do continually bear in mind, as pointed out in Chapter 7, that literature should be used to substantiate and carry forward arguments and to help deal with counter-arguments. A literature survey should not read as a catalogue of vaguely relevant material, even though it is wise to find a way of bringing in all the important works in the field.

Developing the content of a chapter

When developing the material to go into any chapter, the following checklist may be a useful starting point to stimulate thinking:

- Purposes of the chapter
- Links with other knowledge (e.g. earlier or later chapters or the work of other people)
- Constraints (if any, under which the work described had to operate)
- Work carried out
- Outcomes of that work
- Where next?

If you like to work with mind maps (see pages 28–30) the content of a chapter can be developed using the above bullet points as spokes. Probably much of the substance of chapters can be obtained by lifting sections directly out of earlier reports. They will, of course, need suitable editing, to make the thesis read as a coherent whole.

Suggestions and points to ponder

- To get a feel for using a mind map to develop the content of a thesis chapter, look back at pages 28–30. Label the spokes with the above bullet points and see if this takes your thinking anywhere useful.

Having developed the content of a chapter, albeit in draft form, the material needs to be put into a logical order. This is considered in the next section.

Sequencing the content within a chapter

There is no single right way of sequencing material within a chapter, although some students waste considerable time searching for it. What matters is that the sequencing should be acceptable, irrespective of whether it could be done differently. There needs to be an internal logic, which should be stated explicitly, so as to guide readers. If the chapter contains more than one stream of argument, all the streams need to be linked by careful structuring and cross-referencing. Much of the advice on structuring a report in Chapter 16 can be adapted for structuring a thesis chapter.

Over time, amendments to content and structure will suggest themselves – often as a result of the highly productive exercise of arguing with yourself as you write.

Linking chapters into one or more storylines

Chapters of a thesis should link together to make a unified whole with one or more storylines that lead inexorably to make the case or cases for which the thesis is arguing. The technique of developing and demonstrating a storyline was introduced on page 165 in Chapter 16, but for a thesis, being so much longer and almost certainly having several themes, it is even more useful. So it is always worth wording the headings of chapters and sections so that they convey as comprehensively as possible what is in them. Then it is helpful to keep an up-to-date contents list, as you work, to be able to see a developing storyline at a glance. It is here that any lack of coherence is likely to show up first. So the technique can save hours of writing that would later have to be discarded.

It should be clear from a chapter's introduction where that chapter fits into the rest of the storyline, i.e. where it carries on from previous chapters of the thesis. A good technique to accomplish this is to write a few keywords or notes under each of the following headings:

- Setting the scene for the chapter, i.e. the general area(s) that the chapter considers.
- The gap in knowledge or understanding which the chapter addresses – usually as identified as an issue in (an) earlier chapter(s).
- How the chapter fills the gap.
- A brief overview of what is in the chapter.

Then edit the notes together to form the introduction to the chapter. Figure 23.1 illustrates the technique in a simplified way.

The concluding section or paragraph of a chapter (except of course for the final chapter) should show how the theme of the chapter is carried on elsewhere in the storyline/thesis. The technique for doing this consists of writing a few keywords or some notes under each of the following headings:

- What the chapter has done
- What new questions the chapter has identified
- Where these questions are dealt with.

Then edit the notes together. Figure 23.2 illustrates the technique in a simplified way.

Write notes under each of the following

1 Setting the scene for the chapter, i.e. the general area(s) that the chapter considers, e.g.:

   Resource-based learning, universities, Sierra Leone.

2 The gap in knowledge or understanding which the chapter addresses, usually as identified as an issue in (an) earlier chapter(s), e.g.:

   Resource-based learning is not used in universities in Sierra Leone. Could it be, as Chapter 8 shows that it has proved useful in other countries?

3 How the chapter fills the gap, e.g.:

   Suggests ways in which resource-based learning might be used for teaching English as a foreign language in the National University of Sierra Leone.

4 A brief overview of what is in the chapter, e.g.:

   Surveys and draws conclusions from the very limited use of resource-based learning over the last twenty years in other subject areas and at various educational levels in Sierra Leone.

Edit the notes together to form the introduction to the chapter, e.g.:

   Resource-based learning for teaching undergraduates is little used in Sierra Leone, even though the evidence from Chapter 3 shows that it has proved useful in other countries. The present chapter suggests ways in which it might be used for teaching English as a foreign language in the National University of Sierra Leone. The chapter does so on the basis of surveying and discussing the very limited use of resource-based learning over the last twenty years in other subject areas at various educational levels in Sierra Leone.

Figure 23.1   A simplified example of the use of a technique for developing the introduction of a thesis chapter.

Suggestions

- Assume that you are about to write the introduction to a chapter of your thesis. If you are not ready to do this yet, practise the technique on any other piece of writing, such as an essay or report. Write a few keywords or some notes under each of the above headings and then edit them together into an introduction.
- Imagine that you are about to write the concluding section or paragraph to a chapter of your thesis. Write a few keywords or some notes under each of the above headings and then edit them together.

Write notes under each of the following

1 What the chapter has done, e.g.:

> Concluded that resource-based learning could work well for teaching English as a foreign language in the National University of Sierra Leone.

2 What new questions the chapter has identified, e.g.:

> How should the resource materials be developed? How should they be produced? How should the teachers be trained to use them?

3 Where the questions are dealt with, e.g.:

> In Chapters 7 and 8.

Edit the notes together to form the conclusion to the chapter, e.g.:

> This chapter has concluded that resource-based learning could be usefully employed to teach English as a foreign language in the National University of Sierra Leone. The chapter has raised questions about how the resource materials should be developed and produced, and how the teachers should be trained to use them. These questions are addressed in Chapters 7 and 8 respectively.

Figure 23.2 A simplified example of the use of a technique for developing the concluding paragraph or section of a thesis chapter.

Incidentally the technique for developing an introduction is worth considering for any form of writing, although the technique for developing the concluding section or paragraph may not be. It all depends on the purpose of what is being written. The crucially important point to remember about a thesis is that it must gather all loose ends in together to lead to the conclusion of whatever case or cases it is making. A thesis, unlike most other written works should go further than merely being a source of information. It must interpret information.

Cross-referencing in the thesis

A document as large as a thesis will inevitably require cross-references between sections and chapters, but during the drafting stage it is not possible to know what the page or section of the cross-reference will be. In principle, word processors can automate cross-referencing, but this requires working with a single, extremely large file. A more manageable alternative, at least in the early stages, is to work with separate files for each chapter. A low-tech technique is to call the cross-reference 'page ##' or 'section ##' to signify that a number (or something else) is to be put in later. The double symbol is less ambiguous than a single one because it is less likely to have a meaning of its own. When finalizing the thesis, all that is necessary is to use the 'find' command to locate all the ## symbols and replace them with a number (or whatever) which is now known. This is much easier than having to read through to locate all instances where a reference number is needed. The same technique can be used, along with a message to yourself, to indicate anywhere where you need to return to for further work. Microsoft Word's 'comment' and 'bookmark' tools do a similar job.

In the not-too-distant future, libraries will hold theses in electronic form, and when that happens, it will be much more user-friendly to have the entire thesis as a single file. Then cross-referencing can and should be electronic.

The writing process

Writing a thesis is generally a matter of progressively refining chapters in the light of their internal consistency and their relationship to other chapters. This cannot be done quickly, and most students underestimate the time it requires.

It is not usually productive to try to write the chapters of a thesis in sequence. Start with a chapter or several chapters that are currently fascinating you or that you have already come to grips with in your mind. Then develop them in whatever way is easiest for you, be it text on a computer, or scribble on blank sheets of paper, or as a 'mind map'. The emphasis should be on producing a coherent structure, rather than on grammar or style. When you come to do the actual composition, it is most straightforward to do your own typing and then use the 'drawer treatment' as described on page 174.

Ask your supervisors at what stage they would like to see the drafts. A common procedure is for students to write a chapter of a thesis, submit it to a supervisor and then rewrite to accommodate comments, but it is a mistake then to believe that the revised chapter is completely finished, never to need further modification. The 'storyline' of an entire thesis can never be clear from a single chapter. The full thesis is required, at least in draft. No supervisor will finally 'approve' a chapter in isolation. The scene-setting chapters are most likely to remain unchanged, but the analytical and interpretative ones depend too much on one another. The word 'approve' is in inverted commas, because it is the student's, not the supervisor's, formal responsibility to decide when a thesis (or chapter) is ready for submission.

Updating drafts is so easy on a word processor that some students produce them copiously. So negotiate with your supervisor how many drafts he or she is prepared to comment on and in what detail. Most supervisors have to set some limits.

You and your principal supervisor will have been very close indeed to your work for a considerable time. You, in particular, will know it inside out and back to front. So the links between its components may be entirely obvious to you both, while not being particularly clear to those who have met your work recently. It is important to minimize misunderstandings and to find out as early as possible where clarification is necessary. Giving departmental seminars will have helped, as will giving conference presentations and writing journal articles. If you have not done any of these recently, then try to find someone new to your work, who will listen to you explaining it or, ideally, will read the draft thesis and say where they have trouble following your arguments.

You must work through the final draft of the thesis in an editorial mode. Finalizing a thesis is always much more time-consuming than expected. The style must be academic; the text must be written to make a case; chapters have to be linked into a storyline; cross-references and 'pointers' need to be inserted to keep the reader orientated to what is where and why; there should be no typing or stylistic errors; and tables, figures and references should be complete, accurate and presented in whatever format has been agreed with the supervisor. Pay particular attention to the abstract, contents list, beginnings and ends of chapters and the final chapter, as it is these which examiners tend to study first, and it is on these that they may form their impressions – and first impressions count. There may be departmental or institutional guidelines on maximum length, as shown in Box 23.2.

Throughout the writing and editing process, be meticulous about keeping backups. Pages 37–38 made suggestions in this connection.

Box 23.2 An example from one institution of how the requirements on lengths of theses differ from one field of study to another

University of London Ordinance 12 requires that the length of the [PhD] thesis in any field shall not, other than in the most exceptional circumstances, exceed 100,000 words inclusive of footnotes and appendices, other than documentary or statistical appendices, and exclusive of bibliography. This word limit and those below do not apply to editions of a text or texts. In the following fields the thesis shall not normally exceed the number of words indicated, but a candidate wishing to exceed the prescribed limit may apply for permission to the College through his/her supervisor, such application being made in writing at least six months before the presentation of the thesis:

- *Archaeology: 60,000 words, exclusive of maps, bibliography, and data*
- *Biology: normally 65,000 words, exclusive of experimental data, appendices and bibliography*
- *Classics: 80,000*
- *Crystallography: 60,000, exclusive of tables and figures*
- *Geography: 75,000*
- *Geology: 60,000*
- *German: 80,000, exclusive of quotations from primary and secondary texts*
- *Materials Science: 40,000–50,000 and in any event not exceeding 80,000 (exclusive of any accompanying data in microfiche form)*
- *Philosophy: 75,000*

(University of London, Birkbeck 2005)

Box 23.3 Finding an acceptable end-point for a thesis

A dissertation [thesis] is never finished, it is just abandoned at the least damaging point.

(Race 1999: 121)

Most students choose to prepare the final versions of their theses themselves, although professional copy editors and typists can support to varying extents. If you need help, make enquiries well in advance of your deadline, because such individuals inevitably find that certain times of the year are busier than others. The departmental secretary or the students' union should be able to make recommendations.

Although most students underestimate the time that a thesis takes, it is also worth pointing out that many students spend longer on it than necessary, either trying to bulk up the quantity or toying with stylistic refinements. The assertion of Box 23.3 should thus be regarded as highly pertinent advice, as is the quote at the beginning of this chapter.

Producing the abstract

The abstract of the thesis is probably the first place that examiners are likely to look. So it is worth making it good; to provide an enticing and accurate orientation to what is to follow. Abstracts should be written after the bulk of the thesis is written. That is the only way that anyone can write confidently about what is there. Your supervisor will doubtless want to give an input, but you can make a first draft as follows:

1 Write the first sentence on why/how the work described in the thesis is significant and original.
2 Write the last sentence on the implications of the work.
3 Sandwich in between a summary of the work in no more than a few paragraphs.
4 Edit the above together so that the resulting abstract answers the questions of what you did, why you did it, how you did it and the major results in qualitative terms.
5 Edit again to the requirements of length given in the institutional regulations.

You may also like to look at the extract in Box 17.2 in Chapter 17. Although it is about writing an abstract for a conference paper, there is a lot that is transferable.

Presenting the thesis in accordance with institutional requirements

Check carefully what the institutional regulations state about the size of the paper; single or double sided; line spacing; margins; quotations; footnotes; page numbering; figures; tables, style for citing references; appendices; etc. Layout requirements should be easy to accommodate if you have used the 'styles' facility as advised on pages 165–167. Copyright is normally retained by the student.

The institutional guidelines will give a checklist of the 'elements', i.e. the various bits and pieces, that must be included. It will be broadly similar to the list in Box 23.4.

Institutions and possibly departments usually require a specified number of copies for their own records. Decide how many extra copies you will want for yourself and to give to people who have helped you. It is common politeness to give a copy to your supervisor, and to acknowledge him or her formally in the thesis, along with others who have helped, and it is a nice gesture to include a handwritten note of appreciation in the copy that you give your supervisor.

Theses are not cheap to bind, and professional binding takes time. So it is worth finding out early on whether or not the institution requires theses to be hard-bound at the time of any oral examination. Practices vary on this. If regulations allow theses to be unbound or soft-bound, so much the better, as examiners normally require at least a few amendments to be inserted into the final bound copies. Institutions invariably insist on their own binding housestyle and nominate official binders. If there should be more than one, it is worth checking their prices, as costs of binding can vary. Fortunately, from a cost point of view, it will probably not be long before the library copy, at least, can be in electronic, rather than bound, form.

Box 23.4 A checklist for the elements of a thesis, subject to institutional regulations

Not all of the following elements are required in a thesis. Much depends on the norms of the discipline, the level of the thesis and institutional requirements.

- *Consent form of some sort*
- *Title page showing the officially approved thesis title, full name of candidate, title of degree and name of institution*
- *Abstract*
- *Dedication*
- *Preface/acknowledgements*
- *Table of contents*
- *Lists of tables, figures, etc*
- *Main text of thesis*
- *Appendices*
- *Bibliography*
- *References*
- *Glossary*
- *Index*

(Cryer undated)

Suggestions

- Find out the requirements of your institution for thesis presentation in terms of the following:
    1 Numbers of copies
    2 Paper size, colour and weight
    3 Fonts and typefaces
    4 Methods of reproduction
    5 Layout, e.g. margin sizes and line spacing
    6 Pagination, e.g. of front material as well as of main text
    7 Style of title page
    8 Abstract
    9 Table of contents
    10 Illustrations, audio and video recordings, etc.
    11 Binding
    12 Style of print on binding
    13 Corrigenda, i.e. how errors may be corrected without retyping and rebinding

- Do your institutional regulations require the thesis to be bound for the examination?

- How long needs to be allowed for a thesis to be bound, who does the institution allow to do it, and how much does it cost?

24

Handling the oral/viva/ thesis defence

> Ultimately the goal is not just to survive your viva, it is to do well, to do yourself justice . . . to give an excellent performance on the day.
>
> (Murray 2003: 10)

The form of the PhD/MPhil examinations • Submitting the thesis for the examination • The importance of the viva/oral examination/thesis defence • How orals/vivas are conducted • Preparing yourself for your oral/viva • Setting up tokens of appreciation • Dressing for the oral/viva • Conducting yourself in the oral/viva • Preparing for the result

The form of the PhD/MPhil examinations

The examination for the PhD and MPhil awards is in two parts in the UK: first, the submission and preliminary assessment of the thesis, and second, its defence by oral examination, also called a viva. In some countries there is not normally any oral examination, while in others it is a very formal public occasion. This chapter is primarily for PhD and MPhil students who will be experiencing an oral examination of the sort which is standard practice in the UK. In the UK the number and status of examiners depends on the regulations of the institution. There will almost certainly also be an internal examiner and an external one. Students' supervisors can normally attend the examination in exceptional circumstances, and then only as observers and where the examiners unanimously agree.

Candidates for PhDs at institutions outside the UK may also like to scan the chapter as it may suggest additional points to make in the thesis or be useful if a face-to-face examination should be required for any reason. The same is true for candidates on programmes with a smaller research component.

Submitting the thesis for the examination

With good working relationships between supervisors and students, there will be a mutual agreement about when a student is ready to enter for the examination, although institutional regulations normally lay down that the responsibility is with the students. Clearly it would not be sensible to go against a supervisor's advice except in very special circumstances.

It is normally students, not their supervisors, who are responsible for obtaining, completing and delivering entry forms for the examination. So these need to be thought about several months ahead of time. If the thesis is not submitted within a specified time afterwards, the whole entry procedure will have to be repeated.

Some months before your thesis is ready, your supervisor will identify an external examiner to propose to the appropriate institutional committee. That person will have expertise in your field and be from another institution. While few supervisors would be naive enough to suggest a politically or methodologically incompatible examiner, it is in your own interests, where possible, to involve yourself in the selection. You will know the literature in your field, so your supervisor's suggestions should not come as a surprise, and you may even be able to suggest some possibilities yourself. Many supervisors would expect you to, although there are institutions where the regulations prevent students from even knowing the names of their examiners in advance.

The importance of the viva/oral examination/thesis defence

The decision as to whether or not the thesis is up to the required standard is tentatively taken before the oral examination. However, a poor performance in the oral may lead the examiners to question their decision, whereas a good performance can boost a borderline thesis into a pass. This is the main reason why it is in students' best interests to present themselves as well as they can. Other reasons are that the oral examination can be enjoyable, stimulating and useful.

How orals/vivas are conducted

It is normal for oral examinations to take place at students' home institutions, which the external examiners visit. However, some institutions are considering cutting down on the time and costs of travel by arranging the contacts through video link.

There is no such thing as a typical oral examination – see the extract in Box 24.1. However it is likely to last between one and three hours, although it seldom seems this long because everyone gets so involved in the discussion. The external examiner normally chairs and takes the lead. Being an expert in the topic, he or she is concerned primarily with that topic and with ensuring that standards are as near uniform as possible across institutions. The internal examiner's role is normally more one of organizing and administering the examination, ensuring that it is conducted fairly and that appropriate institutional standards are set and maintained. The internal examiner is also likely to be concerned with the student's general knowledge of the wider field and with how the work being examined fits into that field. In some countries the examination is open to the public, and/or candidates may be expected to give seminars on their work.

Box 24.1 Some general points about orals/vivas

There is no such thing as a standard viva, but a few general points should be borne in mind. A candidate will not be expected to answer questions from memory and examiners will specify pages or passages in the thesis and allow time to look at them. Usually an examiner will give a general indication of how he or she feels about the thesis including areas of approval or of possible concern. Questions about what worries an examiner should not be taken as a sign that the candidate will be failed, but it is important that they should be answered directly and backed by references to the text of the thesis itself. Finally a candidate should always be prepared to discuss how the work presented by the thesis might be developed further especially for publication.

(Smith 1991: 56)

Many students prefer not to have their supervisors with them at the oral examination because it can be inhibiting to explain their work in front of someone who knows it so thoroughly already. Supervisors can, however, be present in certain circumstances, depending on institutional regulations. So you should think about whether there are good reasons for this to happen in your case, and then discuss possibilities with your supervisor.

Points to ponder

- It is sensible to find out as much as possible in advance about what is likely to happen in your oral examination. Ask around to find some answers to the following questions.

  1 Where will your oral examination take place?
  2 How long is the examination likely to last?
  3 How is the examination likely to be conducted?
  4 Would you want a supervisor to attend if this could be arranged?

Preparing yourself for your oral/viva

A common suggestion is that students should prepare for the oral/viva through a mock examination with supervisors or others role-playing examiners. This may or may not be a positive thing to do, as the extract in Box 24.2 explains. Only you and your supervisor can decide what is best for you.

Box 24.2 The pros and cons of a mock oral/viva

Mock vivas are not a good substitute for long term preparation . . . Students should not regard a mock viva that examines the whole, or, part, of the thesis as a trial run for the content of the actual oral examination. The specific questions asked in mock vivas and actual vivas are frequently very different . . . Vivas can have diverse content depending on the examiners' views of the standard of the thesis being examined and about what types of knowledge a PhD candidate should possess. So, for example, a candidate whose thesis is judged to be borderline may receive a different type of viva in terms of content from a candidate whose thesis is judged as strong.

(Tinkler and Jackson 2004: 133)

Once you know who your examiners will be, it would be sensible to find out what you can about them, to familiarize yourself with their work and find links between it and your own. If at all possible, ask around to find out their examination style.

Since the date of the oral may be several months after completion of your work, you will have to reread your thesis some days before, so that it is at your fingertips. An oral examination is often called a thesis defence, which may help you to prepare better. Reread your thesis, as if trying to find fault. If possible, solicit the aid of a friend or family member. Then prepare suitable defences. Defending is not the same as being defensive. If criticisms seem valid, prepare responses to show that you recognize this by saying, for example, what you would have liked to be able to do about them if there had been more resources or if you had thought about it at the right time, or what you hope that other researchers may still do about them.

The extract in Box 24.3 suggests some questions to prepare for. It may be helpful to annotate your thesis, using 'Post-It' style stickers, so that you can find key areas quickly. Common early questions are likely to be 'What did you enjoy most about your work?' or 'What would you do differently if you were starting out all over again?' or 'How did your Personal Development Planning or skills training influence your work?'. These questions may appear to be simple pleasantries to put you at your ease, but they may mask skilful probing into how well you can appraise your own work and your personal development as a researcher and scholar. Unless you prepare for them, they may throw you and affect how you conduct yourself in the rest of the examination.

Box 24.3 Some questions to prepare for in the oral examination/viva/thesis defence

a)   The 'context' of your research – which debates, issues, problems it is addressing.

b)   The 'red thread' of your research – the idea that binds it together.

c)   Its main findings, i.e. your (major) contribution(s) to knowledge.

It is one of the classic opening gambits of external examiners, after an initial question to set the candidate at ease, to ask a question along these lines.

(Clark 1991: 45)

Examiners may ask you to present parts of your work orally. They often do this to check that a thesis is a student's own work and to gauge his or her understanding of it. Come prepared to talk through – and possibly also sketch out – the major 'route maps' through your work. This may mean repeating what is already written.

You may also like to prepare some questions for the examiners, although whether or not you use them should be a matter of judgement at the time. You will certainly want to impress with the quality of your thinking, but it would be unwise to raise issues which could seem peripheral and to which examiners might not be able to respond readily. Suitable questions might concern links which examiners might have on recent related work elsewhere or advice on how to go about publishing your work.

You will want to be in good form for the examination. Don't think that drugs or alcohol or chewing gum will relax the tension. They will not. There is some evidence that they make performance worse, and they will probably lower the examiners' view of you. A clean handkerchief or box of tissues is good insurance, to wipe sweaty palms and even tears, although any tension should disappear rapidly once discussion gets under way.

Suggestions and points to ponder

- What can you find out about your external examiner's examining style?
- What can you find out about your external examiner's own work?
- What can you usefully find out about your internal examiner?
- With the aid of staff and other students, develop a set of simple questions that examiners are likely to use to open the proceedings.
- Prepare responses to these questions, orientated towards giving the impression that you are thoughtful and honest and that you appreciate what a research degree ought to be about.
- Read through your thesis as if you were an examiner trying to criticize aspects of it, and develop a defence. Check this out, preferably with your supervisor, to make sure that it is reasonable and not defensive.
- Prepare – with due sensitivity – some questions to ask or issues to raise with the examiners if it seems appropriate.

Setting up tokens of appreciation

In some departments, it may be a normal courtesy to give some small token of appreciation to supervisors, or to put on a celebration for other students. These may have to be set up in advance of the examination, even at the risk of tempting fate.

> ## Suggestions and points to ponder
> - You will probably already know the normal practice in the department for showing appreciation to examiners, supervisors and other staff and students. If not, find out, and then adapt it to suit your own situation.

Dressing for the oral/viva

It is advisable to choose clothes that are smart and businesslike, to show that you appreciate the importance of the occasion. The exception is where the external examiner is likely to dress casually. Whatever style of dress you eventually think appropriate, choose your outfit with care and make sure that it is both comfortable and reasonably cool to wear.

It may help to ask a friend to check over your outfit with you and to spend time discussing options. If you have nothing suitable, consider buying or borrowing. Think about whether you would give a better impression if you did your hair differently – which applies to both sexes!

Conducting yourself in the oral/viva

Although it is understandable that you may be nervous at the prospect of the oral examination, most students find that they enjoy the experience of discussing their work with able and informed individuals. Remember, you are the world's expert on your work, and your supervisor and the resources of your department should have provided you with sound support throughout your period as a research student. If you are not considered ready to be examined, you should have been told – and if you are considered ready, everything should go smoothly.

There are, however, a few guidelines on conducting yourself:

- Take a pen and paper into the examination, along with your thesis.
- Act with composure. Say good morning or good afternoon when you enter the room, but do not speak again until you are spoken to, or until the discussion reaches the stage of exhilarated debate. The examiners will want you to be pleasant but they will not be impressed by gregariousness.
- Sit squarely on the chair, not poised on the edge. If there is anything about the room arrangement that disturbs you, ask politely for it to be changed.

- Show that you are listening attentively to the examiners' questions. They will expect you to argue, but try to do so without emotion, on the basis of evidence and keeping personalities out of it, showing that you take others' points of view seriously, even if you do not agree with them. If you are in doubt about what examiners mean or whether you have answered a question in the way they are expecting, ask for clarification. Don't defend every point; be prepared to concede some, but not too many.
- Don't hesitate to jot points down on paper if this helps you think.

Preparing for the result

It is not unknown for examiners to say at the outset that a candidate has passed. Many examiners, however, would never consider doing so, in that it would invalidate the whole purpose of the examination. Normally if everything goes smoothly, you will be told shortly afterwards that you have passed, subject as always to ratification by the institution.

In even the best theses, examiners often want small amendments. The supervisor, in conjunction with one of the examiners, is usually given the responsibility of ensuring that this work is carried out satisfactorily, without further formal examination.

If more substantial changes are required, or additional work needs to be done, the revised thesis has to be examined again at a later date. The student is given a specified time to conduct the further work and write it up, normally about 18 months – but it is advisable to start as soon as possible while the work is still fresh in one's mind.

The examiners have a number of other options, depending on the regulations of the institution. These include failing the thesis completely or awarding an MPhil instead of a PhD if they feel that the thesis does not merit the award of a PhD.

25

Afterwards!

There is no security on this earth; there is only opportunity.
(Douglas MacArthur at www.quotationspage.com)

Handling the outcome of the examination • Publishing the thesis • Into the rest of your life and career

Handling the outcome of the examination

Having stuck with a postgraduate programme through to completion, it is normal to pass the final examination. However, in the case of a full research degree, such as a PhD, the examiners generally require some amendments to the thesis. These may be so trivial for congratulations to be in order immediately. Or they may take some time to implement. Either way, it is best not to delay dealing with them, because the work is still fresh in your mind. If the examiners award an MPhil instead of a PhD or if anything should have gone seriously wrong, you will want to discuss the matter with supervisors. If necessary, students' unions can normally supply professionals to advise on appeals.

You may expect to feel elated at your success. Other emotions, however, are not unusual, because the emotional build-up has been so great. A common emotion is detachment, as if this great thing has not really happened. Another is lack of purpose because a driving force of your life over a long period has been severed. After a while, though, your main emotion should be pride and a sense of personal confidence at having become uniquely knowledgeable in your chosen area.

It is a good idea, if you can, to take a short holiday, to mark the end of your time as a student and to refresh yourself for getting on with the next stage of your life.

Publishing the thesis

It is likely that you may already have either published your work in journals or made some progress towards doing so, and no doubt supervisors will have given guidance and support. You may even be publishing jointly.

Publishing your research as a book is a very different undertaking, not least because it will need to have at least some appeal to an audience which is wider than merely the academics in your field, who can probably glean most of what they want of it from journals anyway. There are a number of facets to the wider appeal of a book. The title must be short and snappy; the style needs to be reasonably informal; and the results and their implications need more emphasis than how they were obtained. Illustrations are helpful; so is anything which generates emotion. It is probably best to start afresh rather than trying to edit the thesis directly.

The first thing to do is to look around for publishers who publish the type of book concerned. Then talk to the editor. It may be helpful to have a contents list roughed out and a chapter written in draft as a basis for the discussion, but it is a waste of time going any further at this stage. Different publishers have different requirements and once one agrees to publish, its staff can offer very valuable advice.

Into the rest of your life and career

The skills developed during your research programme will prove invaluable in the rest of your professional life. This is not only true where they relate directly to your discipline area. The so-called personal-transferable skills considered in Chapter 12 will also prove their worth irrespective of whether your career develops inside or outside the field of your postgraduate study. They will also help when – not if – you need to adapt to change, as is nowadays a way of life.

It is crucially important to appreciate that you will, like everyone else, need to keep on learning. Professional skills rapidly need to be updated as new practices overtake existing ones. That is generally appreciated. Perhaps less appreciated, though, is the ongoing need to re-appraise and improve how you are interacting with the people and situations around you, to discern and handle internal politics and to recognize and grasp opportunities which may arrive unexpectedly and last only fleetingly. The extracts in Boxes 25.1, 25.2 and 25.3 make these points well.

In general terms, perhaps the two most important skills for your future are those of identifying what your next learning requirement is and then finding a way to accommodate it. The term 'lifelong learning' encapsulates the idea.

Box 25.1 Skills for succeeding in your career

The following comment is from the co-author of 'Skills for Graduates in the 21st Century', a report by the Association of Graduate Recruiters:

Will graduates need IT skills? Of course they will. Will they need foreign language skills? Of course they will. But will those skills be the defining skills of the 21st century? I don't think so. The skills for the future include self-promotion, action planning, networking, coping with uncertainty and 'political awareness' – or an understanding of the hidden tensions and power struggles within organisations.

(Jonathan Winter, as reported by Simon Targett in *Times Higher Education Supplement* 1995: 5)

Box 25.2 Recognizing the obstacles to career advancement

The first step in dealing with obstacles to career advancement is to recognize them, for which the following list is revealing. It was written for women, but minor adaptation can make it useful, either generally or for specific disadvantaged groups.

- *Old-school tie network*
- *People staying in positions a long time*
- *Barriers in larger traditional, male-dominated organisations*
- *Less mentoring (formal and informal) for women*
- *Lack of confidence*
- *Dislike of playing office politics*
- *False assumption that competence and ability are enough*

(Bogan 1999: 9)

Box 25.3 Planning the direction of a career path

Career planning for those in the fast lane is not scientific. It is mostly to do with spotting and taking advantage of opportunities.

(Mileham 1995)

There is no such thing as a career path – it's crazy paving, and you have to lay it yourself.

(Robin Linnecar, as quoted in Association for Graduate Recruiters 1995: 12)

Appendix

Skills training requirements for research students: Joint statement by the UK Research Councils*

Taken from the *Code of Practice for the Assurance of Academic Quality and Standards in Higher Education*, Section 1: Postgraduate Research Programmes (QAA 2004).

Introduction

The research councils play an important role in setting standards and identifying best practice in research training. This document sets out a joint statement of the skills that doctoral research students funded by the research councils would be expected to develop during their research training.

These skills may be present on commencement, explicitly taught, or developed during the course of the research. It is expected that different mechanisms will be used to support learning as appropriate, including self-direction,

* Originally the joint statement was from the UK Research Councils and the Arts and Humanities Research Board (AHRB), but now, as the AHRB is itself a research council, the statement has been amended at the request of Communications at QAA.

supervisor support and mentoring, departmental support, workshops, conferences, elective training courses, formally assessed courses and informal opportunities. The research councils would also want to re-emphasize their belief that training in research skills and techniques is the key element in the development of a research student, and that PhD students are expected to make a substantial, original contribution to knowledge in their area, normally leading to published work. The development of wider employment-related skills should not detract from that core objective.

The purpose of this statement is to give a common view of the skills and experience of a typical research student, thereby providing universities with a clear and consistent message aimed at helping them to ensure that all research training is of the highest standard, across all disciplines. It is not the intention of this document to provide assessment criteria for research training.

It is expected that each council/board will have additional requirements specific to their field of interest and will continue to have their own measures for the evaluation of research training within institutions.

A) Research Skills and Techniques – to be able to demonstrate:

- the ability to recognise and validate problems
- original, independent and critical thinking, and the ability to develop theoretical concepts
- a knowledge of recent advances within one's field and in related areas
- an understanding of relevant research methodologies and techniques and their appropriate application within one's research field
- the ability to critically analyse and evaluate one's findings and those of others
- an ability to summarise, document, report and reflect on progress

B) Research Environment – to be able to:

- show a broad understanding of the context, at the national and international level, in which research takes place
- demonstrate awareness of issues relating to the rights of other researchers, of research subjects, and of others who may be affected by the research, e.g. confidentiality, ethical issues, attribution, copyright, malpractice, ownership of data and the requirements of the Data Protection Act

- demonstrate appreciation of standards of good research practice in their institution and/or discipline
- understand relevant health and safety issues and demonstrate responsible working practices
- understand the processes for funding and evaluation of research
- justify the principles and experimental techniques used in one's own research
- understand the process of academic or commercial exploitation of research results

C) Research Management – to be able to:

- apply effective project management through the setting of research goals, intermediate milestones and prioritisation of activities
- design and execute systems for the acquisition and collation of information through the effective use of appropriate resources and equipment
- identify and access appropriate bibliographical resources, archives, and other sources of relevant information
- use information technology appropriately for database management, recording and presenting information

D) Personal Effectiveness – to be able to:

- demonstrate a willingness and ability to learn and acquire knowledge
- be creative, innovative and original in one's approach to research
- demonstrate flexibility and open-mindedness
- demonstrate self-awareness and the ability to identify own training needs
- demonstrate self-discipline, motivation, and thoroughness
- recognise boundaries and draw upon/use sources of support as appropriate
- show initiative, work independently and be self-reliant

E) Communication Skills – to be able to:

- write clearly and in a style appropriate to purpose, e.g. progress reports, published documents, thesis
- construct coherent arguments and articulate ideas clearly to a range of audiences, formally and informally through a variety of techniques

- constructively defend research outcomes at seminars and viva examination
- contribute to promoting the public understanding of one's research field
- effectively support the learning of others when involved in teaching, mentoring or demonstrating activities

F) Networking and Teamworking – to be able to:

- develop and maintain co-operative networks and working relationships with supervisors, colleagues and peers, within the institution and the wider research community
- understand one's behaviours and impact on others when working in and contributing to the success of formal and informal teams
- listen, give and receive feedback and respond perceptively to others

G) Career Management – to be able to:

- appreciate the need for and show commitment to continued professional development
- take ownership for and manage one's career progression, set realistic and achievable career goals, and identify and develop ways to improve employability
- demonstrate an insight into the transferable nature of research skills to other work environments and the range of career opportunities within and outside academia
- present one's skills, personal attributes and experiences through effective CVs, applications and interviews

References

The 'official Harvard' style for referencing websites is to quote the full web address (URL) and the date viewed. For many of the web references here, however, this would be of the form:

Prospects. http://www.prospects.ac.uk/cms/ShowPage/Home_page/Funding_my_further_study/Institutional_funding_and_employment/p!eFdkk; $E8$C3$F#Employment%20conditions, viewed 25 March 2006

where the single line URL has been arbitrarily broken to fit onto the page. Such referencing is open to misinterpretation, mistyping and seems unduly cumbersome, particularly as no-one would realistically try to get to the page by retyping. Consequently, the book references websites in the much more accessible form of:

Prospects (undated) Accessible at www.prospects.ac.uk through a search on keywords, checked March 2006.

Association of Graduate Recruiters (1995) *Skills for Graduates in the 21st Century*. Cambridge: The Association of Graduate Recruiters.

Bargar, R. and Duncan, J. (1982) Cultivating Creative Endeavour in Doctoral Research, *Journal of Higher Education*, 53(1): 1–31.

Becher, T. Henkel, M. and Kogan, M. (1995) *Graduate Education and Staffing: Report of a Research Seminar*. London: Committee of Vice-Chancellors and Principals/Society for Research into Higher Education.

Bell, J. (2005) *Doing Your Research Project* (4th edn). Maidenhead: Open University Press.

Bellaby, P. (undated) Accessible at the University of Salford website http://www.rgc.salford.ac.uk through a search on *Bellaby ethics*, checked March 2006.

Berry, R. (1986) *How to Write a Research Paper*. Oxford: Pergamon.

Bogan, M. (1999) Is the workplace a level playing field? in S. Tyler (ed.) *Career Women Casebook 2000*. London: Hobsons.

Bowrick, P. (1995) Blowing the whistle on referees, *Times Higher Education Supplement*, 10 February, p. 11.

British Academy (1992) *Postgraduate Research in the Humanities*. London: British Academy.

Cameron, I. (2004) PhDs push for status change, *Times Higher Education Supplement*, 26 November, p. 6.

Clare, J. (2006) Internet Plagiarism is rife at Oxford, *Daily Telegraph*, 14 March, pp. 1–2.

Clark, J. (1991) Personal views, in G. Allan and C. Skinner (eds) *Handbook for Research Students in the Social Sciences*. Brighton: Falmer Press.

Coe, E. and Keeling, C. (2000) Guide 6: Setting up peer-mentoring with postgraduate research students, *Issues in Postgraduate Supervision, Teaching and Management*. London: Society for Research into Higher Education/*Times Higher Educational Supplement*.

Community Learning Network (undated) Accessible at the Community Learning Network http://www.cln.org through a search on keywords, checked March 2006.

Council for International Education (UKCOSA) (undated) Accessible at http://www.ukcosa.org.uk through a search on keywords, checked March 2006.

Cryer, P. (1997) How to get ahead with a PhD, *The Times Higher Education Supplement: Research Opportunities*, 16 May, p. i.

Cryer, P. (ed.) (1998) *Guide 3 Developing Postgraduates' Key Skills*. London: Society for Research into Higher Education/*Times Higher Education Supplement*.

Cryer, P. (undated) Workshop handouts. Unpublished.

Deakin University (undated) Accessible at http://earth.its.deakin.edu.au through a search on keywords, checked March 2006.

Delamont, S., Atkinson, P. and Parry, O. (2004) *Supervising the Doctorate*, 2nd edn. Maidenhead: SRHE and Open University Press.

Denicolo, P. (1999a) Discussion document used in training supervisors of postgraduate research students at the University of Reading. Unpublished, University of Reading.

Denicolo, P. (1999b) Guide 5: Supervising students from public sector organisations, *Issues in Postgraduate Supervision, Teaching and Management*. London: Society for Research into Higher Education/*Times Higher Educational Supplement*.

Denzin, N. and Lincoln, Y. (eds) (1994) *Handbook of Qualitative Research*. Beverly Hills, CA: Sage.

Economic and Social Research Council (1986) *The Preparation and Supervision of Research Theses in the Social Sciences*. Swindon: Economic and Social Research Council.

Ehrenberg, A. (1982) Writing technical papers or reports, *The American Statistician*, 36(4): 326–9.

Elton, L. (1999) Personal communication.

Engineering and Physical Sciences Research Council (1995) *Postgraduate Research: A Guide to Good Supervisory Practice, Consultative Document*, August. Swindon: Engineering and Physical Sciences Research Council.

European Ministers of Education (1999) *The European Higher Education Area*. Joint Declaration of ministers convened at Bologna, 19 June, accessible at the Ministero dell'Istruzione, dell'Università e della Ricerca website, http://www.murst.it/convegni/bologna99/dichiarazione/english.htm (checked March 2006).

Ewing, J. (undated) Accessible on the National Postgraduate Committee website, http://www.npc.org.uk through a search on keywords, checked March 2006.

Eysenck, H. (1994) Past masters: Hans Eysenck describes his unsympathetic mentor, Sir Cyril Burt, *Times Higher Education Supplement*, 14 October, p. 17.

Fairbairn, G. and Winch, C. (1996) *Reading, Writing and Reasoning*, 2nd edn. Buckingham: Society for Research into Higher Education and Open University Press.

Flinders University Library (undated a) Accessible at http://www.lib.flinders.edu.au through a search on keywords, checked March 2006.

Flinders University Library (undated b) Accessible at http://www.lib.flinders.edu.au through a search on keywords, checked March 2006.

Fontana, D. (1993) *Managing Stress*. Leicester: British Psychological Society and Routledge.

Francis, S. (2005) D in PhD does not mean dogsbody, *Times Higher Education Supplement*, 21 January, p. 56.

George Mason University (undated) Accessible at its Technology Across the Curriculum website http://tac.gmu.edu website through a search on keywords, checked March 2006.

Heisenberg, W. (1971) *Physics and Beyond: Encounters and Conversations*, A. J. Pomerans (trans.). New York: Harper & Row.

JISC Plagiarism Advisory Service (undated) Accessible at http://www.jiscpas.ac.uk through a search on keywords, checked March 2006.

MacAleese, M. (1998) Keynote address at the International Postgraduate Students Conference, Dublin, 20 November.

Martin, J. (1982) A Garbage can model of the research process, in M. McGrath et al. (eds) *Judgment Calls in Research*. Beverly Hills, CA: Sage.

Mathews, E. H. and Taylor, P. B. (1998) *Making the Researcher's Life Easier with Research Toolbox* (the manual for Research Toolbox Software). Web published, no longer available online.

Medawar, P. (1981) *Advice to a Young Scientist*. London: Pan.

Mileham, P. (1995) Executive cases in brief, *Times Higher Education Supplement*, 24 November, p. 32.

Murray, R. (2003) *How to Survive Your Viva*. Maidenhead: Open University Press.

Ochert, A. (1999) A time and emotion study, *Times Higher Education Supplement*, 4 June, p. 20.

Oliver, P. (2003) *The Student's Guide to Research Ethics*. Buckingham: Open University Press.

Parry, S. and Hayden, M. (1994) *Supervising Higher Degree Research Students: An Investigation of Practices across a Range of Academic Departments*. Canberra: Australian Government Publishing Service.

Phillips, E. and Pugh, D. (2005) *How to get a PhD*, 4th edn. Maidenhead: Open University Press.

Premkamolnetr, N. (1999) Accessible at the International Federation of Library Associations and Institutions website http://www.ifla.org through a search on keywords, checked March 2006.

Prima Magazine (1994) Repetitive strain injury, October, p. 57.

Prospects (undated) Accessible at the www.prospects.ac.uk website through a search on keywords, checked March 2006.

QAA (Quality Assurance Agency for Higher Education) (2004) *Code of Practice for the Assurance of Academic Quality and Standards in Higher Education*, Section 1: Postgraduate Research Programmes (September). London: Quality Assurance Agency in Higher Education.

QAA (Quality Assurance Agency for Higher Education) (undated) Accessible at http://www.qaa.ac.uk through a search on keywords, checked March 2006.

Race, P. (1999) *How to get a Good Degree*. Buckingham: Open University Press.

Roberts, G. (2002) *Set for Success: The Supply of People with Science, Technology, Engineering and Mathematical Skills*. The report of Sir Gareth Roberts' Review. London: HMSO.

Salinger, D. (undated) Accessible at http://www.llas.ac.uk website through a search on 'Bologna agreement' PhD, checked March 2006.

Salmon, P. (1992) *Achieving a PhD: Ten Students' Experiences*. Stoke-on-Trent: Trentham Books.

Sanders, C. (2004) PhDs push for status change, *Times Higher Education Supplement*, 26 November, p. 6.

School of Advanced Study, University of London (undated) Accessible at http://www.sas.ac.uk through a search on keywords, checked March 2006.

Science and Engineering Research Council (1992) *Research Student and Supervisor: An Approach to Good Supervisory Practice*. Swindon: Science and Engineering Research Council.

SCONAL (Society of College, National and University Libraries) (2005) Accessible at http://www.sconul.ac.uk through a search on keywords, checked March 2006.

Shatner, W. (1993) *Star Trek Memories*. London: HarperCollins.

Smith, A. and Gilby, J. (1999) Guide 4: Supervising students on industrial-based projects, *Issues in Postgraduate Supervision, Teaching and Management*. London: Society for Research into Higher Education/*Times Higher Educational Supplement*.

Smith, D. (2005) D in PhD does not mean dogsbody, *Times Higher Education Supplement*, 21 January, p. 56.

Smith, J. (1991) What are examiners looking for? in G. Allan and C. Skinner (eds) *Handbook for Research Students in the Social Sciences*. Brighton: Falmer Press.

Taaffe, O. (1998) Labours of love, *Guardian Higher*, 29 September, p. vi.

Targett, S. (1995) More money than job skills, *Times Higher Education Supplement*, 13 October, p. 5.

Times Higher Education Supplement (1999) Explicit ideas on sex, *Times Higher Education Supplement*, 27 August, p. 11.

Times Higher Education Supplement (2005) 29 July, p. 42.

Tinkler, P. and Jackson, C. (2004) *The Doctoral Examination Process*. Maidenhead: SRHE and Open University Press.

UK Council for Graduate Education (UKCGE) (1999) *Preparing Postgraduates to Teach in Higher Education*, p. 2.

UK Grad Programme (undated) Accessible at http://www.grad.ac.uk through a search on keywords, checked March 2006.

University College London Graduate School (1994) *Graduate Society Newsletter*, Issue 1.

University of Kent (2005) Accessible on its website http://www.kent.ac.uk through a search on keywords, checked March 2006.

University of Leicester Careers Service (undated) Accessible at http://www.le.ac.uk through a search on keywords, checked March 2006.

University of London, Birkbeck (2005) Accessible at http://www.bbk.ac.uk through a search on keywords, checked March 2006.

University of Manchester (2005) Accessible at http://www.manchester.ac.uk through a search on keywords, checked March 2006.

University of Warwick (2005) Accessible at http://www2.warwick.ac.uk through a search on keywords, checked March 2006.

Wainright, T. (2005) PhDs praise quality effort, *Times Higher Education Supplement*, 12 August, p. 2.

Wikipedia Free Encyclopaedia (undated) Accessible at http://en.wikipedia.org through a search on keywords, checked March 2006.

Wong, P. (1997) Accessible at the University of Texas at Dallas website http://www.utdallas.edu through a search on keywords, checked March 2006.

Index